FOREIGN SERVICE

FOREIGN SERVICE

*Five Decades on the Frontlines
of American Diplomacy*

JAMES F. DOBBINS

THE RAND CORPORATION
Santa Monica, California

BROOKINGS INSTITUTION PRESS
Washington, D.C.

Foreign Service is a copublication of the Brookings Institution Press and the RAND Corporation.

THE BROOKINGS INSTITUTION is a private nonprofit organization devoted to research, education, and publication on important issues of domestic and foreign policy. Its principal purpose is to bring the highest quality independent research and analysis to bear on current and emerging policy problems. Interpretations or conclusions in Brookings publications should be understood to be solely those of the authors.

THE RAND CORPORATION is a research organization that develops solutions to public policy challenges to help make communities throughout the world safer and more secure, healthier and more prosperous. RAND is nonprofit, nonpartisan, and committed to the public interest.

RAND Corporation, 1776 Main Street, Santa Monica, CA 90401-3208
Tel.: 310-393-0411; Fax: 310-393-4818; www.rand.org

Library of Congress Cataloging-in-Publication data are available.
ISBN 978-0-8157-3004-0 (cloth : alk. paper)
ISBN 978-0-8157-3020-0 (ebook)

9 8 7 6 5 4 3 2 1

Typeset in Granjon

Composition by Westchester Publishing Services

Contents

vi   *Contents*

Foreword

ROBERT B. ZOELLICK

JIM DOBBINS'S MEMOIR IS THE story of an exemplary Foreign Service officer during an extraordinary time.

Jim's tenure spanned ten presidents and thirteen secretaries of state. He showed up for work at the State Department in 1967; he closed the door on his diplomatic service, after being recalled to duty, in 2014. The half-century in which Jim worked as an American envoy encompassed an incredible range of events, and Jim was a witness or deeply involved in many of them. Those five decades also comprised major transformations for the United States, at home and abroad.

Jim's earliest experiences signaled the possibility of a career on America's international frontiers. He spent his early teenage years in the Philippines, where his father worked for the Veterans Administration. After graduation from Georgetown University's School of Foreign Service, Jim was commissioned in the U.S. Navy, where his duty station aboard the aircraft carrier *Bon Homme Richard* in the Tonkin Gulf in 1965 enabled him to listen to garbled messages of patrol boat attacks that helped lead to America's long trial of battle in Vietnam.

This memoir is a diplomatic version of John Keegan's landmark *Face of Battle* (1976), an account of warriors' struggles in the vanguard, not of generals studying maps at headquarters. This story is that of an individual soldier of diplomacy, a recounting of the tactics and operations on the frontlines of foreign policy. And there is no doubt that as a fresh FSO, Dobbins skirmished over unusual terrain; at his first posting in Paris, as "third secretary," Jim not only supported the frustrating Paris Peace Talks on Vietnam, but also wandered the tumultuous streets of Paris in 1968 as Ambassador Sargent Shriver's "Special Assistant for Youth Affairs."

Jim's assessment of his role in the Foreign Service is too modest. In my experience, most U.S. Foreign Service officers were one of three types. There were Americans who enjoyed living abroad to encounter different people, cultures, languages, and perspectives. Other FSOs viewed themselves as analysts and foreign reporters, seeking opportunities to understand other governments and then to communicate back to audiences of compatriots in Washington, and, on occasion, to top officials. Then there was a relatively small caste of which Jim was a premier member: These FSOs wanted to make U.S. policy. An FSO seeking a policy career must, of course, serve abroad, but will be drawn to privileged assignments with senior officials, often presidential appointments on the storied Seventh Floor of the State Department. If fortunate, the FSO might develop a reputation as a valuable contributor in shaping or executing policy. With experience, a reputation might grow within the Foreign Service, but also with those people of both parties who work closely with presidents, secretaries of state and defense, and national security advisers. Yet a career officer's association with political appointees runs risks, too.

One of the State Department's great ironies is that its Foreign Service—so schooled in understanding the complexities and even foibles of other countries' political systems—recognizes only the most basic processes, personalities, and prerogatives of the U.S. Congress. Given congressional and political jabs about the "striped pants set" at the State Department, one can understand the wariness of most Foreign Service officers to adapt to Congress's ways; unfortunately, that distance can lead to conflicts that interfere with policies and careers. Jim encountered this problem, too.

Beyond the first three types of officers, the U.S. Foreign Service now includes a fourth group, and Jim's book explains the events that defined the experience of this cohort. Over the past decade or so, many FSOs have been posted to states in conflict or societies struggling to recover, where on-the-ground duties involve more "reconstructing" than "reporting." As Jim points out, many FSOs now "find themselves in countries with no effective government and thus little opportunity for normal diplomatic discourse. Even more difficult than shaping the behavior of foreign states is influencing the development of other societies." Ironically, these assignments recall the early service of some of Jim's peers who were posted to Vietnam.

Jim's role as a policymaker—and as a senior U.S. representative in societies in conflict—is worth special note. One of his bosses and friends, Rick Burt, and I recently compared our experience of working with Jim. We agreed that when Jim helped solve problems, he offered breadth and insight by analyzing and presenting issues within the context of history and wider considerations. A discussion with Jim was also seasoned with his sharp wit. Moreover, Jim Dobbins was always willing to explain his case patiently and was never afraid to push back; even if he could not change minds, he would fulfill his tasks with all his skill and tenacity. In addition, unlike some senior FSOs, Jim was not partisan or political and avoided being branded as a Republican or Democrat; he thrived under administrations of both parties and was a consummate professional. Finally, Jim always believed the United States could make a difference, perhaps even stretching that influence at times and in places where others might make different but equally well-reasoned calculations. I hope this book will help make Jim's service a model for future Foreign Service professionalism, not serve as a reminder of a vanishing breed.

During the first half of Jim's career, his friends would joke that he could only be posted to countries where one could drink the water. We knew of Jim's skill in the Cold War world of transatlantic diplomacy during the long East-West struggle. His natural State Department home was the well-established, buttoned-down European Bureau, or perhaps the smaller, intellectually sharp Bureau of Politico-Military Affairs. But then Jim underwent a conversion to the messy labors of security, power sharing, reconstruction, humanitarian support, and development in broken countries struggling through conflicts. Ambassador Dobbins became the go-to guy for the new diplomacy of nation-building—in Afghanistan, the Balkans, Haiti, and Somalia. That's a tour one will find only in guidebooks for the extremely intrepid! Therefore, Jim's memoir also identifies a major shift in U.S. foreign policy priorities and experience.

During eleven years with RAND, after Jim's first retirement from the State Department, he wrote and edited a series of superb and practical books that analyzed America's experience with nation-building. Even though, today, the United States has grown weary and skeptical of such missions, Dobbins' assessments of policy, possibilities, and requirements for success offer a treasure of experience and judgment for those facing similar challenges in years to come.

This memoir is a colorful complement to Dobbins' books of analysis. *Foreign Service* is Jim's personal after-action report, a human and even affectionate tale of the face of diplomacy by one of America's foremost diplomats during eras of trial, triumph, tragedy, and transition. I hope you enjoy the book as much as I did. The author is a man with whom anyone would be proud to share a diplomatic foxhole.

ROBERT B. ZOELLICK

Former Deputy Secretary of State, Under Secretary and Counselor of the Department of State, U.S. Trade Representative, and President of the World Bank

Preface

THE PACE AND MODALITIES OF diplomacy have changed a great deal since I first went abroad as an American representative nearly fifty years ago. Travel now is by jet plane, not steamship. Contact between responsible officials is often direct rather than through local intermediaries. Text, voice, and even visual communications are instantaneous, nearly always available, and essentially cost-free. These developments speed individual transactions, but they also add complexity to the system. There are many more nodes on the network than there used to be, and at the most basic level, there are many more countries. American and most foreign bureaucracies are much larger, and outside actors have more access and more influence. The voracious demands of the twenty-four-hour news cycle compel reactions without time for reflection. The secretary of state is in near constant motion, as are many subordinate officials. This produces a good deal of wear and tear.

Technology has introduced some efficiencies. The world still doesn't stop over the weekend, but now some work can be done from home, allowing occasional time with family, even if much of it is spent on a smartphone communicating with some counterpart half a world away or devising press guidance for some breaking development.

Life in the foreign service has become harder. International travel was once infrequent, even for diplomats, and the government could afford to make it comfortable. Now, travel is just another commodity, and the government joins in driving the price down and the discomfort up. Assignments to difficult, distant, and dangerous places are more frequent, and an increasing number of postings require employees to leave their families behind. American representatives sometimes find themselves in countries with no effective government and, thus, little opportunity for normal diplomatic discourse. Even more difficult than shaping the behavior of foreign states is influencing the development of other societies.

Even so, greater frequency of travel and ease of communications have altered the nature of statecraft less than one might think. Diplomacy is still largely about getting other governments to do what your government wants, and all governments are made up of people. Identifying the right people to talk to and establishing a degree of mutual trust are the first steps toward almost any objective. All governments, democratic or authoritarian, are also bureaucracies, and the successful diplomat must maneuver within his own government to secure adequate resources and realizable objectives, and within other governments to achieve those objectives.

My intent is to show American diplomacy as it was and as it has become. While this volume follows my individual career, most of the stops along the way have been trodden by many. Many of my experiences are representative of the profession as it has developed. The early decades of my career passed largely in the structured world of transatlantic and East-West relations, where I engaged in work that would have been familiar to the participants in the Congress of Vienna. That world still exists, and the patterns of diplomacy within it have changed only in outward form. With the end of the Cold War, however, my own career path shifted from traditional statecraft to state building, from seeking to influence the policies of other nations to seeking to fashion and improve the capacity of new governments and influence the behavior of nongovernment actors.

I am grateful to the many companions on this journey, some of whom read my manuscript and helped shape this account. John Negroponte was an early role model, first encountered during the Vietnam peace talks. Robert Blackwill brought me onto Henry Kissinger's "Seventh Floor," opened the way to a London posting and then to eight years as a deputy to

Assistant Secretary, later Ambassador, Richard Burt, first in Washington and then in Germany. Robert Zoellick, Raymond Seitz, and Robert Blackwill were leading figures in diplomatic action surrounding German unification. David Gompert was my White House counterpart as the post-Cold War order in Europe began to take shape. Charles Ries twice served with me, at our mission to the European Union and in State's European Bureau. Strobe Talbott was a friend and mentor throughout the Clinton administration, and Zal Khalilzad was my partner in putting together the first post-9/11 Afghan government. Khalilzad and Gompert were both instrumental in my move to the RAND Corporation.

I am particularly grateful to RAND for providing me time and encouragement to write this memoir and to Brookings for offering to join in its publication.

In recent years, spurred by the success of *The Face of Battle*, John Keegan's 1976 look at war from the perspective of the individual soldier, other military historians have sought to portray and understand the actual experience of combat rather than concentrating exclusively on decisions of the high command. This volume, too, focuses on the tactical and operational levels of diplomacy, describing what individual American diplomats actually do, how policies are made and executed, and what it is like to be caught up in the process. Just as military strategy cannot be fully understood or successfully formulated without an understanding of the forces it sets in motion and the frictions that obstruct its execution, so a better grasp of the actual techniques and pitfalls of diplomacy may aid in the evaluation of past foreign policies and the formulation of future ones. I hope this account can offer the reader a look at the true "face of diplomacy," the usually incremental and often painstaking process by which nations move and are moved.

FOREIGN SERVICE

ONE

Pacific Youth

I WAS TEN YEARS OLD when we left for Manila. In 1953 international travel was rare, slow, and comfortable, and our family crossed the country by train and the Pacific by ship. In those distant days even very junior government employees like my father traveled first class.

Till then my universe had been a Brooklyn neighborhood evenly divided between Catholics and Jews. I walked to the nearby parochial school, and the Jews and the few Protestants attended the local public school. We all played stickball together in the street, pausing to let the occasional auto pass by. My mother, the tenth of eleven children, had been raised by older siblings after her own mother died and her father abandoned the family. My dad was raised in more prosperous circumstances, his father having risen from office boy to chief operating officer of a major American corporation. More than a dozen aunts and uncles and an even larger number of cousins lived within a few subway stops of our home, and relatives were constantly coming and going. One uncle occupied the third-floor apartment in our house. A cousin spent weekdays with us while his mother worked. Christmas and Thanksgiving celebrations were tumultuous, and each summer the Dodgers faced off against the Yankees in the World Series. We could stand outside the local appliance store and watch the game through the window via the wonder of television.

Our family left from Grand Central Station, and arrived in Chicago the next morning. There we spent half a day sightseeing before boarding the California Zephyr. Once aboard, we dined on white linen as the country rolled by. As night fell I gazed out the window by my darkened bedside while the rhythm of the rails slowly brought on sleep, only to awaken as the train pulled into stations with place names hitherto encountered only in Saturday matinee Westerns.

In San Francisco we boarded the SS *President Cleveland*, one of the American President Line ships that sailed every few weeks from the West Coast to Hawaii, Japan, Hong Kong, and the Philippines. The voyage to Manila took almost three weeks, with a day or two spent in each of the preceding ports, but there were movies, competitive sports, swimming, and other children to play with. This was not a cruise ship filled with vacationing retirees, but an ocean liner carrying businessmen, missionaries, and government officials and their families to and from their overseas postings.

My father was a lawyer with the Veterans Administration (VA). The Philippines had been an American colony until 1946, and thousands of Filipinos had fought at Bataan and Corregidor, and in subsequent resistance to Japanese occupation. These were all American veterans, and as a result, the VA's largest office was outside the United States.

During our voyage my two sisters and I heard our parents speak about the dangers posed in the Philippines by the presence of guerillas, which we assumed to be large simians. On arrival in Manila we moved into temporary quarters, a ground-floor apartment that backed onto a busy street. As each dawn approached, we could hear the calls of cocks, donkeys, and other less identifiable creatures. These, I assured my younger sisters, must be the beasts of which our parents had spoken.

In truth, the city proved quite safe, particularly for Americans. The United States had gained prestige and the affection of the Filipinos by liberating the country from a disagreeable Japanese occupation and then immediately granting it independence. Even the Communist insurgents (yes, there were guerillas) operating not far from Manila generally avoided targeting Americans, including those at the nearby U.S. air base at Clark Field. During our five years in the country, I never encountered anything but courtesy and good humor from the local population, and I soon mastered the rather chaotic system of buses and jitneys that served as public transportation so was free to roam the city at a very young age.

After a few weeks, we moved into a walled compound with some half dozen houses surrounding a communal swimming pool and tennis court. We acquired a cook, two maids, a driver, and, after a younger brother was born, an amah. This establishment was pretty standard even for a quite junior American civil servant. In the early 1950s, the United States was very rich and the rest of the world very poor. The dollar was almighty.

I still remember the impressive names of our staff. The cook, Romeo, was soon replaced by Cornelius when the former's efforts to live up to his name discomforted the maids. The drivers were, successively, Ivanhoe and then Estolastico.

For two years I attended a Christian Brothers elementary school with one other American and one English boy. The rest of the students came from well-to-do Filipino and Spanish families, but instruction was in English. Although all my classmates were pleasant, helpful, and well able to converse in English, the three Anglos and the few native Spanish speakers formed a somewhat separate group. Thus to the extent I gained entry into local society at this stage, it was mostly among the country's former Spanish elites.

When I completed eighth grade my parents switched me to the local American school, called, appropriately enough, the America School. It was Manila's only international school and the students came from many countries, but instruction and social life were based on the American model. I joined a Filipino Boy Scout troop, but otherwise the next few years were spent largely in the company of my compatriots.

Because Manila was the VA's only foreign post, there was no regular rotation of personnel. Many of the American employees had been hired locally after World War II and were free to stay as long as they wished. Several had married Filipinas, raised families, and settled in for life. Certainly my parents had no desire to leave. We received six weeks of home leave every two years and, given the month-long travel time each way, the result was an extended break.

But in 1958 the VA decided to join other government agencies in rotating its overseas personnel every two to four years. This was disagreeable for my parents, and much more so for those who had put down deeper roots.

I was happy enough to be going home, as I would be able to spend my last year in a real American high school. I prevailed upon my parents to let me fly to New York alone several months ahead of the rest of the family. As I look back I wonder at their allowing a child just turned sixteen to set off on flights that took him to Wake Island, Midway, Honolulu, San Francisco, and, eventually, New York.

The transpacific leg of the journey was aboard a Pan American clipper, the interior of which was configured much like a Pullman rail car, with pull-down bunks that allowed one to sleep under sheets and blankets behind drawn curtains. Unfortunately, this comfortable and commodious aircraft had to refuel repeatedly, which meant that no sooner had one dozed off than it was time to get up and prepare for another landing.

I spent two nights at a beachfront hotel on Waikiki, and then several days in San Francisco at the home of a girlfriend whose parents had also been part of the VA community in Manila. My aunt and uncle met me when I arrived in New York, where I remained for the summer.

Our family returned not to Brooklyn but to Washington, D.C., where my father took a position at the VA headquarters. My senior year was straight out of *American Graffiti*; or rather, *American Graffiti* was straight out of the Eisenhower-era high school experience. Mine was in the Maryland suburbs, where students and teachers all were white, and the student body was divided socially between those headed to college and those taking shop.

I took a part-time job that allowed me to buy a ten-year-old Ford for $100, which opened up the social world of dating, drive-in restaurants, and movies. The work was door-to-door magazine sales and this had several benefits. It familiarized me with neighborhoods all over the city and its suburbs, it taught poise and instilled self-confidence, and it required maintaining a sunny disposition in the face of repeated rejection. I stuck with this job for most of the next five years, emerging with the knowledge that I was rather good at persuading people to buy things they did not need or even want—not a bad qualification for the world of diplomacy.

The mother of a friend asked me what I wanted to do with my life. Something involving overseas travel, I responded, recalling our Manila swimming pool and household staff. She suggested I consider applying to Georgetown University, which then had the country's only undergraduate school of international affairs. I did so and, in the fall of 1959, I joined the freshman class at the Edmund A. Walsh School of Foreign Service.

Like almost everyone who passed through that school between 1941 and 1976, I was most impressed by the year-long course on the development of civilization taught by Carroll Quigley. He was a spellbinding lecturer who, by the time I got there, had thoroughly mastered his technique and his subject matter. For three hours every week he maintained the rapt attention of more than 100 freshmen as his discussions ranged from the ancient world to the twentieth century without ever consulting a note or pausing for breath. He made us read Homer, Plato, Thucydides, and other foundational books of Western civilization. His obituary, written some fourteen years after I took his course, said that Walsh school alumni found his "the most influential course in their undergraduate careers." Bill Clinton, who arrived at Georgetown the year I graduated, cited Quigley in his acceptance speech to the 1992 Democratic Convention.

With its heavy emphasis on history, economics, and political science, the Walsh school provided a good grounding for a career in diplomacy, and in the summer before my senior year, I took the written entry exam for the Foreign Service. To my surprise, I passed, and some months later I entered the State Department for the first time, to take the oral part of that exam.

The building occupied by the department, called New State, was but a year old and the second largest federal office structure in the country after the Pentagon. Like most other government agencies at the time, it was open to the public. On entry, visitors could consult the receptionist in the lobby or not, as they chose, before venturing further into the building. Today visitors are warned to allow at least fifteen minutes for screening before gaining entry.

My oral examination was conducted by a three-man panel made up of two senior Foreign Service officers and one public member. After ninety minutes of mild grilling I was asked to step outside. When called back in, I was told I had passed and would be offered a commission. Their only criticism, based on the written exam, was that I needed to improve my spelling, a deficiency never remedied.

I explained that I had already enlisted in the Navy and expected to attend Officer Candidate School on graduation. They assured me that the department would hold open the appointment until my military service was completed. I was twenty years old and it would be forty years before I had to look for another job.

Getting into Officer Candidate School (OCS) was comparatively easy. Getting out successfully was the single hardest thing I have ever done. I reported for duty in July 1963, and for the next four months my classmates and I were subjected to relentless pressure. Contrary to the depiction in the film *An Officer and a Gentleman*, no physical hardship was involved; no runs, hikes, or calisthenics, and certainly no instruction in hand-to-hand combat. We did march in formation everywhere, and for punishment marched some more, but that was the extent of the physical demands.

The pressure was, in part, academic. Courses in engineering, navigation, and seamanship were pretty daunting for liberal arts majors, or, in my case, international affairs. After a few frightening weeks, however, it became clear to me that I would pass academically by a safe margin. Of more enduring concern was the steadily increasing number of demerits I was accruing, which could eventually preclude graduation.

Demerits were awarded for every imaginable infraction: a single thread out of place on a uniform; a speck of tarnish on a belt buckle; books and underwear not arranged in the precisely mandated order in one's locker; shoes not shined to the prescribed level of refraction; marching out of step; arriving five seconds late for any event or movement. The system was one of extreme, apparently pointless regimentation, combined with inadequate sleep, voluminous course work, and endless harassment from only slightly more senior cadets.

There was, of course, a point to all this. The intent was to apply maximum mental pressure with a view to washing out a significant proportion of aspiring officers and teaching the remainder habits of order, discipline, and stress management. Washing out held no mild consequences. We were already in the Navy. Those who failed to complete the course did not go home; they went to boot camp at the Great Lakes Naval Training Center, and then on to the fleet as a lowly seaman apprentice. The prospect of this fate led one of my classmates to attempt suicide, not an unusual occurrence. In this respect the similar incident portrayed in *Officer and Gentleman* was quite accurate.

That movie reflected another, happier reality. Newport, Rhode Island, a lovely summer resort, lay just outside the gate, and we were set loose after parade each Saturday morning and not expected to be back before Sunday evening. Hundreds of young ladies descended on Newport Beach from Boston and beyond each Saturday night to socialize with aspiring naval officers. Woe to any of us who failed to reappear at the barracks by Sunday evening, but until then we were on our own. The contrast between the freedom and possibilities of a Saturday evening and the stress and regimentation behind and before us only heightened the exhilaration of the moment.

Another feature of our apprenticeship was a particularly unpleasant form of peer rating. We were all required to respond, in writing, to a questionnaire that had us comment on the failings of our classmates. Some days later we were each interviewed by the officer responsible for overseeing the military aspects of our development. The setting was strange, like a confessional, in which the aspirant was directed into a closet-size room to be grilled by his superior through a sort of transparent screen. After reviewing my less than spotless record for military punctilio, this officer informed me that my classmates found me to be an arrogant, supercilious jerk. This was disconcerting, as doubtless was the intention. I became more subdued and deferential for a few weeks, but I doubt this revelation improved my social skills for any longer than that.

The OCS experience was much like pledging a fraternity, something I had done at Georgetown. There was the same hazing by more senior classmates, the same effort to break down one's self-regard to instill solidarity in hardships overcome and pride in entry into an exclusive society. And it worked. Toward the end of the course, a physician told me I had flat feet and offered to have me classified 4F; that is, physically unfit for military service. Since I had already passed the Foreign Service exam, this meant I could avoid any military obligation and embark directly on my chosen career. But I was hooked, determined to graduate and don the uniform of a naval officer, and I begged the doctor to do no such thing.

I was commissioned on November 22. My parents came for the event. Following the ceremony we drove into Newport to visit the summer homes of the Gilded Age rich, but as we pulled up in front of Commodore Vanderbilt's "cottage," The Breakers, the car radio reported that President Kennedy had been shot. The sun went out, my parents went home, and I spent what should have been a celebratory weekend looking out at a cold rain and watching somber television coverage.

I spent the following three years aboard the USS *Bon Homme Richard*, an attack aircraft carrier in the Pacific. I was able to visit, once again, the places I had known as a child—Hawaii, Japan, Hong Kong, and the Philippines. We also spent a month sailing through the Indian Ocean, the first carrier to do so since World War II. The Shah of Iran flew aboard the carrier at one point, and our pilots put on an air show, bombing the open ocean and breaking the sound barrier a few hundred feet overhead. The

Shah was duly impressed and purchased American weapons throughout the rest of his reign.

By mid-1964 the conflict in Vietnam was heating up and we spent more of our time sailing around the Gulf of Tonkin launching what were called "armed reconnaissance flights." Our planes took off with full bomb loads and returned empty, or didn't return. A young aviator in the bunk above mine was one of those who didn't come back.

On August 4 I stopped by the ship's Combat Information Center on my way to the bridge, where I was to stand the mid-watch. Two days earlier North Vietnamese torpedo boats had attacked an American destroyer, the USS *Maddox*, that had been operating in the gulf under the overall command of our captain. On this evening I overheard the highly confused voice communications between the *Maddox* and a second destroyer, the *Turner Joy*, operating deep in the gulf. We listened as these two ships maneuvered and fired at what they believed to be North Vietnamese torpedo boats.

Before the sun set again President Johnson had gone on national television to announce that the North Vietnamese had twice attacked our ships. He asked Congress for authorization to respond militarily, and this was quickly granted in what became known as the Tonkin Gulf Resolution. A couple of days later the *Maddox* came alongside the *Bon Homme Richard* to refuel, by which time the episode and the ship had become world famous.*

After the Gulf of Tonkin incidents, all pretense of restraint was abandoned; thereafter, a new rhythm developed. We would spend a month off Vietnam launching combat missions, then three days in Subic Bay, the big U.S. Navy base north of Manila, following which we would resume bombing North and South Vietnam. Our six-month deployment extended to ten. When we finally returned to San Diego, ours had been the U.S. Navy's longest cruise since the end of World War II. Four months later we returned to the war.

The very monotony of this life at sea had its appeal. Every day was the same; the same horizon, the same routine, the same people. We had no newspapers, no radio, no television, and certainly no Internet. Life was

---

*Subsequent inquiry revealed that, while a North Vietnamese attack had occurred on August 2, the incident two days later was more likely a case of overly jumpy commanders responding to ambiguous radar and sonar signals.

comfortable enough. Each stateroom contained two desks, two chairs, and two bunks. Laundry and linen service were provided by the ship's stewards, who were all either African American or Filipino. Stewards also cooked and served meals in the wardroom where we dined each night on white linen, and there was a movie every night for those not standing watch.

We junior officers headed divisions of fifty to one hundred men. Since most of the men knew their jobs much better than we did, our responsibilities were not very onerous. I was in charge of the division that controlled the ship's antiaircraft guns. Some of these weapons were of World War II vintage, guided by a mechanical computer the size of a small automobile. Other guns were newer; their computer systems might have fit into a large steamer trunk. At one point, I decided I should have some basic understanding of what my men did and, accordingly, got hold of the textbook used to train aspirant fire controlmen third class, the lowest rating. Two chapters in, I gave up. The material was much too complex for me.

The most challenging of our duties was watch standing. This task came with progressively more responsibility as one moved from subordinate positions to become qualified as officer of the deck. For the duration of a four-hour watch this individual was in effective control of the ship, subject only to the orders of the captain or the executive officer. The captain spent much of his day on the bridge; the executive officer spent nearly all of his below decks, and, normally, neither was on the bridge at night. For these hours, the officer of the deck maneuvered the ship and its accompanying escorts according to plans provided him when he assumed charge. As the largest ship in the battle group, and with the most senior captain, the carrier was always in tactical command of its escorts. These included three or four destroyers, and often one or two auxiliary ships from which we were to refuel or replenish stores and ammunition. The newer, larger carriers often carried an admiral who controlled the movements of the formation; but the *Bon Homme Richard* was a less commodious, World War II vintage vessel so we went through the war without a flag officer aboard.

One morning while the captain was attending to business far below decks, the Combat Information Center alerted me that two unidentified radar contacts, surface ships, were closing on our task force, traveling a speed of fifty knots. If these were North Vietnamese torpedo boats I did not want them to get anywhere near the carrier. I ordered one of our accompanying destroyers to intercept and investigate, even as I called for the captain to return to the bridge. We soon learned that these were American, not North Vietnamese craft. I was later told that I had caused the cancellation, or at least the postponement, of a clandestine operation to insert agents into North Vietnam. I was also assured that it was their fault, not mine, for not alerting us that they would be entering our area of operations.

Conning an aircraft carrier accompanied by up to half a dozen other vessels through the night only a few dozen miles off the enemy shore; passing not infrequently through swarms of North Vietnamese fishing boats; assigning newly arriving ships their place in the formation; steering a complex zigzag course; determining how many of the ship's boilers would need to be lit to provide adequate wind over the deck for flight operations as dawn approached; watching the colorful choreography as the flight deck crews, in multihued jerseys, armed and maneuvered the F-8 Crusader fighters, the A-4 jet bombers, and the A-1 prop attack aircraft for takeoff; then increasing speed and turning the entire formation into the wind as the captain came on the bridge: these were awesome responsibilities for a twenty-three-year-old lieutenant junior grade. It would be decades before I would experience anything comparable.

Our ship spent the last six months of my active duty in dry dock at Long Beach, a suburb of Los Angeles. There was little work for the crew to do, and, like many others aboard, I moved to a nearby beach community and pursued an active social life. Several nights a week, I drove up to Beverly Hills to see the girl I had met more than a decade earlier in Manila and had visited on my way back from there in San Francisco.

The ship eventually completed its repairs and went out to sea for an initial shakedown cruise, and as the senior and most experienced watch stander aboard, I had the honor of taking the ship out into the Pacific one last time. On our return to port a few days later I saluted the quarter deck and walked down the gangway for the final time.

TWO

Apprenticeship

IN THE SPRING OF 1967 I joined four dozen other newcomers in the State Department's A-100 class. This six-week course derived its name from a room in the old State Navy War Office Building next door to the White House where an introductory class for newly commissioned Foreign Service officers was first organized back in 1924. My classmates were all young and white, and mostly male. Some were straight out of undergraduate school; others had spent a year or two with the recently established Peace Corps. Only a few had an advanced degree. At twenty-five, with three and a half years of military service, I was among the more experienced.

Washington was an exciting place to be that year. The anti-war and civil rights movements were gaining momentum. This was the "summer of love." Haight-Ashbury, in San Francisco, was its epicenter, but the streets of Georgetown were filled with hippies, discos, and shops selling tie-dyed T-shirts. The city was home to thousands of idealistic young volunteers in LBJ's war on poverty, eager to build the Great Society. On warm evenings we would congregate on the stoops of group homes clustered around Dupont Circle talking of new responsibilities and stirring aspirations. It was hard not to be affected by the pervasive sense of new possibilities, even for someone like myself, already a very junior member of the establishment. The times were, indeed, a-changing. Fifty years on, that decade's anthems of protest, progress, and optimism still evoke a strong tug of nostalgia for me.

At the A-100 course we learned about the Department of State: how it was organized, how it functioned, and how it fit into the larger government apparatus. We were taught nothing about U.S. foreign policy; not what it was, or even how it was made. That was to be learned on the shop floor. Each of us was interviewed regarding our interests and aspirations, and on the last day of class there was a small ceremony. One by one, as our names were called, we filed to the head of the room to receive orders to our first posting. About a third of my classmates were assigned to Vietnam, where they would staff a new countrywide rural assistance program just being launched. This came as an unpleasant surprise to most, as we had been told earlier in the course that first-tour officers would not be assigned to Vietnam.

When my turn came, I walked forward with some trepidation, only to learn that my orders were to Paris. There was a murmur of appreciation and, I expect, envy. Decades later, at a lunch for retirees, I sat next to the officer who had made this assignment. He, too, had served in the U.S. Navy before entering the Foreign Service, and he admitted that this common experience may have played a role in his awarding me the class's plum posting.

Before departing Washington we had calling cards made. These contained only our names and title, "third secretary," with an embossed American eagle; no phone number or other locator information. Following long-established protocol these cards were to be left at the homes of more senior embassy officers on arrival at our post in the hope of subsequent invitations. We were told that the cards needed to be engraved, not printed. I ordered 500, passed out no more than half a dozen over the next couple of years, and never ordered more.

After four months of instruction in French, I set off for Paris. Once again travel was by sea. I loaded everything I owned into my car, a mechanically unreliable but highly presentable Jaguar sedan, and drove to the Brooklyn dock where the USS *United States* berthed. This was the fastest ship to cross the Atlantic, a record it holds to this day. As I walked on board, my car, with all my worldly possessions in the trunk, was lifted into the hold.

Two of my A-100 classmates were also on board, on their way to Germany. The three of us were assigned a table in the dining room with an attractive young lady of our age and her mother. Breakfast and lunch were informal but, for dinner, male guests wore black tie and the women wore long dresses, and after dinner we adjourned to the lounge for drinks and dancing to the ship's orchestra. Four days and nights later the ship docked at Le Havre. The Jaguar was offloaded while my passport was being stamped; the car was waiting on the pier when I disembarked. Three hours later I pulled up in front of the American embassy in the heart of Paris.

In those days, first tour officers were expected to rotate among the embassy's four main elements, spending roughly six months in each. My first posting was to the consular section, then heavily overstaffed. I was placed in charge of notarizing American legal documents, a responsibility that required only that I be able to sign my name. Nobody seemed interested in teaching me the slightly more complex steps needed to issue passports or visas. Following some halfhearted attempts to solicit instruction, I stopped asking. After three months I moved to my next rotation, as an aide to the American ambassador to the Organization for Economic Cooperation and Development (OECD). His was a separate mission housed in a lovely eighteenth-century chateau on the Avenue Foch. Many of its rooms retained their original woodwork and elaborately painted ceilings. My cubicle had minimal floor space, but the ceiling fifteen feet above was filled with nymphs, clouds, and blue sky.

The OECD had its roots in the Marshall Plan. Originally it was the forum that brought the donor, the United States, together with all the recipients. The organization had transitioned into a Western club in which issues common to highly developed economies were studied and strategies for dealing with them agreed upon. My job was to help coordinate the flow of information to and from the head of our mission, Ambassador Philip Trezise, accompany him to meetings, and report the results to Washington. The organization's work was highly technical and its discussions arcane, which made the job a good introduction to international economic policy and to multilateral diplomacy.

Next came something wholly unexpected. On March 31, 1968, President Johnson announced he was halting the bombing of most of North

Vietnam in a bid to open peace talks. Johnson added, "I shall not seek, and I will not accept, the nomination of my party for another term as your president." Six weeks later Averell Harriman and Cyrus Vance arrived in Paris to head the American delegation to these very talks. I met them at the airport and became the only Paris-based officer assigned to what was then the world's highest-profile diplomatic endeavor.

Harriman, who had been FDR's ambassador to Moscow throughout World War II, was the delegation's head. Cyrus Vance, formerly the deputy secretary of defense, had reportedly been assigned by Johnson to keep an eye on Harriman, who had a reputation for independence. The other delegation members were Dan Davidson, an adviser to Harriman, Major General George Seignious, representing the Pentagon, a National Security Council staffer from the White House who handled press affairs, and a senior Foreign Service officer (FSO), Philip Habib. These six were supported by several junior FSOs, a CIA analyst, and a couple of Army colonels.

Initially I was assigned to assist the officer responsible for managing paper flow: routing incoming official traffic; clearing and dispatching outgoing reports; reviewing and forwarding relevant news items; and assembling briefing books for each meeting with the North Vietnamese. After a couple of months the officer returned to Washington and I took over the delegation's secretariat, with a staff of half a dozen clerks and couriers.

This position gave me access to the voluminous background material the delegation had brought with it, and all the subsequent communications back and forth with Washington. Before this I had never seen a top-secret document. Now I pored over hundreds of them. Many had cover pages stamped "Limited Distribution" or "Extremely Limited Distribution," or even "No Distribution." This was all very exciting, and in my spare time I read voraciously, learning a little about Vietnam and a lot about how embassy reports and Washington staff studies were written.

Harriman, seventy-six years old on his arrival in Paris, was a vigorous leader. Perhaps to counter any suggestion of failing capacity, he always eschewed the elevator and took all stairways two steps at a time. He was a somewhat aloof figure focusing on big policy issues. It was Vance who chaired our morning staff meetings and Phil Habib who oversaw the reporting and substantive preparations for each session with the North Vietnamese. Phil had been head of the political section of our embassy in Saigon, and he was a tough, plain-spoken, warm-hearted curmudgeon who inspired equal measures of fear and affection in his junior staff. He remained in Paris with the delegation long after everyone else had moved on, eventually became its head, and subsequently served as under secretary of state for political affairs, the top career position at State.

In addition to me, there were two other junior Foreign Service officers working for Habib, John Negroponte and Richard Holbrooke. John and Dick were a year or two older than I, but both had entered the Foreign Service several years earlier and were, as a result, several grades my senior. Both served in Saigon during the years I had been sailing off that country's coast. Consequently, they knew a good deal more than I about Vietnam, our policies toward it, and the process by which these were made. John was friendly, with a cool, wry, slightly patrician air reflecting his British birth, wealthy family, and an American prep school education. Dick was loud, boisterous, pushy, and supremely self-confident, exhibiting all the traits at twenty-five that would later make him the best-known American diplomat of our generation.

John arrived with Harriman and Vance. Dick's arrival a few weeks later stimulated some muttering among the original team who groused that he had employed his connection with the number two official at State, Under Secretary Nicholas Katzenbach, for whom he had worked, to get himself attached to the delegation. Jealousy was further stimulated when Dick arranged to accompany Harriman on a flight back to Washington some weeks later, affording him hours of uninterrupted access to the boss.

Late one evening Habib came into my office, where Dick was consulting some documents. Phil instructed Dick to complete a minor task before leaving and Dick declined, saying he had dinner plans. Phil erupted loudly at this presumption, gruffly telling Dick to do as he was told. As soon as Phil left, Dick told me to perform the chore. I refused. Dick became visibly annoyed, but then, in an offer of friendship and patronage, said, "Jim, I think you're a lot like me. We shouldn't quarrel." I still refused. Dick departed for his dinner date in a huff, leaving the task undone. There were no repercussions as far as I could tell.

One of my duties was to accompany Harriman and Vance to their meetings with the North Vietnamese. These were held at the Hotel Majestic, a French government conference center near the Arc de Triumph. The building had served as the German Army's headquarters during its occupation of Paris. These meetings were stiff and sterile, each side reading long, prepared speeches and then trading rebuttals. There were occasional breaks for tea, during which the two sides engaged a bit more informally. On departure we would make our way through a scrum of journalists waiting for whatever revelations the participants might offer. For the first few weeks, these meetings were the world's biggest news story, bringing several thousand journalists to Paris. Standing behind Harriman as he replied briefly to inquiries from the likes of Walter Cronkite and other prominent journalists was a thrill, even if I was just carrying his briefcase.

My usual post at the Majestic was a small anteroom adjoining the main conference chamber. Here I monitored message traffic and news tickers, slipping into the adjoining room to bring to Harriman's attention any items I thought he should see. On April 4, as Harriman sat listening to his North Vietnamese counterpart, I handed him the news report that Martin Luther King had been assassinated. I could see his shoulders sag. Five weeks later, in the same room, at the same point in the proceedings, I handed him another news item; this one reporting that Bobby Kennedy had been shot to death.

All of us were wondering what was happening to our country—first Jack, then Martin, and now Bobby. Between the civil rights movement, the anti-war demonstrations, and the youth revolution, America was in turmoil. So was Paris. During these same months France was undergoing an even more massive social upheaval, sparked by university students protesting overcrowded classrooms, uninspiring teachers, deteriorating facilities, and the rising costs of a supposedly free higher education. Demonstrations escalated; students took over the medieval Latin Quarter in the heart of Paris, barricading the streets and fighting nightly battles with the police. I found these confrontations more folkloric than life-threatening. The students waved red-and-black banners while defending hastily erected barricades against charges of baton-waving police. No shots were fired, no bulldozers brought in, and no one was killed.*

I was still young enough to pass for a student, so after work I would take the Metro to the Latin Quarter and roam through the crowded streets and university lecture halls listening to the impassioned speeches. I would stand behind the students' barricades as the police worked themselves up for the next charge. Then I would walk down a few blocks, cross the Seine

---

*The only fatality throughout that turbulent month was that of a student who, running from the police, jumped into the river and drowned.

at one of the many bridges, and come around behind the police lines as they formed up on the Ile de la Cite just across from the Place St. Michele where the main barricade stood.

One Saturday morning after a particularly spectacular night of rioting had been caught on national television, I traveled down to the Latin Quarter, along with many respectable Parisians, to gauge the damage. The students had uprooted a number of the trees along the Boulevard St. Michele to reinforce their defenses. I came across a well-to-do couple of late middle age being harangued by a young student explaining their *revindications*, that is, their grievances. "Yes, yes," the old gentleman responded. "That is all very well, but look what you have done to that tree. It will take twenty years to replace." The student, visibly crestfallen, replied, "You are right. That was unforgivable." It struck me then that this revolution was not entirely serious.

The revolt became more consequential when it was taken up by the labor unions. The largest of these, the Communist-controlled Confederation General de Travail, called a general strike, which the other unions supported. Eleven million workers walked off the job. Soon practically every business in the country was closed. No planes flew, no public transport moved, and pretty soon neither did any private automobiles, as there was no gasoline to be had. Clearly the students had tapped into a much wider malaise. As the crisis intensified, President de Gaulle left the country, traveling secretly to Germany where he consulted with the leadership of the French Army on the Rhine. Assured he had the military's backing, he returned to Paris and called for a massive counterdemonstration.

On May 30 a crowd of some 800,000 marched down the Champs-Élysées and assembled directly in front of the embassy on the Place de la Concorde. Looking out our windows at a sea of people waving French flags, John Negroponte commented that I was fortunate at this early stage of my career to witness the fall of a regime. He was quite serious; in the 170 years since the adoption of the American Constitution, France had passed through two monarchies, a consulate, two empires, and four republics. But the Fifth Republic would endure. De Gaulle went on national television later that day to announce that he had dissolved the parliament and was calling early elections. The air went out of the revolutionary balloon and de Gaulle's party went on to win the largest majority in French parliamentary history. De Gaulle himself was diminished by the experience, however, and resigned a year later.

My parents arrived a few days after this massive demonstration. We spent a week touring the chateaus of the Loire Valley, greeted by all with relief as the first tourists to return following the resumption of normal life.

Meanwhile, months went by with no apparent movement in the Vietnam negotiations. Back home the presidential election campaign, pitting Richard Nixon against Vice President Hubert Humphrey, was moving into high gear. Vietnam was, of course, a major issue. One morning I arrived at the office to find several of my colleagues poring over a stack of outgoing reports that I had never seen. This was disconcerting, as one of my jobs was to review all outgoing message traffic. As I joined in reading these telegrams, it became evident that a parallel negotiation had been taking place for some weeks, alongside the formal talks at the Majestic. Vance had been meeting in out-of-the-way locales with his North Vietnamese opposite, the number two on their delegation. No breakthrough had occurred, but the discussions had become more businesslike.

Reports on the negotiations had previously been sent in a designated channel labeled NODIS-HARVAN, the distribution of which was limited in Washington to a small group with a "need to know." The reports of Vance's talks were labeled NODIS-HARVAN Plus, and distribution at both ends had been even further restricted. Those on our small Paris team who had been excluded were naturally miffed at the implied slight, it having been determined, at least for a while, that we had no need to know. This was my first exposure to a practice that was the norm in sensitive negotiations, by which access to the contents of such talks was progressively restricted as they moved toward some sort of outcome. Later that year Harriman and his North Vietnamese opposite number joined these secret meetings. Another compartment was created, HARVAN Double Plus, further limiting those in the know. Eventually, during the Nixon administration, the real negotiations were conducted by Henry Kissinger, then a senior White House staffer, entirely outside the framework of the Paris talks, and these continued for years as an empty facade.

President Johnson had gotten the Paris negotiations started by announcing a partial halt to the bombing of North Vietnam. Harriman and Vance offered a complete halt to the bombing in exchange for an expansion of the peace talks to include representatives of the South Vietnamese government, then headed by President Nguyen Van Thieu. Eventually, after months of stalling, the North Vietnamese agreed. But now the South Vietnamese balked at sitting down with representatives of the Viet Cong.

Harriman and Vance were eager to announce this agreement and begin the larger talks before the upcoming American presidential election on November 8. At one delegation meeting several participants expressed frustration at Washington's inability to secure President Thieu's agreement. One of us asked how it was possible that anyone so dependent on the United States could refuse such an urgent demand, to which Harriman responded that client regimes like that in Saigon "always have one threat that trumps anything their patrons can bring to bear; they can threaten to collapse."

Johnson announced a complete halt to the bombing of North Vietnam on October 31, a week before the American election. But still the South Vietnamese refused to send a delegation to Paris. Hubert Humphrey lost, and rumors circulated that Richard Nixon had encouraged Thieu's intransigence, promising that South Vietnam would get a better deal under his administration. Henry Kissinger was allegedly implicated in this effort. Kissinger had visited Paris three times that summer, where he met with Harriman, Holbrooke, and Davidson. Davidson kept Kissinger abreast of the talks by telephone, and Kissinger passed this information on to the Nixon campaign, warning that Johnson was likely to announce a full bombing halt shortly before the November 8 election. Nixon supporters had encouraged Thieu to drag his feet, although Kissinger was not involved in that initiative. I was still green enough to find all this shocking.

The remaining months of the Johnson administration were occupied with coaxing the South Vietnamese into the talks. This involved labored negotiations between Saigon, Washington, and the North Vietnamese delegation in Paris on the shape of the negotiating table (round); the speaking order (chosen by lot); and the presence or absence of flags (no flags). The first expanded meeting of the talks was not held until January 18, two days before Richard Nixon's inauguration.

By then our small negotiating team was breaking up, with members returning to private life or other government jobs. Harriman was replaced by Henry Cabot Lodge. Negroponte stayed for a while and then went to work for Kissinger at the National Security Council. John remained with Kissinger until the negotiations were completed in 1973. Disappointed with the outcome, which he believed had conceded too much to Hanoi, John returned to State. Habib stayed in Paris and eventually succeeded Lodge as head of the delegation, tasked with maintaining the facade behind which Kissinger's negotiation took place.

The Johnson administration spent its last year and its remaining diplomatic capital in an effort to bring the South Vietnamese government into these negotiations only to find that its ally in Saigon did not actually want to participate. I would repeat this same experience with Hamid Karzai four decades later. The Nixon administration would ultimately move in the opposite direction, conducting secret talks with North Vietnam that excluded not just Saigon but also the State Department. This effort eventually produced an agreement, but one that neither South nor North Vietnam proved willing to implement.

I moved on to a position in the embassy's political section. The American ambassador to France was Sargent Shriver, a Kennedy by marriage and temperament. Under JFK, Shriver had been the founding head of the Peace Corps, an organization that epitomized Kennedy's inaugural injunction, "Ask not what your country can do for you, but what you can do for your country." Like his brother-in-law, Shriver was young, handsome, and charismatic. During the "events of May," as the previous spring's uprising had come to be called, Shriver had been photographed sitting on the curb in the midst of a demonstration conferring with student protesters. Similar demonstrations had shaken both the United States and Germany. Briefly, at least, youth were being taken seriously as a source of political change, and I was assigned to be Shriver's assistant for youth affairs.

Shriver was genuinely interested in young people, seemed to enjoy exposure to them, and also saw this as a means of establishing a distinct image. My principal responsibility was to arrange events at which Shriver and other senior embassy officers could mingle with representative French youth. Other embassy officers thought these events a waste of time, and engaged in them only to humor their chief. My proposal that each section head should host one youth-oriented event each month met with little enthusiasm and only grudging, limited acquiescence. The deputy chief of mission, the embassy's top career official, commended my zeal but cautioned against excess. "Remember," he said, "the impressions you leave here among your colleagues and superiors will follow you throughout your career." How true.

Among my duties was to supply a leavening of youthful faces to join in Ambassador Shriver's larger receptions. One of these events was attended by Jane Birkin, a young American actress making her name in the French cinema. She was in a well-publicized relationship with Serge Gainsbourg, an even more famous French singer, composer, and actor. Miss Birkin chatted with everyone very cordially and, when it came time to leave, asked me whether I knew the location of the café where she had arranged to meet Serge. I did and offered to show her the way, as it was nearby. We, accordingly, made our farewells together, to the wonder of several of my colleagues, who concluded that I had made a remarkably rapid conquest. I walked Miss Birkin to the café where Serge was waiting and then made one of the great mistakes of my life. Instead of simply going home, allowing the story of my departure with Miss Birkin to spread, I returned to the reception to sighs of disappointment.

Winning over a generation of French youth one at a time was not, as my older colleagues perceived, likely to greatly benefit American foreign policy. For me, nevertheless, the experience was fun and instructive. I got to work with an engaging and famous chief while meeting a number of interesting visitors to Paris, including two Apollo astronauts just back from deep space. I sat in the embassy political section and participated in its work. The economic, consular, and administrative units were all larger, but the political section was located directly adjacent to the ambassador's office and tended to get more of his attention than any other. In those days most top department officials were former political officers. Experiencing the rhythm of political work at the heart of one of our largest and most important embassies was a great opportunity.

So was simply living in Paris. If there is a better place to be young, single, and gainfully employed, I've not found it. I was able to take advantage of the city's social and cultural life and to travel widely throughout France and surrounding countries. Weekends were spent with the *Michelin Guide* in hand, walking through historic neighborhoods, evenings with friends sampling the capital's nightlife and the country's cuisine, and vacations touring the countryside or visiting colleagues from the A-100 course in Germany and Italy. I managed to go through four automobiles—one wrecked, one stolen, one left abandoned by the roadside, and one sold—and several romantic relationships of shorter or longer duration. One observant boss noted that nightlife was impinging on my professional performance and recommended marriage as a corrective.

My memories of these two years are more crowded and intense than of any other time, but the pace could not be sustained. At a party given by the embassy Marine detachment each Friday evening, a fashion designer I had earlier met offered to introduce me to one of his models. I chatted with her for some time in French, only finally grasping that she spoke not a word. I had enough foresight to learn she was Toril Kleivdal from Oslo, and did get a phone number. I telephoned the next day and made a date for dinner. The girl I remembered had long blond hair, but when I arrived at the address she had given me, I was met by someone with hair no longer than mine. And she was living with two men. She assured me that her roommates were romantically entangled with each other, not her. We married on a snowy New Year's Eve in Oslo, Norway, a year later.

THREE

The Seventh Floor

ANY MEMBERS OF THE FOREIGN Service who intended to marry a non-American, even one from a stalwart ally like Norway, were required to submit their resignation upon their engagement. Prospective brides were vetted and the officer's resignation was either accepted or rejected depending on the results of the investigation. Suitability rather than security seemed to be the prime criteria, since the vetting was conducted by the embassy's human resources staff, not by security officers. In the case of female FSOs seeking to marry, their resignation was automatically accepted; no need for an interview. Female officers were required to leave the service even if they were marrying an American; indeed, even if the prospective groom was another Foreign Service officer. The logic of this requirement was that no respectable man could be expected to follow his wife around the world and no married woman could be asked to leave her husband behind.

Toril had no difficulty passing inspection, and my offer to resign was duly rejected. Marriage to a non-American did have one lasting impact on my career, however. With my assignment in Paris drawing to a close, I had applied for Japanese language training, hoping to return to the Far East, where I had spent much of my youth. On my arrival in Washington, I began what was to be an eighteen-month course of Japanese instruction, the last year of which was to take place in Japan. One day into the course I was contacted by the office of personnel. They had realized I intended to marry a foreigner, and the rule at that time, and perhaps still today, was that non-American spouses needed to become American citizens before they could accompany their husbands abroad, since the husband's diplomatic immunity could only be extended to his spouse if she were of the same nationality. This process of naturalization took at least a year, so my assignment to Japan was broken.

I have not regretted this diversion in my career trajectory. Japanese is a very hard language to learn. It is spoken in only one country, and any FSO who takes the time to learn it can expect repeated assignments to that country. But leadership of our Tokyo Embassy is almost exclusively reserved for prominent political figures; Japanese language officers, thus, spend their careers laboring up a steep incline whose summit they can never hope to reach.

Instead I found myself assigned to the department's policy planning staff, a perch with broader perspective. This organization had been set up by George C. Marshall in 1947. Under George Kennan, its first task had been to design what became the Marshall Plan for European reconstruction. Originally made up of only half a dozen members, its size had tripled by the time I arrived. It had also taken on wider responsibilities, to include intradepartmental and interagency coordination. Its director served as one of two State representatives on the National Security Council committee that reviewed studies prior to their submission to the president.

The staff was composed of quite senior officers, many of whom would have preferred to be in more operational positions in the department or in the field. There was no real hierarchy among them; each had his or her (there was one woman) own area of responsibility. I worked directly for the director, Bill Cargo. He had two quite senior deputies, but they were more interested in high policy than integrating the efforts of the staff as a whole. As a result, much of the day-to-day administration fell to me. While I didn't personally plan much policy, I had an unusually wide-ranging view of how others did so, at least within State.

In those days the department was a smaller and less top heavy organization than it has become. It had no deputy secretary, whereas now it has two. It had two under secretaries, whereas now there are five. It also had many fewer assistant secretaries and no special envoys. The planning staff occupied a suite along Mahogany Row, the paneled offices on the building's seventh floor adjacent to that of the secretary. Our principal responsibility was less to actually plan policy and more to strengthen the department's influence over a White House-led planning process. In this we were largely unsuccessful. President Nixon wanted policy to be made in and executed by the White House, and his national security adviser, Henry Kissinger, ensured that it was.

State's tactic for maintaining its autonomy was to engage with Kissinger and his staff only at fairly junior levels. Kissinger's tactic was to launch numerous broadly conceived and time consuming interagency studies that seldom came to any conclusion, while secretly conducting diplomacy on the key issues. These studies were initiated by something called the National Security Study Memorandum, the response to which was a National Security Study, and eventually these studies were supposed to result in a National Security Decision Memorandum. The number of studies underway soon multiplied to more than 100, covering virtually every major foreign policy issue confronting the United States. In theory this process assured that all relevant agencies had an opportunity to contribute to the formulation of policy and, because Kissinger emphasized the need for options rather than recommendations, to provide the president the opportunity to impartially review all the reasonable alternatives.

In fact the process had several additional effects. First, it robbed the State Department and other executive agencies of initiative. By forcing every important issue into a study and, thus, into the National Security Council system, individual agencies were prevented from taking any decisions on their own authority that might foreclose options under consideration. Second, while the process by which these studies were conducted was, in principle, led by the agency with the major interest—for the most part the State Department—in fact, as consideration of the issues moved to higher levels, they were brought before committees chaired by Henry Kissinger. Third, the staff time needed to prepare these documents diverted resources and attention of the executive departments from the actual conduct of foreign policy, which Henry Kissinger increasingly appropriated. Fourth, these studies, when completed, went to the president through Henry Kissinger. He, naturally, relieved the president of reading these lengthy tomes, which could number hundreds of pages, by providing a summary and recommendations for action. Finally, a decision, when it came, was promulgated through Henry Kissinger, sometimes in a National Security Decision Memorandum signed by the president, but increasingly in memos signed on the president's behalf by Henry Kissinger. Many of the studies never resulted in such decisions, however, at least not in decisions that were ever relayed back to State. Rather, Kissinger mined the assembled material for his own diplomatic initiatives.

Among my responsibilities was tracking this whole process for State and maintaining an up-to-date status report on each of the many studies underway. In retrospect this was an empty exercise, but it did require that I familiarize myself with virtually every foreign policy issue on the administration's agenda.

Secretary William Rodgers decided he would issue a public report on American foreign policy, and our staff was assigned responsibility for gathering and integrating the contents from all the relevant bureaus. Before we got very far we learned that the White House would issue the report and we were asked only to provide material for it. Now that this was to be a White House product no one on our staff showed any interest, so it fell to me to spend a Saturday editing the submissions from every bureau in the department into a reasonably coherent product. Henry Kissinger took great pride in the annual reports that eventually emerged, but no one else paid these much heed.

My two years with the planning staff passed agreeably. Toril and I took a one-room apartment directly across the street from the department. We had to move the dining table each night to lower our bed, but I could return home every day for lunch, and I was, perhaps, the only person in the department to have that luxury. Toril went to Americanization school, brushed up her English, and took a part-time job selling Scandinavian furniture. We did our grocery shopping in the basement of the soon-to-be-infamous Watergate Apartments, and on weekends we often took a train to Philadelphia to go see my parents.

The anti-war movement was reaching its apogee and Washington was awash with protesters and police. From our apartment window we could watch the resultant confrontations and even smell the teargas. Walking downtown we would pass the White House; on one occasion it was completely barricaded by a wall of buses parked head to tail around its entire periphery. Weekend evenings we mingled with the more prosperous among the visiting forces of disorder in the bars and restaurants of Georgetown.

In 1967 Secretary Dean Rusk directed the creation of an Open Forum Panel, originally conceived of as a vehicle through which junior officers could devise and bring to his attention innovative policy ideas. Oversight of this panel, originally made up of ten members but later opened to anyone who was interested, fell to the planning staff. None of our senior officers had any interest in this institution, so I became its effective overseer. Inevitably Vietnam was the main topic of discussion and the panel became a vehicle through which dissent could be safely voiced. These expressions had no affect whatever on Vietnam policy, which was not, in any case, being made at State, but it did allow officers to let off steam without ruining their careers.

At this stage I was still green enough to assume that our country's leadership knew what it was doing. I was proud of my military service and knew from my experience in Paris that the United States had made a serious effort to negotiate an end to the war. It was only several years later, after the Pentagon Papers had been published, that I began to realize that even very smart and well-meaning people could make bad decisions.

Another issue raised in the forum was the role of women in the Foreign Service. Alison Palmer was an FSO who had been denied several African postings by ambassadors who said they did not want a woman officer on their staff. When Allison came to speak to the Open Forum Panel session she was in the early stages of organizing a class action suit against the department. At the time I wondered why anyone would fight to go to the places from which she had been excluded. After years of litigation Allison eventually won her suit, and the department was compelled to institute a number of reforms, though by then she had resigned.

Another insight into the role of women in American diplomacy came from a review of officer performance records. Periodically, the personnel system would send my boss the files of individuals they proposed to assign to our staff. Cargo asked me to review these and forward to him only those worthy of consideration. Officers then did not have access to their own performance files, so these evaluations tended to be much more candid than they would become once such access became required. It was quite common for supervisors to comment on the wife of the rated individual. (Female Foreign Service officers, as noted, could not have spouses, and in any case, no women were referred to us for placement, probably because there were none in the service of the necessary rank.) Although unpaid, wives abroad were expected to assist the ambassador's spouse and other more senior wives in charity work and the organization of large social affairs. Doing so gracefully and cheerfully could advance their husband's career. Shirking such duties could have the opposite effect. Supervisors, thus, commented in these performance reviews on the spouse's social graces and even her physical appearance.

Eventually the department responded to mounting protests from younger, perhaps even professionally employed, wives by issuing new guidance forbidding any mention whatsoever of spouses in performance evaluations. It also forbad any effort to pressure spouses into social or other duties. This new guidance initially disconcerted as many as it satisfied, since it meant that wives were henceforth deprived of any recognition for their often substantial and unpaid contribution to our country's representation abroad. They were even sometimes denied the opportunity to contribute, since the more senior spouses now felt inhibited from inviting their assistance. Toril saw both sides of the argument. She happily engaged in official entertainment and was disappointed at not being able to receive recognition for so doing, but she never experienced, and would doubtless have resisted, any compulsion to participate.

As the end of my time with the planning staff neared I was offered an assignment to the American Consulate in Strasbourg. Without the slightest reflection I agreed. One assignment to France had been outrageous good luck. How could two not be even better?

FOUR

Provincial Interlude

SADLY, TRAVEL BY OCEAN LINER had become a thing of the past. The SS *United States* was laid up and would never sail again. I flew to Paris, spent a day at the embassy, then proceeded to Strasbourg. There I discovered that my prospective chief, George Andrews, had just been sacked by our ambassador to France, Arthur K. Watson. It was a sad case. Andrews' father had once been consul general in Strasbourg, and George had spent his early youth here, so he was, naturally, looking forward to filling his father's shoes. He had only just arrived at the post when Watson came for a visit, took an unexplained dislike to him, and insisted he be withdrawn. He and his wife were to depart the day after my arrival.

They kindly had me over for drinks on their last night and passed on what they could in the way of advice. I, thus, became the acting principal officer, and it looked like I would remain such for a while. Fortunately the consulate's local French staff were all highly knowledgeable. There were seven of these—a receptionist, a person handling visas, one preparing passports, another managing general correspondence—all under the direction of the consulate's chief clerk. We also had a combination driver, gardener, and general handyman. The routine business of the consulate was handled by these experienced staff who required little oversight.

This left me a good deal of time for the social and representational aspects of the job. I spent several days each week traveling through Alsace and Lorraine, meeting with mayors, prefects (appointed governors), business leaders, and other local notables. Provincial France was then still very traditional and highly rank conscious. Even a lowly vice consul was to be courteously received, particularly one from the United States; these two provinces had been liberated twice over the past sixty years with the help of American troops. There were a number of beautifully maintained American military cemeteries throughout the region, and one of the most touching aspects of the job was speaking at annual memorial day commemorations. The local French population took these seriously, turning out in large numbers to express their gratitude.

Toril joined me in Strasbourg after spending a few weeks with her family in Norway. Only after several months did George Andrews' replacement arrive. The new consul general, Ron Woods, came out of the Paris political section. He and his wife were only a few years older than Toril and me, and we all became close friends. Several of his former colleagues from Paris visited frequently. Ron and these friends provided me with role models and mentors for what I hoped would be the next stage of my career, while Ron's wife, Judy, introduced Toril to the ways of diplomatic entertainment.

Ron and Judy had a large house a couple of blocks from the consulate where they regularly hosted dinners and receptions. Toril and I lived even closer to the office; in fact, directly above it. We had a well-proportioned apartment on the second floor of the consulate building. In Washington I had been able to come home for lunch; now I could return whenever my coffee cup needed refilling.

Strasbourg was the seat of the Council of Europe, a pan-European (or at least West European) institution. Founded shortly after World War II, the council had been overshadowed by the European Community, which had fewer member states but far more power. Nevertheless, the council had its own parliamentary assembly, which met periodically. It issued reports and produced accords on a range of social, legal, and human rights issues that had application to its wider membership. I reported assiduously on these developments, as I did on local politics, not that anyone in Paris or Washington was very interested in either. Still, it was excellent practice.

After some months we were told our ambassador would be making another visit. Arthur Watson was the oldest son of Thomas Watson, the founder of IBM. Arthur had a reputation as a boozer and a lecher, which may explain why his younger brother was running the family firm while he had been shipped off to Embassy Paris at the cost of some significant campaign contributions. He was known to be an arbitrary and choleric boss. Given that his last visit to Strasbourg had ended the tenure and blighted the career of Ron's predecessor, we awaited his arrival with some trepidation.

The visit could not have gone more smoothly. Watson clearly enjoyed the company of our young and attractive wives, but he was a complete gentleman. He took the four of us to dinner at the best restaurant in eastern France, where we all drank in moderation, and I wondered whether rumor had maligned him. Apparently not. A few months later Jack Anderson, the well-known muckraking columnist, reported in the *Washington Post* that, on a flight from Paris to Washington, Watson "kept shouting for more Scotch, grabbing the stewardesses and trying to stuff money down the front of their blouses" before passing out "sprawled across the first class lounge." In response to a congressional inquiry, Watson admitted he had been "exceedingly but unintentionally rude," though he denied being drunk. He left his post in Paris shortly thereafter. A year later he took a fall and died at age fifty-five.

Life in Strasbourg was pleasant and undemanding. Alsace was a major wine producing region and there were frequent opportunities, official and otherwise, to sample the many varietals it produced. The city bordered the Rhine between two low mountain chains, the Vosges in France and, on the German side of the river, the Black Forest. Hillside vineyards overlooked quaint towns full of timbered houses, and the cuisine combined the best of French and German. Many weekend evenings were spent over meals in quaint towns above the Rhine valley. We had our first child, a son named Christian.

Idyllic as this was, the posting to Strasbourg was neither challenging nor particularly career-enhancing. Progress in the Foreign Service depends heavily on the reputation one establishes, and no matter how spectacularly I performed here, the only person I was going to impress was Ron, who was only a few years more advanced in the service than I. While promotion is based on written evaluations, assignments are based almost entirely on word of mouth. Good assignments well executed led to accelerated promotion, whereas too much time in backwaters like Strasbourg could result in career stagnation.

Two years into what was supposed to be a three-year assignment, I was presented with an unusual opportunity when the European Bureau invited officers in the field to submit papers with new ideas for American policy. The winner would have his contribution circulated throughout the department. Having lots of spare time, I produced a thirty-page paper arguing that the United States should support the emergence of European institutions for foreign and security policy collaboration to promote a more balanced transatlantic partnership. My recommendations were quite premature, anticipating developments and opportunities that were still decades in the future. But the bureau liked the paper and they offered to publish it provided I dropped one proposal. I declined to make the deletion and the paper was, consequently, not circulated.

One of the officers who had read and liked the paper subsequently moved to the Office of Personnel; there he fielded a request from our newly appointed ambassador to the United Nations, John Scali, who asked the department to send him a speechwriter. Recalling my paper, this officer called to ask whether I was interested. On getting a positive response, he advised me to drop whatever I was doing and drive the very next morning to Geneva.

Scali was in Geneva for a meeting of the UN's Economic and Social Council. He greeted me on the lawn of an official mission residence located on a bluff overlooking the city. Lemonade was served. It was a sunny, late-summer day and we watched the huge jet of water, some fifty meters high, spurt from the middle of the harbor. Scali handed me a draft of a speech he was to give. He was unhappy with what his staff had prepared and challenged me to do better. I was given an office in the U.S. mission, where I spent most of that night producing a new version. Despite my almost complete lack of familiarity with the subject matter, this effort passed muster and Scali told me to report to New York forthwith.

FIVE

On Turtle Bay

JOHN SCALI HAD BEEN A reporter for the Associated Press and then ABC News. In this latter capacity he had played a minor role in the diplomacy surrounding the Cuban Missile Crisis of 1962, where he acted as go-between, conveying messages between the Kremlin's top intelligence official in Washington and the White House. These communications played a role in eventually defusing the confrontation. Some years later President Nixon, unhappy with all the unfavorable press attention his national security adviser was receiving, brought Scali into the White House to help burnish the president's own image as the real architect of American foreign policy. In this capacity Scali orchestrated the public aspects of Nixon's breakthrough visit to China. This performance landed him the UN job and, with it, a seat in the cabinet.

Scali had spent thirty years as a diplomatic correspondent, more than ten years of that on network television. I was, therefore, surprised to find him remarkably insecure before any sort of audience. In circumstances where others might have adlibbed a presentation, Scali required a script, which he generally stuck to word-for-word. As long as he had a prepared text, he was a powerful speaker, which is a good thing, as public speaking was a big part of his job. Preparing several such scripts each week became a big part of mine.

Writing these remarks was hard work. It required some familiarity with the topic, a facility with words, and a lot of rewriting. There was a satisfaction, however, in having one's prose become the public expression of American policy. There was also an occasional ability to shape the content of these pronouncements in meaningful ways. The political and economic sections of the mission chafed at my refusal to allow them to review the final drafts I provided Scali. I could, therefore, occasionally slip in a phrase or two that took things a bit further than my more cautious colleagues would have preferred.

I was eager to do more than write speeches, and I persuaded Scali to extend my portfolio to the full range of staff duties. This involved me, albeit largely as an observer and facilitator, in everything the mission was doing. As with the tour in the policy planning staff, my two years in New York provided and, indeed, demanded familiarity with the broad sweep of American foreign policy.

The United Nations was an exciting place to work. The site, with its world famous glass slab overlooking the East River at Turtle Bay, was striking. The building hosted dozens of meetings daily and was filled with an exotic mix of diplomats from the world over. During the General Assembly each September the corridors teamed with heads of state. The delegates' lounge and dining room were elegant settings with river views, open to even the most junior of those accredited to the organization. General Assembly meetings were one boring speech after another, but debates in the smaller Security Council chamber could be unscripted, spirited, and consequential.

I found multilateral diplomacy more varied and eventful than the conduct of relations in a single country. Even in a large and prestigious post like Paris the ambassador was essentially a messenger. Important negotiations were handled directly between officials dispatched from capitals. Even senior embassy staff were either reporting on local events or preparing the ambassador for his next meeting. At the United Nations, by contrast, real bargains were being struck in multiple venues on many different topics each day. Some of these bargains were procedural in nature, or of trivial importance, but the sheer volume of committee meetings meant that relatively junior officers could find themselves representing the United States and negotiating on its behalf. Most decisions were taken by majority vote, which meant that one's side either carried the day or not. It was, thus, possible to tally successes and failures in a way not generally possible in a bilateral post.

Toril and I arrived in New York in the spring of 1973 with our six-month-old son. We were fortunate to secure a city-subsidized apartment in Brooklyn Heights, located minutes by car from the UN. We even had a partial view of the Manhattan skyline from our balcony. With the luxury of underground parking both at home and at work, I also had one of the shorter commutes in New York: over the Brooklyn Bridge, up FDR Drive, and into the UN garage. I was surprised someone at my level of income would qualify for subsidized housing until I learned that one of the U.S. mission's five ambassadors was also in a "middle income" city-subsidized building. Only in New York!

The United Nations did not normally work on weekends, and my position carried with it no entertainment duties. Toril and I, thus, had plenty of time to enjoy the city and surrounding countryside. I particularly enjoyed revisiting places recalled from my childhood: Prospect Park, the Botanical Gardens, and the Brooklyn Museum. Parts of the borough were in severe urban decline, but it still had some lovely show pieces.

There were a few all-absorbing crises during my tenure, including the 1973 Middle East Yom Kippur War and the 1974 Turkish invasion of Cyprus. The Security Council and, thus, Scali were heavily involved in the diplomacy that ended both conflicts. The Yom Kippur War sparked the Arab oil embargo, which caused brief but painful gasoline shortages in the United States. It also resulted in a major and enduring spike in oil prices. In the midst of this embargo, Yasser Arafat, the head of the Palestinian Liberation Organization, chose to visit New York and address the General Assembly. Arafat personified for Americans the Palestinian terrorist attacks on Israeli, European, and American targets, including, most notably, the previous summer's attack on the Munich Olympics that killed eleven Israeli athletes. Police authorities were so concerned for his safety they closed the Long Island Expressway during both the morning and evening commutes to get him in and out of town safely, thereby further endearing him and his cause to New Yorkers.

The American people paid more attention to the hostile rhetoric in the General Assembly than the quiet diplomacy in the Security Council.

Negotiations in the latter forum had been essential in heading off a U.S.-Soviet confrontation during the Yom Kippur War, and keeping the peace between two American allies, Greece and Turkey, during the Cyprus crisis. But Arafat's visit more than undid any credit the UN might have received for successes of this sort.

These international crises were overshadowed by the emerging Watergate scandal and the slow unraveling of Richard Nixon's presidency. Scali had come out of that White House and kept in touch with many of his former colleagues, including Chuck Colson, who was personally implicated in the break-in and cover-up, and Henry Kissinger. Scali nominally worked for Secretary of State William Rodgers, but he often turned to Kissinger when he didn't like the guidance he was getting from State. Divided oversight gave Scali considerable freedom of action, but this changed in September 1973, when Kissinger replaced Rodgers as secretary of state while retaining his White House position. Now Scali had one boss, and a demanding one at that.

Kissinger visited the UN shortly after taking up his new office, and I was asked to greet and chat with his eighty-six-year-old father, Louis Kissinger, who lived in the city, while he waited to see his son. I also had my first encounter with the secretary, sitting in as the note-taker in one of his meetings. I was forewarned that Kissinger insisted on verbatim records of his conversations, jokes and all. Forty years later, when I called on Kissinger in his New York office, there was still a young man in attendance taking down every one of our inconsequential words.

With Nixon's resignation Scali's friends in the White House went back into private life or to jail. Not long thereafter Scali himself was replaced. Shortly before this occurred I received a call from a young Foreign Service officer I had never met. Robert Blackwill introduced himself, said he was an assistant to Kissinger's top Soviet and European adviser, Hal Sonnenfeldt, and asked if I would replace him in that position. Bob painted a glowing picture of Sonnenfeldt's importance and the responsibilities I would inherit, so I agreed.

Scali kept in touch thereafter, taking me to lunch in his favorite Italian restaurant once or twice a year. I admired him for the tireless efforts he had made to explain the importance of the United Nations to skeptical American audiences. This was a thankless task, and one many of his successors failed to take up. On the contrary, Daniel Patrick Moynihan, Scali's immediate replacement, began a tradition of UN bashing that was continued by Jean Kirkpatrick and, much later, by John Bolton. This was bad diplomacy but good politics. It certainly served Moynihan well. After only seven months on the job, he resigned to run for senator from New York, succeeding in large measure on the basis of his performance at the UN.

SIX

Upstairs

WHEN I ARRIVED BACK IN Washington in 1975 Henry Kissinger was both secretary of state and national security adviser. He kept offices in both the White House and State and ran both institutions through a small cadre of trusted aides, to the extent that he trusted anyone. One of these was Helmut (Hal) Sonnenfeldt, counselor of the department. Hal oversaw relations with Europe and the Soviet Union. Under Secretary for Political Affairs Joseph Sisco handled the rest of the world. I was one of three assistants to Sonnenfeldt. I was responsible for Western Europe, Bill Shinn for the Soviet bloc, and John Kelly for arms control issues, most notably the ongoing Strategic Arms Limitation Talks (SALT).

All communications between the secretary and the bureaus, which were located on the sixth floor and below, came through either Sonnenfeldt or Sisco. The latter had more countries and issues, but Sonnenfeldt handled the matters that Kissinger cared most about. Depending on the topic, one of Hal's three aides would prepare a note from Sonnenfeldt to go on top of any memo to Kissinger from the floors below. This note would summarize the content and recommend a response. If Sonnenfeldt was not around and the matter urgent, we would initial the memo for him and send it on to the secretary. Kissinger's responses went through a reverse process, being passed back to us and then on to the relevant bureau or not, depending on the contents.

Our approval was also required for any outgoing policy instruction to the field. One of us would screen, approve, or, more rarely, hold each outgoing telegram for Sonnenfeldt to review.

Our office also handled initial arrangements for Kissinger's travel. Sonnenfeldt would come back from a meeting with the secretary to say, for instance, "Henry wants to go to Paris, Bonn, and London next week. Check on availabilities." I would then call the three relevant Washington ambassadors and ask them to confirm that their ministers and government heads would be available. Only once the itinerary was set and the most important appointments confirmed would the European Bureau and the relevant American embassies be informed of the forthcoming travel.

Layering and secrecy are characteristic of any organization, particularly ones conducting diplomacy, but Kissinger took these to extremes not seen before or since. A level of clandestine behavior that may have been appropriate when slipping into Paris for assignations with the North Vietnamese or traveling undetected into Red China had become standard practice. This affected the morale of everyone in the department, who knew their judgment and discretion were not trusted. There was, nevertheless, some utility to his approach to bureaucracy. Kissinger tended to be indiscreet in conversation, both with his staff and with foreign officials. Wider dissemination of some of his wittier sallies or, in the case of contacts with his staff, enraged rebukes could be embarrassing. Restricting access allowed Kissinger to give wider range to this wit and ire. Filtering staff policy recommendations through another level of review also provided him a crisper product more attuned to his actual needs. Subjecting all outgoing instructions to centralized clearance ensured that these reflected his unacknowledged as well as his admitted intentions.

However unhappy this made the rest of the building, it clearly gave my junior colleagues and me great access and unusual influence. The record of Kissinger's conversations with Soviet Ambassador Anatoly Dobrynin, for instance, would be sent to our office but disseminated further only in bits and pieces. For particularly sensitive meetings only Sonnenfeldt or one of his assistants would attend and take the notes. Often enough the follow-up and resultant diplomacy would also be handled by Sonnenfeldt, leaving the rest of the building and our missions abroad in the dark.

Helmut (Hal) Sonnenfeldt was a difficult boss. He was under enormous pressure, and Kissinger was famously impatient, not to say intemperate. He regularly harangued and even humiliated his closest associates. Hal often came back from a session with the secretary in an irritable and demanding mood. He never yelled at us, despite having likely been subjected to such treatment himself, but he did complain, criticize, and press for better, faster performance.

Sonnenfeldt was often referred to as Kissinger's Kissinger. They were both Jewish refugees and had both fled Germany in 1938. They both had German as their first language, although only Kissinger, who was a few years older, retained the accent. Both became American citizens in 1944, both joined the U.S. Army, and both served in Germany. After the war both became military intelligence agents there. Both went on to get advanced degrees, after which Kissinger joined the faculty at Harvard while Sonnenfeldt became head of the Soviet division in the State Department's intelligence bureau. They first met in Germany and kept in touch thereafter, and Sonnenfeldt was among the first recruits to Kissinger's National Security Council staff.

Despite these similarities in background and early connections, I never had the sense that the relationship was particularly close. Certainly it did nothing to shield Hal from Kissinger's impatience, which was regularly passed on to us in a somewhat muted form.

My most important task was to write several memos every day to Kissinger, often covering something from the sixth floor, but sometimes they stood on their own. These notes had to be prepared quickly, to avoid the delay of necessary decisions or not to miss deadlines imposed by Kissinger or his immediate staff. Often Hal was not readily available to review and approve our work, in which case we were empowered to forge his signature and send the memo on. This was particularly necessary on Saturday mornings, when Hal played tennis while the rest of us, not just in his office but throughout most of the sixth and seventh floors, were at work. We did our best to conceal Hal's absence from Kissinger by having the office perform as if he were present.

This ruse may have fooled Kissinger, but not his immediate staffers, who helped preserve the illusion that everything important was being done personally by the secretary's top subordinates even as they worked with the wider circle of more junior officials to keep the policy machine functioning. Kissinger, though a demanding and frequently abusive boss, was able to recruit and retain an extraordinarily bright and competent staff. Larry Eagleburger, his closest aide, had recently been moved from running Kissinger's immediate office to become under secretary for management, thus putting him in charge of the department's administrative apparatus. Jerry Bremer moved up to head Kissinger's personal staff, assisted by David Gompert and Alvin Adams.

These junior officers exercised considerable power, occasionally to the discomfort of their nominal superiors. Bremer and Gompert would schedule meetings with Kissinger on Sonnenfeldt's issues for Saturday mornings when they knew Hal planned to play tennis. They would even tease Kissinger. One morning Gompert ostentatiously handed Sonnenfeldt a paper, in front of the secretary, saying, "Hal, here is the memo for your meeting with the president this afternoon." As expected, Kissinger grabbed the memo away from Hal and insisted on rearranging his schedule so he could attend the session with the president instead of Hal.

Eventually fed up with this high-handed treatment, Sonnenfeldt and Sisco jointly complained to the secretary about the disrespectful behavior of his junior staffers. After hearing out his two most senior advisers, Kissinger called Bremer, Gompert, and Adams into his office. "I don't know what you three are doing," he said in his deep, sonorous voice, "but I want you to keep it up."

Hal never took exception to anything written and sent in his name, nor did he often modify work prepared for his signature. I liked to think this was a credit to my judgment and insight, but I also recognized that Hal's overarching priority was to retain the privilege of being the last and most influential contributor to anything going to the secretary, even if he was not personally available to provide it.

As I took up my new responsibilities, the thirty-five-nation Conference on Security and Cooperation in Europe was nearing completion of an agreement that had been under negotiation for the preceding three years. The Kremlin had sought implicit recognition of the then-European borders, including the parts of Germany, Poland, Finland, and the totality of the three Baltic states annexed by the Soviet Union after World War II. The West Europeans had secured in exchange Soviet and East European undertakings to respect basic human and civil rights. Kissinger had never been enthusiastic about the process. It was something the Soviets and the

Europeans wanted, with which he went along grudgingly, extracting such concessions as he could on the way. As these talks moved toward a conclusion, the looming accord became more controversial in the United States, particularly among our East European ethnic lobbies.

Within days of my arrival I was being asked to clear final instructions to our negotiators. Kissinger, in his usual fashion, was conducting parallel conversations on the topic with Dobrynin, the contents of which were shared only with our office. Our task was to make sure that the U.S. representatives in the multilateral negotiations then underway in Geneva were acting in conformity with Kissinger's private undertakings with Moscow without our revealing that these existed.

In late July I flew to Helsinki to await the arrival of President Ford, Kissinger, Hal, and other White House staffers. Ford was to join thirty-four other leaders for two days of speeches expected to conclude with the signature of what came to be known as the Helsinki Final Act. My function on trips with the president or secretary was to staff Hal for any issues that might arise, and relay his and Kissinger's instructions to officials in Washington or elsewhere that emerged from whatever conversations ensued. This required that I wake well before Hal to review all the overnight communications and be ready to brief him on the most important issues before he went off to do the same for his superiors. This also meant staying up after the end of everyone else's day to carry out whatever assignments Hal imparted on his return from official dinners or late-night meetings. During the day there was a lot of waiting around to be available between meetings for new instructions that might emerge.

This routine could become tedious; hurry up and wait all day and only a few hours of sleep each night. On this trip, however, there were compensating diversions. Helsinki was an attractive, compact city built on the water. The weather was the perfection of a Scandinavian summer, with crystal clear skies and warm sun moderated by a gentle sea breeze. Most of my day was spent at the conference center, where I was able to rub shoulders with the world's most prominent statesmen; at one point I literally bumped into Canadian prime minister Pierre Elliot Trudeau. Watching the arrival of Soviet leader Leonid Brezhnev was a special treat. His motorcade of half a dozen identical, long, black ZILs swept into the circle fronting the conference center and stopped simultaneously in a beautifully synchronized movement. A dozen doors opened simultaneously, from which emerged a small, carefully choreographed army of identically dressed, gun-toting security men followed by the general secretary.

Kissinger took the view that his staff should not travel with their own staff. Hal was at pains, therefore, to disguise from Henry that anyone from his own office was in attendance. At one point I was walking from our hotel to the conference center carrying Sonnenfeldt's briefcase when I saw Kissinger, surrounded by half a dozen staffers and security agents, walking toward me. Striding alongside him was Hal, who, I was momentarily confused to see, was also carrying a briefcase. The future flashed before me. If I were fortunate enough to reach the height of my profession, thirty years hence, I might graduate from carrying the counselor's briefcase to carrying the secretary's.

Hal, seeing me approach, made surreptitious hand signals warning me to sheer off. We passed in the street as if strangers, with Henry, Hal, and the others going in one direction while I continued in the other until they moved out of sight. Years later I recounted this story to Kissinger. "Pure paranoia," he replied, implying that this was Hal's failing rather than his.

Hal asked me to work with Kissinger's speechwriter, Peter Rodman, on the draft of President Ford's remarks to the conference. Peter, not surprisingly, deflected my offer to assist. I secured a copy the following morning, and after a quick perusal I informed Sonnenfeldt that it was hopelessly soft, a paean to détente without a trace of support for greater freedoms and respect for human rights. These latter issues had become a hallmark of the Conference on Security and Cooperation in Europe (CSCE) negotiations and occupied a significant place in the document Ford was there to endorse. Hal took the draft and, along with one of Ford's top aides, Robert Hartman, spent the morning toughening up the language.

In later years the Helsinki Final Act was to become an important touchstone for dissidents throughout the Soviet empire, giving them a document they could cite, signed by their top leaders, that committed them to standards that were not being met. The CSCE process continued, one review conference after another, throughout the Cold War and beyond, providing a continuous forum for advancing human rights, promoting the peaceful settlement of disputes, and fostering European-wide arms control.

Kissinger's commitment to détente did not extend to West European communists. He was concerned, not without reason, that one or more of these parties might ride the wave of improving East-West relations into power. The strongest and also the most moderate of the Western Communist parties was the Italian group. Its leadership had criticized the 1968 Soviet invasion of Czechoslovakia, sought alliances with the non-Communist left, and managed to gain more than 34 percent of the vote in the 1976 Italian elections. Next in strength was the French Communist Party, which routinely racked up more than 20 percent of the vote while hewing much more closely to the Moscow party line. Communists also controlled both countries' strongest labor union confederation. It had been the French Communist-run trade union that initiated the general strike in 1968 that nearly toppled the Fifth Republic.

Kissinger's immediate concern was Portugal. A year earlier a group of junior military officers had staged a bloodless coup, overturning the authoritarian government that had ruled the country since the 1930s. These officers ranged from left to far left in political orientation, and they brought both the Socialist and Communist parties into the government. Kissinger saw the entry of Communists as a profound threat to the North Atlantic Treaty Organization (NATO), of which Portugal was a founding member. He went so far as to say that he would prefer a Communist-dominated Portugal outside NATO to a Communist-influenced one inside. Accordingly, the United States began to insist on excluding Portugal from more sensitive NATO discussions. Another, probably even greater, concern was the effect American toleration of a Communist or Communist-Socialist government in Portugal could have on the political dynamics of Italy and France, where a similar development could have far more serious implications for Western cohesion.

Kissinger tended to see events in Portugal through the lens of Salvador Allende's rise in Chile, which was cut short by a military coup that had received some American support. To his face he accused Mario Soares, then Portugal's foreign minister and head of its Socialist party, of being "another Kerensky," the Russian revolutionary leader who preceded Lenin. "I don't want to be a Kerensky," protested Soares. "Neither did Kerensky," responded Kissinger.

Frank Carlucci, the American ambassador in Lisbon, sought to dissuade Kissinger from further efforts to punish and isolate Portugal, arguing that the situation was very fluid, the Communists were not in a dominant position, and that, given time, more moderate forces would prevail. Our office became the buffer between the secretary and Embassy Lisbon. I was busy drafting and occasionally signing Hal's name to memos to Kissinger explaining what was going on in Lisbon and urging that Carlucci be given further time and leeway to manage the situation. Sonnenfeldt was of the same view and successfully moderated Kissinger's behavior, undoubtedly enduring several tirades in the process.

This was Sonnenfeldt's usual role. Far from being Kissinger, as he appeared to many, he was a more pragmatic and steady version of his chief. Of course he could not allow this to become widely known and so, for most, he remained simply a junior version of his boss.

Sonnenfeldt led efforts to persuade key allied governments to aid the Portuguese Socialists, which, like Carlucci and unlike Kissinger, he saw as an essential counterweight to the Communists. Of particular utility in this regard were those allies that had Socialist governments of their own, notably the United Kingdom and Germany. These governments could funnel aid to the Portuguese Socialists on a party-to-party basis, in a quiet but overt fashion. Providing assistance in this manner avoided the risks inherent in covert funding via intelligence agencies, which often became public to the discredit of both recipient and donor. Such party-to-party assistance to Portugal was the beginning of a much wider and still very active effort to assist democratic parties in countries emerging from dictatorship by employing political party channels. In subsequent years, such assistance would become important first in Spain's transition to democracy and later throughout Eastern Europe. Eventually both American political parties and all the major German political parties established independent but government-funded institutes explicitly designed for the support of democratic movements abroad.

In November the Portuguese fever broke. An abortive coup by far left officers was parried by a counter-coup led by more moderate military leaders, one of whom was, subsequently, elected president. Parliamentary elections were held early in 1976 in which the Socialists came out ahead. Soares became prime minister and Portugal was on its way to becoming a fully consolidated democracy.

Transatlantic consultations over the crisis in Portugal highlighted once again the lack of any channel other than the bilateral for concerted Western action on sensitive issues that fell outside the essentially military purview of NATO. With the opening to China behind him and peace thought to be at hand in Vietnam, Henry Kissinger declared 1973 to be the "Year of Europe," and proposed the drawing up of a new Atlantic Charter. European leaders found having a year set aside especially for them rather patronizing, as if every year were not the year of Europe, and they did not respond with enthusiasm. The United States and Europe took divergent paths during that year's Yom Kippur War. The Europeans sought to remain uninvolved while Nixon and Kissinger went all out in support of Israel, even to the point of placing American nuclear forces in Europe on high alert without any prior notice or consultation with the countries where these weapons were located. European leaders were further nettled by a query attributed to Kissinger: "If I want to talk to Europe, who do I call?"

The Year of Europe was a bust. Two years later, however, while we were all in Helsinki, French President Giscard d'Estaing and German Chancellor Helmut Schmidt had a private word with Kissinger suggesting the convening of an exclusive summit meeting involving only Britain, France, Germany, the United States, and Japan. Giscard and Schmidt saw this as an opportunity to coordinate economic and financial policies, as both their countries were in the midst of their worst economic recession since the 1930s.

Kissinger responded favorably and instructed Sonnenfeldt to follow up. Hal, accordingly, began consultations that led to each of the five leaders appointing a personal representative to prepare for the summit. Kissinger persuaded George Shultz, former secretary of the treasury under Richard Nixon, to represent President Ford. Shultz was at the time head of the Bechtel Corporation, one of the world's largest construction companies. He was willing to attend a few meetings on behalf of the president but not to do the reporting and the follow-up. Accordingly, Sonnenfeldt would attend the meetings with him. The other Sherpas, as those who prepared these summits came to be called, attended alone, so only the United States was allowed two participants.

Before preparations for the summit advanced very far, the Italians got wind of what was afoot and mounted an intense campaign to be included. The French and British were resistant, but there was more sympathy in Washington. In the end it fell to me to inform a very relieved Italian ambassador that his prime minister would be welcome to attend. This led the Canadians, the next largest Western economy, to mount their own campaign. Canada did not make the first summit, but was included in subsequent ones. Thus, the G-7 was born.

The main point of controversy at this first summit was a Franco-American debate over fixed versus floating exchange rates; the French preferred the former, the Americans the latter. These and other issues on the largely economic agenda were well beyond my comfort zone. Sonnenfeldt insisted on overseeing preparations for the meeting, however, and I was his instrument to do so. This meant dealing with government officials far more senior and knowledgeable than I, but once Hal seized an issue, he never let go.

The final Sherpa meeting was to take place in London two days before the summit. Hal wanted to stay in Washington for a preparatory meeting with the president, so he dispatched me to accompany Shultz to London. The Sherpas met in Admiralty House, the former residence of the First Lord of Admiralty, located a few hundred yards from the prime minister's residence on Downing Street. Again, all the Sherpas except Shultz were unaccompanied, and all were very senior. One, Raymond Barre, went on to become prime minister of France. I was interested to see how they all deferred to Shultz. After several hours of discussion, the group agreed they should provide their chiefs with a draft communiqué for the forthcoming meeting. Looking around for someone to set pen to paper, our British host suggested I should produce a text for them to work from. Shultz sensed this was well beyond my capacity, and he offered to do the draft himself. He withdrew to an adjoining room, returning fifteen minutes later with a draft that was only modestly revised before being issued two days later by the five leaders at the French president's country chateau of Rambouillet.

As we drove back to our hotel I reviewed with Shultz how I proposed to report the discussion. He nodded, suggesting no amendment. Throughout our day and a half together, I found him taciturn and perhaps a bit distracted. After dropping Shultz off, I went to the embassy to file my report of the Sherpas' discussion and transmit the draft communiqué. By the time I arrived back in Washington, President Ford and his party, including Sonnenfeldt, were on their way to France.

The Rambouillet meeting became the first of annual summits that continue to this day. Over time preparation for these has become much more elaborate, the Sherpas meeting frequently throughout the year, supported by sub-Sherpas and teams of experts. I am not sure the results are any more substantial, but the communiqués are certainly much longer. Though these meetings have become somewhat formulaic, they continue to offer an opportunity for the West's top leaders to meet and discuss the most pressing issues of the day, and this alone is probably worthwhile.

Hal was also responsive for institutionalizing a second, even more exclusive and very confidential forum for transatlantic consultation alongside the G-7. The foreign ministers of the United States, the United Kingdom, France, and Germany began meeting twice a year, supported by more frequent meetings of their four political directors, the position in most European foreign ministries responsible for overseeing political and security relations. The American equivalent was the under secretary of state for political affairs, but that official, at least during Sonnenfeldt's tenure, was not even told that this new forum had been created.

These Quad meetings, as they came to be called, were held in great secrecy lest other European governments learn of their existence and clamor for participation, as had already happened with the economic summits. So great was the sensitivity that the first several meetings of the four political directors were held not in any of the foreign ministries but rather in the private homes of the host political director. Again the three European officials came unaccompanied, but Hal insisted on bringing me. In exchange for this privilege, Hal agreed I would provide a record of the discussions to all four participants.

Political directors began to meet every couple of months, while the ministers gathered in this format on the fringes of a semiannual gathering of NATO foreign ministers. Efforts were made to keep the minister meetings quiet, but this was more difficult, as they all had large entourages and accompanying journalists. As cover, it was explained that their discussions were restricted to Berlin-related issues, the city still technically being under four power occupation and, thus, outside NATO territory.

These Quad talks ranged widely across the whole field of East, West, and transatlantic relations, actually spending little time on Berlin issues. Two matters in particular occupied the early discussions: Euro-communism and Yugoslavia. It was in this setting that the four governments began discussing what might be done if Communists came to power in a NATO country, and also how to help their democratic opponents, notably in Portugal and later in Spain.

Related to Yugoslavia, the issue was what might happen on the death of its long-serving president, Josip Broz Tito, then eighty-three years old. The concern was less for the internal stability of the country than for the Soviet reaction. A Soviet military invasion, on the models of its 1956 intervention in Hungary and 1968 invasion of Czechoslovakia, was thought a distinct possibility. Kissinger wanted to get the major European allies thinking about how they might react in such circumstances, so he enlisted General Alexander Haig in this effort. Haig had been Kissinger's top deputy at the National Security Council. He had gone on to become Nixon's last chief of staff and, subsequently, supreme allied commander of Europe, the top American and allied officer in Europe. Haig sent an American general from his staff to brief the political directors on the military options in responding to a Soviet thrust into Yugoslavia. Neither Kissinger nor Haig seemed to have informed anyone in the Department of Defense of these discussions, although some of the political directors probably consulted with their own militaries. Interestingly, it was the French director who proved the most robust, frankly acknowledging the possibility of French military participation in such an operation. Given that France had several years earlier withdrawn from NATO's military command structure, this was an encouraging evolution.

These conversations continued for a couple of years, during which Tito showed no signs of expiring. I noted after several such discussions that we faced three possibilities. Either Tito would die and the Soviets would invade, or Tito would die and the Soviets would not invade, or Tito would not die. Ultimately, of course, he did die, in 1980. Fifteen years later it was not the Soviet Union but NATO that invaded.

It is a truism of Foreign Service reporting that no one ever comes off second best in his own record of a conversation. The note-taker's job is to capture the brilliance of one's superior's presentation while summarizing the main points of the others. Since I was the common reporter for these conversations, I had the harder task of making all four of the principals look good. The German political director told me that his foreign minister regularly requested and read the transcripts of these meetings, and he thanked me for reporting not what he actually said but what his minister would have wanted him to say.

This forum remained the principal channel for sensitive transatlantic consultation throughout the Cold War. In the 1990s, as the disintegration of Yugoslavia became the dominant issue, Italy was added and the Quad became the Quint, serving as a Western steering group throughout that decade's Balkan wars.

Accompanying Hal on his travels taught its own lessons. On one occasion, landing in Europe with a tight onward connection, he was exasperated to discover I had checked my bag. Impatient as always, he left me at the carousel. It took me half a day to finally catch up with him. I have not checked luggage since.

The first few times we accompanied Kissinger Hal sent me ahead, flying commercially, to meet him at the destination so as to conceal from the secretary that he was traveling with a staffer of his own. This became very cumbersome on multi-stop trips, as I would either have to leave one place early to get to the next on time or arrive at the next destination quite late. Eventually Sonnenfeldt relented and allowed me to join him on the secretary's plane. He warned me, however, to stay out of the secretary's way. Kissinger, he explained, was wont to walk down the plane's aisle pointedly asking anyone he did not recognize, "Who are you?"

Eventually such a moment arose. I was in the back of the plane playing liars poker with several of the accompanying journalists. Kissinger walked back, knelt facing rearward on the seat directly in front of me, and struck up a conversation with the group. Either he thought I was a new addition to the press pool or, more likely, concluded that the journalists had befriended me. He smiled, included me in the conversation, and never objected when he encountered me on later trips.

Back in Washington, State received a request from the White House to provide a draft speech by President Ford on foreign policy. Writing speeches normally fell to Winston Lord, head of the policy planning staff. Winston was unwilling to spend time on a draft that the White House speech writers would almost certainly redo, so he tried to pass the task off to Hal, who demurred but volunteered me. This done, the two of them walked off to lunch together, having provided no guidance whatsoever regarding the contents. For the rest of the day I struggled to compose a credible exposition of the Ford administration's foreign policy, feeling quite inadequate to the task. My effort was shipped off to the White House unmodified. Several days later I was pleased that a sentence or two survived in Ford's actual address.

During my early months with Sonnenfeldt, Henry Kissinger continued to serve as both secretary of state and national security adviser. Sonnenfeldt still functioned as a member of both organizations, and our office stocked both White House and State Department stationery. Hal sent memos to Kissinger on one letterhead or the other depending on where he wanted the resultant paper delivered.

This arrangement was clearly disadvantageous to James Schlesinger, secretary of state, who found Kissinger the national security adviser adjudicating his differences with Kissinger the secretary of state. This was particularly galling when it related to ongoing nuclear arms negotiations with the Soviet Union. Schlesinger felt Kissinger was making too many concessions in his effort to conclude a successor agreement to the original strategic arms accord that had been signed in 1972. Sonnenfeldt was Kissinger's principal adviser on these issues, and our office would craft the State position. Then, working through Hal's former colleagues on the National Security Council (NSC) staff, we would formulate NSC staff advice to the president. Ford would, thus, get a package containing dueling memos from Schlesinger and Kissinger covered by a memo from Kissinger advising him which course to choose.

The conflict between Kissinger and Schlesinger eventually reached an intensity that caused President Ford to fire Schlesinger and deprive Kissinger of his White House position. In his place Ford elevated Lieutenant General Brent Scowcroft, who had been serving as Kissinger's deputy. That this was more than just a nominal transfer of power became evident in a conversation I overheard between Kissinger and Scowcroft as a group of us moved from one meeting to another. Kissinger explained how he wanted an issue handled. Scowcroft quietly but firmly demurred, explaining how the president wished it managed differently.

By this time Kissinger's star was waning. South Vietnam had fallen earlier in the year, and Kissinger was now being attacked by liberals for having prolonged that war, by conservatives for having ended it on disadvantageous terms, and by both sides for his efforts at rapprochement with the Soviet Union.

In early 1976 Kissinger convened a meeting in London of American ambassadors from across Europe. On the second day, after Kissinger had departed, there was a further discussion of Soviet and American policy toward Eastern Europe led by Sonnenfeldt. Hal expressed regret that the Soviet Union had not achieved an "organic" relationship with the Eastern European states such as the United States had with Western Europe. Hal argued that Europe would be more stable if the USSR did not have to hold its satellites down by force, that a consensual relationship between the Soviet Union and its East European neighbors based on perceived mutual interest would lead to a more peaceful environment. "So it must be our policy to strive for an evolution that makes the relationship between the East Europeans and the Soviet Union an organic one," Hal concluded.

This was a controversial argument, but not as controversial as the one with which he was eventually charged. Some days later, back in Washington, the European Bureau brought for my clearance a telegram to all European posts reporting this discussion. I found the account accurate but, nevertheless, brought it to Hal's attention, pointing to the passage referring to his expression of regret that the Soviet Union had not formed a more organic relationship with the states of Eastern Europe. I asked him whether he really wanted this included in the report. Hal read through the relevant passage and initialed his approval.

Before returning the cable to the European Bureau for transmission, I checked to ensure that it was classified Secret and designated for extremely limited distribution (EXDIS, in department parlance). This would offer some protection against it falling into the wrong hands. I did not, however, think to also have it also marked STADIS, which would further limit distribution to State Department addressees only. Without that marking the message would also go to the White House, Defense Department, and the CIA.

On March 22, three months after the London meeting, Rowland Evans and Robert Novak, two prominent Washington newspaper columnists, published an article quoting, or rather misquoting, from this telegram. The article stated that "Henry Kissinger's right hand man declared in a secret briefing that permanent organic union between the Soviet Union and Eastern Europe is necessary to prevent World War III." The story went the twentieth-century equivalent of viral. Sonnenfeldt, Kissinger, and Ford were lambasted from both right and left for selling out Eastern Europe for the sake of détente with Moscow. The 1976 presidential election campaign was already heating up, and Ford's opponents in both parties would make good use of what became known as the Sonnenfeldt Doctrine to characterize Ford as soft on communism. Later in the year Ford compounded his problem by inexplicably declaring, in a debate with Jimmy Carter, that Poland was free of Russian domination.

The Evans and Novak story was intentionally inaccurate. The reporters had a copy of the cable and knew exactly what Hal said. Sonnenfeldt never used the words *permanent* or *union*, nor did he mean to imply either. The term *organic* can have several meanings; one is *unitary* as in an organic whole, but another is *natural* as in organic foods. Hal clearly meant *natural*, in the sense of voluntary, not enforced. Nor had he said that such a relationship needed to be permanent, nor that it was necessary to prevent World War III. Hal had employed a poor choice of words to put forward a debatable proposition, but he had not said or meant what Evans and Novak alleged.

Yet the damage was done. To their credit neither Kissinger nor Ford disowned Hal or his remarks. Kissinger explained that Hal had been misinterpreted and that he, Kissinger, had no disagreement with what Hal had actually said. He added, during a press conference, that "if there were truly a new doctrine of this administration it wouldn't be named after Sonnenfeldt."

Many years later I recalled these events to Kissinger, and he confirmed that he had no disagreement with what Sonnenfeldt had said. He went on, however, to comment that Hal need not to have said it. He felt he had adequately dealt with the topic during the first day of the chiefs of mission conference, he told me, but had acceded to Sonnenfeldt's desire to address the issues as well, suggesting Sonnenfeldt hold another session with the assembled ambassadors on the second day to do so.*

As a result of this controversy, Hal became a non-person for the rest of the Ford administration. He continued to do his job as usual, but was kept rigorously out of the public eye. An early sign of his pariah status was his exclusion from the state dinner Ford held for visiting German Chancellor Helmut Schmidt, an invitation that would have been automatic pre-Sonnenfeldt Doctrine.

I was also distressed to see the eclipse of détente over the last year of Kissinger's tenure. The Soviet Union had become a status quo power in Europe, more concerned with holding what it had than with extending its influence westward. But in the third world, Moscow remained revisionist, moving opportunistically to recruit allies and destabilize pro-Western regimes when the occasion offered. The collapse of the Portuguese empire in southern Africa offered one such opening. Soon Kissinger had the United States supporting a South African intervention in Angola in an effort to beat back Soviet and Cuban influence. Because Nixon and Kissinger had

---

*In his 1994 book *Diplomacy* Kissinger wrote: "In the long run the Soviet Union would have been safer and economically stronger if it had surrounded itself with Finnish style governments in Eastern Europe . . ." Sonnenfeldt was arguing that it would also have been safer for the West had this occurred.

sold détente as a global phenomenon rather than just a regional European stand-down, this Africa sideshow was presented by Ford and Kissinger's critics as evidence of its failure.

Early in 1977, a few days before Jimmy Carter's inauguration, I was invited to Hal's retirement ceremony. Although he was only fifty, Hal knew the incoming Democratic administration was unlikely to offer a position of any influence to someone so closely identified with Henry Kissinger. The previous day Joe Sisco, the under secretary for political affairs, and Graham Martin, our last ambassador to Vietnam, had retired. Their departure was celebrated in the department's largest reception hall, attended by hundreds of former colleagues and officiated by the department's top leadership. Hal's ceremony was held in the office of the head of personnel, attended only by his family and a few former aides. This reflected, I believe, a view that Hal was not a real Foreign Service officer since he had never served abroad.

Sonnenfeldt took up an appointment at the Brookings Institution where he remained until his death in 2012. Free from the pressures of office, Hal became a much warmer person. He took an interest in my career and that of his other former assistants. Henry Kissinger spoke at Hal's memorial service. This event was very well attended, with many prominent personalities and familiar faces, a striking contrast to the low-key, poorly recognized fashion in which he had left the State Department thirty-five years earlier.

SEVEN

Downstairs

MY YEAR WITH SONNENFELDT HAD been stressful, alternately exhilarating and frustrating, and when I was offered a job in the European Bureau overseeing relations with France, I was ready for the move. Hal grumbled but let me go, and the next couple of years were more relaxed. Toril and I bought a house on a tree-lined street in a quiet neighborhood near the city's border with Maryland. We had our second son, Colin, and Ron and Judy Woods had returned to the area. We all socialized regularly with other veterans of the Paris Embassy, and family, home, and work were in happy balance.

The European Bureau had chaffed at the one-way relationship with Sonnenfeldt's office; it was all direction and little feedback. Happily, this was not held against me. To the contrary, my Seventh Floor experience proved an advantage, as I had become familiar with the full range of recent relations with Europe, much of which had not been fully shared with the bureau. Assistant Secretary Arthur Hartman began to assign me responsibilities well beyond running the French desk. The most significant of these was staffing him as the successor to Sonnenfeldt in the Quad political directors forum. This meant accompanying him on his travels, keeping abreast of transatlantic and East-West issues, pulling together briefing materials for each session, sharing the results of these still-confidential discussions with those who needed to know, preparing the material for Secretary of State Cyrus Vance's participation when the Quad met at his level, and attending those sessions, as well.

Early in 1977 Hartman sent me to brief President Carter's recently installed staff on the origin of the G-7 summit and on what to expect at the next meeting, which would take place that May in London. When I arrived at the White House it struck me that everyone in the room was younger than me. Two boyish assistants to the president, among the most senior of presidential aides, spent the first few minutes of our session comparing the times that President Carter had allocated to each on the White House tennis court. Access to this facility had long been a valued perk; Hal's Saturday morning tennis games, for instance, had always been on the White House court. (Hal also continued to get his hair cut by the White House barber, although the State barber shop was much closer.) Carter, nevertheless, seems to have been the only president to have personally assigned court times.

Hartman had been Bill Cargo's deputy when I was on the planning staff. He was then, and remained, my model of an American diplomat. Tall, dignified, elegant, soft-spoken, personable, and smart, he went on to become ambassador in Paris and then Moscow. I was sorry to see him leave the European Bureau in the summer of 1977 but delighted to have him in Paris, to which my responsibilities brought me regularly. His successor, George Vest, continued to involve me in the bureau's wider policy work.

Euro-communism remained a major preoccupation. The country believed at that time to be in greatest danger was France, as the French Socialists and Communists had formed an electoral alliance and were leading in the polls. The Communists were the larger party and by far the more disciplined. They were also, in contrast to the Italian Communists, closely aligned with Moscow. The Socialists were looking for some sign of approval, or at least non-disapproval from the Carter administration, and they tried hard to persuade Washington they would be able to control the Communists and keep them away from the national security apparatus if and when they both came to power. Secretary of State Cyrus Vance seemed inclined to respond positively, and I found myself on the opposite side of this argument from where I had been during the Portuguese political crisis.

The operative question was whether the head of the Socialist Party and its candidate for prime minister, Francois Mitterrand, would be received at a senior level if he visited Washington prior to the French election. Vance's senior staffer, Peter Tarnoff, favored a positive, if perhaps conditioned, answer. We discussed the matter while crossing the Atlantic on a trip with Vance. Peter urged that we, the bureau, trust him and Vance to handle the matter. I continued to argue against the Mitterrand visit. The Socialists must have detected where the hold-up was, as several of their American handlers began to cultivate me. I enjoyed the attention but remained unconvinced. In the end, after much debate, the administration decided against welcoming Mitterrand. I was chosen to go to Paris and deliver the unwelcome news.

As the March 1978 French parliamentary elections loomed, a "Union of the Left" victory seemed increasingly probable, and I was asked to prepare a paper for NSC discussion outlining options for American policy if this were to occur. The alternatives were either to stick with Henry Kissinger's hardline preference to cold shoulder any such regime or to try to make the best of what would be a difficult relationship. I argued for something in between. I felt the United States could afford to allow relations with a small country like Portugal to suffer to send a signal to more important societies, like Italy and France. But I felt it made little sense to create a major breach with France to set an example for less important countries.

We met in the White House Situation Room, where I made my case, urging that we should refuse to deal with ministries headed by Communists, which would in any case be largely domestic in nature, but seek to work normally with the president, prime minister, and the non-Communist ministries, which would include the foreign and defense ministries. In the end we did not have to choose. The Socialist-Communist alliance lost the 1978 legislative election by a razor-thin margin. The Socialists had out-polled the Communists, however, and this proved the beginning of a steady decline of the latter's voting strength. Three years later Mitterrand won the presidential election and immediately dissolved the national assembly. The Socialists triumphed in the resultant legislative election, receiving more than double the Communist vote. This effectively ended Washington's preoccupation with Euro-communism.

Whether U.S. policy had any effect on the political dynamics of France during this period is unclear. Given the very narrow margin by which the Union of the Left lost in 1978, even a tiny boost in its vote could have carried these two parties over the top. More tolerant signals from Washington might have had such an effect. Even less clear is whether Washington's concerns regarding Communist participation in a coalition with the French government were well grounded. Perhaps not, given the experience with just such a government three years later. But by then the Communists had been much weakened.

This was the first assignment in which I had not only my own secretary but also an FSO deputy. She was a young, bright, eager to learn, and industrious young woman on her second tour. After we had spent most of a year together, she announced she was going to resign, explaining to me that there was no future for a woman in our service. She insisted she was very happy in her current position and firmly assured me that nothing I had done or failed to do had led to her decision. I, nevertheless, felt in some way responsible and did my best to dissuade her, but she left a few weeks later. Had she remained, I think she would have found her prospects brightening, as the department soon began to move more aggressively to recruit and promote women, stimulated in part by the successful lawsuit Alison Palmer had initiated a decade earlier.

Bob Blackwill, who three years earlier recruited me to succeed him in Sonnenfeldt's office, telephoned from London in early 1978 to suggest I succeed him again. I arranged to pass through London on my next visit to Europe, interviewed with Deputy Chief of Mission Ed Streator, and got the nod of approval. Before taking up my new post I called on Sonnenfeldt at Brookings, and Hal advised me to treat the assignment as an extended seminar in geopolitics. Like Kissinger, and unlike most Foreign Service officers, Hal was a national security intellectual who valued the theoretical as well as the practical aspects of diplomacy. London was then preeminent among European capitals for a vibrant network of private institutions and individuals writing on international security issues. During our travels together Hal had introduced me to this community of think tanks, journalists, and university dons, and he urged I take advantage of this new assignment to explore this world further.

EIGHT

Postgraduate Studies

KINGMAN BREWSTER, THE FORMER PRESIDENT of Yale, was Jimmy Carter's ambassador to the Court of St. James. Brewster was also a close friend of Secretary of State Cyrus Vance. This connection gave him more latitude in filling the embassy staff than most chiefs of mission enjoy. London was then, and still is, regarded as a plum assignment. As a consequence it tends to be staffed by officers with a lot of seniority. For instance, the head of senior officer assignments at State had assigned himself to head that embassy's political section. But Brewster did not want his embassy to become a retirement post for officers near the end of their careers; he wanted to recreate the atmosphere of youthful enthusiasm, open debate, and new ideas he had left behind at Yale. So he sent this newly arrived section chief home and, instead, installed the two most junior officers in the section to become its head and deputy head. He then had his experienced deputy chief of mission, Ed Streator, recruit the rest of the staff. The overall quality of these efforts may, perhaps, best be measured by the fact that every member of the resultant political section went on to become an ambassador. Even a junior civil servant seconded by the

Pentagon became ambassador to Malta some years later. Ray Seitz, the young officer Brewster raised to become deputy head of the section, returned to London four years later as deputy chief of mission, and two years later, still an ambassador, the only FSO to ever hold that post.

My portfolio in London included issues of defense, security, and East-West relations. To get me started Streator allocated to me a generous share of the post's entertainment fund with the proviso that it be spent before the end of the fiscal year, then only a few weeks away. I also inherited from Blackwill a membership in the Travellers Club, one of those traditional bastions of privilege that line Pall Mall, only a short walk from the government offices on Whitehall. I mounted a lightning campaign of lunches with foreign and defense ministry officials, journalists, and foreign policy academics. Recalling Sonnenfeldt's advice, I became a member of the London-based International Institute of Strategic Studies, introduced myself to the other local think tanks, and took a two-week course at Oxford on grand strategy.

There were then two major security policy issues before the British government. One was whether to replace Britain's aging Polaris nuclear missile submarine fleet and, if so, with what. The second was whether to invite the United States to deploy American nuclear-armed missiles capable of reaching Moscow on British territory. These two issues would dominate the defense debate in Britain for the next several years, and both were also being debated in Washington. I became the principal interface between the two defense establishments. These issues were highly charged politically in the United Kingdom, which then had a center-left Labor government. The Labor Party was deeply divided on issues of defense, particularly nuclear defense, and the dialogue between the two governments on these issues was, accordingly, held closely so as not to spill out into British public debate.

Replacing the Polaris system was going to be costly, requiring the United Kingdom to build a new fleet of nuclear-powered submarines, acquire a new generation of long-range ballistic missiles, and develop new nuclear warheads to go on them. There were cheaper options involving land-based missiles or aircraft-delivered weapons, but these would be less secure against a disarming first strike. The small group of Labor ministers involved in considering these options was moving toward acquisition of Trident, America's newest submarine-launched missile. My position allowed me the rare opportunity to sit in on a number of discussions about nuclear weapons cooperation between the responsible scientists from the two governments. Both sides were somewhat uncomfortable having a diplomat in the room, but Brewster had been very supportive of the view that the embassy should be represented in any exchanges between the two governments. I was, thus, able to keep abreast of one of the most closely held policy debates underway in the British government.

The transatlantic dialogue over the possible deployment in Europe of American intermediate-range nuclear forces (INF) was more public. It became, indeed, the signature transatlantic issue of the 1980s. The Carter administration was in talks with Moscow about a further reduction of strategic nuclear arsenals on the two sides. SALT I, negotiated by Kissinger and Nixon, had capped the increase in strategic missiles and bombers but it had not halted the proliferation of deliverable warheads. The Carter administration's objective was to begin actual reductions of both missiles and warheads. These talks were intended to limit only intercontinental-range systems, but the Soviet Union was beginning to deploy a new nuclear-armed missile, the SS20, which could reach all of Europe but not the United States. German Chancellor Helmut Schmidt, head of a Social Democratic government and a former defense minister, proposed that the United States should seek in its negotiations with Moscow to limit this threat, as well. After some considerable transatlantic debate in which the British were actively involved, Carter agreed to seek such limitations but only in a separate follow-on negotiation once SALT II was concluded. In addition, Washington insisted that the Soviet Union would have no interest in agreeing to any limits on its SS20 force unless NATO was ready to deploy comparable systems of its own. Consequently, Washington proposed to deploy a new generation of nuclear-armed missiles to Europe as a counterbalance to the SS20s and a bargaining chip for their removal.

By this point Helmut Schmidt was beginning to regret ever having raised the subject. Few West Germans were keen to have additional nuclear weapons deployed on their soil and even fewer from within his center-left party, the Social Democrats. But the debate had widened and deepened, and the issue would continue to dominate the transatlantic agenda well beyond the life of the American, British, and German governments.

Much of my time was spent tracking developments in Washington and London on this issue. I was able to insert my own ideas at both ends, to the point where one visiting U.S. official commented jokingly to his British counterpart that Washington was having trouble distinguishing between

British and Dobbins' ideas. There was also a lively debate in the media and the think tank world on these issues that I followed and contributed to.

McGeorge Bundy, who had been Kennedy's and Johnson's national security adviser, was dispatched to London as a Carter emissary to discuss these issues with the British. Bundy had become a super dove on issues of nuclear policy, perhaps in an unconscious effort to compensate for his role in escalating American involvement in Vietnam. I was assigned as his escort, and difficulties arose when it became clear that Bundy did not, in fact, support the emerging policy, opposing as he did the deployment of American missiles to Europe. I found myself quietly correcting him as he made the rounds of British officials and defense intellectuals.

For an American diplomat, Britain is the most accessible of societies. What had become known as a special relationship had developed during World War II and resulted in unique sharing of secret intelligence, nuclear weapons design, and broader defense collaboration. British officials and nonofficials alike regarded the American relationship as their country's most important one. My interlocutors along Whitehall were eager to hear the latest from Washington and to share their own perspectives. I was given free rein to wander the halls of the Foreign Office and Defense Ministry and was treated almost as one of the staff.

My daily round was extraordinarily agreeable. On arriving in the office I would review any instructions from Washington that had been received overnight. Sometimes the resultant messages could simply be passed to the right official by telephone, with the response noted and sent back to Washington without even leaving my desk. Several days a week I would host someone for lunch, most often at the Travellers. We would take sherry in the wood-paneled library, then traverse a long stairway, leaning on a banister originally installed to assist the elderly Prince de Talleyrand, Napoleon's foreign minister and, in his later years, King Louis-Philippe's ambassador to London, on his way to the club's dining room. A bottle of wine would accompany the meal, then we'd go back down to the library for coffee. My guest would then walk back to the Foreign Office or Defense Ministry on the other side of St. James's Park, while I would make my way through Piccadilly and Berkeley Square to the embassy, perhaps browsing in Hatchard's bookshop or one of the Jermyn Street haberdasheries on the way. Back in the office I would write up anything interesting from the lunch and dispatch the result to Washington. Then, in nice weather, I'd take a bicycle ride through Hyde Park to home, a townhouse in South Kensington that came with the job.

One of the more tedious forms of diplomatic social life is the national day reception. Nearly every country holds such an event, and each host ambassador naturally invites his American counterpart. Brewster almost never accepted; otherwise, he would have had to attend such an affair every other night. Rather than simply decline, however, Brewster passed these invitations down through the embassy hierarchy until, in many cases, they reached me.

I accepted the first of these and went to the reception. There were several hundred people milling about, none of whom I knew and none of whom knew me. Thereafter, I adopted the practice of accepting such invitations and then not going, on the theory that the host might take offense if no one from the American Embassy accepted their invitation but would never notice the absence of someone he had never met.

Of all my postings London came closest to a classic image of nineteenth-century diplomacy. I even once wore striped pants for an evening at Buckingham Palace. In the spring Toril and I attended the Queen's Garden Party on the palace lawn, and our son Christian was enrolled in a very proper day school that, years earlier, Prince Charles attended; the curriculum involved as much time on the playing fields as in the classroom. Christian acquired a posh British accent, which I am sorry to say faded away over time. Toril, already a talented seamstress, enrolled in the Royal School of Needlepoint and took up riding in Hyde Park.

Career diplomats generally take a skeptical view of politically appointed ambassadors. Kingman Brewster was one of those who gave this odd American practice a good name. A New England aristocrat whose ancestor had come over on the Mayflower, Brewster was accomplished, thoughtful, dignified, amusing, and widely respected. He was also very well connected, staying with Cyrus Vance when visiting Washington. On one occasion I explained to him some difficulty we were having with the department and, to my astonishment, he buzzed his secretary and said, "Get me Cy." I was even more surprised when he was connected with the secretary a few moments later and my concern was quickly dealt with.

Brewster had supported academic freedom at Yale through the years of civil rights and anti-war tumult. He took much the same attitude toward his embassy; he never interfered in its reporting. On one occasion he complimented me on a telegram I had sent the previous day. "I don't agree with your conclusions," he said, "but it was well argued." When he had something to say on an issue, he would draft and send his own message to Washington, employing the first person singular. These would occasionally contradict something the embassy had sent, in the first person plural, a day or two earlier, and he left it to Washington to distinguish his personal views and those of the embassy staff.

Still the headmaster, Brewster organized regular seminars. Most weeks he would invite some visiting luminary or a prominent British figure to meet with selected embassy staff. Guests included British and American cabinet ministers, members of Congress and Parliament, journalists, and other well-known figures, including ones like George Will, the conservative columnist with whom Brewster disagreed.

Streator also entertained regularly. He liked to host small luncheons of eight to ten people organized around a common theme. He had a first-rate chef and an excellent wine cellar. I was asked to identify topics and knowledgeable guests to gather around the table, and between Brewster and Streator, I was able to meet and talk with a much wider circle of London's political and intellectual leadership than I could ever have done on my own, while enjoying many first-rate meals.

One of Brewster's less welcome innovations was to insist that each political officer should have internal as well as external responsibilities. More normally, a political section would be divided between those who reported on a country's domestic politics and those who worked on its foreign and defense policies. Consistent with Brewster's preference, in our section the Africanist also followed the Labor Party and the Asianist the Conservative Party. I was assigned the Liberal Party, the least important of the three.

Shortly after my arrival Brewster organized a lunch for me to meet the leaders of that party. David Steel, then its head, arrived on time, but we had to wait a while for his immediate predecessor, Jeremy Thorpe. Some days later we learned from the press that Thorpe had been late because he was being officially informed by the police that he was about to be charged with the attempted murder of a former homosexual partner. Steel had himself been forewarned of this development earlier that very morning. It was a tribute to the British stiff upper lip that Steel and Thorpe both carried through our lunch with easy grace.

A few weeks later I attended the Liberal Party's annual convention. It was held in a drab seaside town with only one decent hotel that was, unfortunately, fully booked. There were two days of discussion about what the Liberals would do should they come to power, a most unlikely eventuality. The only point of interest for the media present was whether Jeremy Thorpe, now out on bail awaiting trial, would put in an appearance.

The Liberals were pleased to have foreign observers attend their annual gathering and had scheduled a small reception for those who had come. Thorpe, it turned out, was still the party's spokesman on foreign affairs, and much to the annoyance of his party's leadership, who had urged him to stay away, Thorpe appeared. He explained to the press that he had come to host the reception for the foreign observers. It was not a large or lengthy affair, the only foreign guests being myself and a couple other even more obscure visitors. Thorpe circulated, said a few words to each, and left town having made his appearance and his point. He was eventually tried and acquitted.

Britain was then entering what came to be known as its "winter of discontent." The economy had been weak for some time, and London, when compared to Paris, had a dirty, run-down look. The country had been rocked by a series of labor disputes, and in the embassy we were working on a series of reporting telegrams collectively titled, "The Decline of Britain." In these we debated whether Britain's descent resulted from the loss of empire, sluggishness of management, rigidity of labor, or the persistence of the class system. In the spring of 1979 there were general elections, and the Conservatives won. Margaret Thatcher became prime minister. We scrapped our series.

Months later I visited 10 Downing Street to call on one of Thatcher's private secretaries. Despite recurrent IRA bombings in London, including one attack in the Houses of Parliament, visible security at the PM's residence remained remarkably light. One could simply walk up to the door and knock. When I did so, the door was opened by a uniformed butler, who bade me wait while he sent for the person I was there to see. A few moments later there was another knock. It was the milkman. The butler ordered and received two bottles of milk and one of cream. Before the milkman could leave, the prime minister herself arrived through the same door. She greeted the milkman, obviously a familiar figure, nodded pleasantly to me, and continued on into her home and office.

Shortly before the 1980 American presidential election I participated in a transatlantic conference focused on the SALT II Treaty that had just been signed and was awaiting ratification. We met at Ditchley Park, an English country house that Churchill had used on weekends during the war. Black tie for dinner was *de rigeuer.* The American contingents were mostly right of center political figures, former officials, and journalists, many of whom were critical of the treaty and the Carter administration. At least one of these participants, John Lehman, found my defense of both to be too spirited. On his return to Washington he spoke of me as a "left wing firebrand."

My London assignment still had eighteen months to go and, pleasant and stimulating as this life had been, I was becoming increasingly restless. Although I had up to this point been exceptionally fortunate in my postings, promotion had come no faster than the norm. I was still a mid-grade officer with several thresholds to cross before assuming any real responsibility. I began angling for an early departure and a new job in Washington, but the election of Ronald Reagan seemed to dash my hopes, as the Republicans would inevitably replace most of the department's top and middle leadership, many of whom I knew, with people I did not. Alexander Haig was named secretary of state, and he chose Richard Burt to head the Bureau of Political-Military Affairs (PM). Burt, in turn, named Robert Blackwill as his principal deputy, and Blackwill convinced Burt to bring me back as head of the office handling European security issues.

NINE

Missile Diplomacy

RICK BURT WAS THEN A thirty-three-year-old prodigy. During Black-will's tenure in London, Rick had been the head of studies at the International Institute of Strategic Studies. He had gone from there to become the national security correspondent for the *New York Times*, a plum assignment not normally given to someone devoid of journalistic experience. In this capacity Rick saw a good deal of Zbigniew Brzezinski, Jimmy Carter's national security adviser. Zbig was reputed to be the source of some of Burt's most newsworthy scoops. During these years Blackwill was also back in Washington, working for Brzezinski on the National Security Council staff.

Rick and I had met at several conferences, often finding ourselves on opposite sides of whatever was being discussed, and Rick had also been warned off me by John Lehman, who had just been named secretary of the Navy. Eventually Bob prevailed and Rick agreed to hire me, "against my better judgment," as Rick noted to me on my arrival.

Every new administration has difficulty getting organized. This is particularly true when there is also a change of parties, since there is, then, an even bigger purge of experienced personnel. Normally, the new group is made up of people who had held office four, eight, or twelve years earlier. But the Reagan wing of the Republican Party had never held the presidency. Many of the new crop of officials, including the president, had denounced the national security policies not just of Carter, but of Nixon, Ford, and even Eisenhower. Thus, in addition to the usual turbulence as newly appointed officials learned their jobs and maneuvered for turf, there was also a policy vacuum as long-established practices were swept away while new ones had yet to be defined.

Nowhere was this turbulence more acute than within the staff of the National Security Council. Ronald Reagan eventually went through six national security advisers, more than any other president. The first, Richard Allen, resigned after being accused, perhaps unfairly, of taking a bribe. His successor, William Clark, had no experience in and little affinity for foreign affairs. He was in due course replaced by Bud McFarlane, who became caught up in the Iran-Contra scandal, attempted suicide, and was subsequently convicted of withholding information from Congress. His successor, Admiral William Poindexter, was convicted on five counts of lying to Congress. Only late in Reagan's second term did the White House management of national security stabilize under Frank Carlucci, a former Foreign Service officer, and Colin Powell, a serving Army general.

Each new administration adjusts the system of committees through which national security issues proceed upward to decision. Al Haig, like most secretaries of state, wanted to make, not just carry out, American foreign policy. Richard Allen was not a strong or particularly well connected competitor, nor was international affairs an early area of concentration for Reagan personally. Haig, therefore, largely prevailed in defining an expansive role for State in the new National Security Council system. One result was that our bureau was assigned chairmanship of the interagency committees responsible for developing arms control policy. Two of these groups fell to my office, those dealing with chemical weapons and with intermediate-range nuclear forces.

Multilateral negotiations on a treaty to ban chemical weapons had been underway in Geneva since the previous year. The actual use of these weapons had been prohibited since 1925 by international convention, but states were allowed to build and stockpile chemical weapons and many countries were doing so, including the United States. One of our tasks in PM was to craft higher-level decision alternatives for the American objectives in these negotiations. In principle this should not have been that hard. All we needed was for agencies to define their preferences, which we would capture in a paper and forward for discussion at the cabinet level and for a decision by the president. Haig himself wanted the United States to manufacture a new generation of chemical weapons, so the State and Defense positions should not have been too far apart. As a practical matter the alternatives before us were either to walk away from the current negotiation or to condition any ban of such weapons on verification requirements so intrusive that the Soviet Union would never agree and so become the proximate obstacle to agreement. But the Defense Department (DOD) did not want to bring the issue to a decision at all. The National Security Council staff, freed of any responsibility for forging interagency consensus, joined the DOD in frustrating agreement on any set of alternatives, and meetings, whether chaired by Rick or me, descended into petty bickering. Only after a year of bureaucratic trench warfare did the administration choose the only practical alternative, pursuit of an agreement prohibiting the production and stockpiling of such weapons conditioned on provisions for extensive on-site verification.

Even more difficult were interagency discussions over intermediate range nuclear forces (INF). The Carter administration had forged an agreement with its NATO allies under which the United States would deploy a new generation of such weapons to Europe while at the same time seeking Soviet agreement to put mutual limits on them. The Reagan team was loath to move forward on this or any other arms control path laid out by their predecessors. Yet here again, given the strength of European opinion, the choice was simple: either abandon the deployments or embrace the negotiation. Defense and the NSC again slow-rolled the process of policy formulation.

The resultant uncertainty rattled the Europeans, who were already unhappy that the Reagan administration had decided not to seek ratification of the SALT II Treaty. European leaders worried that Reagan was about to move the Western alliance into a much more confrontational stance with the Soviet Union. As a result our bureau became the recipient of a good deal of allied hand wringing.

Finally, in September 1981, President Reagan announced that the United States was ready to negotiate with the USSR, not just to limit INF systems but to eliminate them altogether. In fact Reagan insisted that elimination was the only outcome the United States would accept. Either we would deploy hundreds of new missiles into five European countries or the Soviet Union would agree to eliminate all of the SS20 missiles it had already deployed.

The inspiration for this "zero option" proposal came from Rick Burt's opposite number in the Pentagon, Richard Perle. As an aide to Democratic Senator Henry (Scoop) Jackson, Perle had organized congressional resistance to Henry Kissinger's détente policies. Now, in a Republican administration, he began using his formidable bureaucratic skills and slightly sinister charm to undo what little was left of that effort. As with the administration's stance on chemical weapons limitations, the zero option for INF was designed to be unachievable and, therefore, an obstacle to any agreement. As such it was resisted by all of us at State. We argued, to no avail, that almost any mutually agreed level of deployments was better than no agreement at all, so why let the best become the enemy of the good?

Perle, sometimes referred to as "the Prince of Darkness," was soft-spoken, amusing, and very sharp; in short, a formidable adversary. He and Rick became at once both friends and competitors. Perle was the original neoconservative while Rick was an only slightly right-of-center moderate. On issue after issue they were in opposite corners to the point where the press began writing about the battle between "the two Richards" for the soul of the administration. In any better-run regime, the dueling egos of two mid-level officials would have been kept in check and their differences sorted out one or two rungs above them. In Reagan's first term, however, the secretaries of state and defense were also at loggerheads, the initial succession of national security advisers was weak, and the president was less engaged in international affairs than he would later become. The two Richards, thus, gave color to the broader competition that was underway within the administration and personified two very distinct visions for American policy: one based on unremitting hostility to Soviet Union, the other on a more tempered version of Kissinger-style détente; one ready to stoke up East-West tensions, the other seeking to cool them down.

Rick also had a competitive relationship with Lawrence Eagleburger, a former aide to Henry Kissinger, who had just been named assistant secretary of state for Europe. On issues of European security, Rick's bureau was responsible for developing policy, via its chairmanship of the relevant interagency committees, while Eagleburger's staff were responsible for executing it, overseeing as they did relations with Europe and the Soviet Union. This division of labor was a formula for conflict, since the European

Bureau (EUR in State parlance) naturally wanted a role in setting the policies it was to execute, and the PM equally sought a role in the execution of the policies it was charged with fashioning.

This was not a clash between equals. EUR was the largest and most powerful bureau in the department. It oversaw the world's most important embassies, controlled a huge share of the department's budget, and enjoyed the ability to reward or punish anyone aspiring to a European assignment, which included just about everyone in the Foreign Service. PM had no overseas dependencies, could not send out instructions without EUR's concurrence, and could not promise attractive ongoing assignments. Its staff was less numerous and more junior. But like Avis, we tried harder. We staged periodic raids on EUR turf, set up parallel channels to European governments, and bypassed the European Bureau whenever possible.

In early 1982 this world turned upside down. Eagleburger moved up to become under secretary for political affairs, the department's third-ranking position. To everyone's surprise, Haig chose Rick to take over EUR. Blackwill followed Rick as his principal deputy, and Richard Haass, a colleague of Rick's from his IISS days, took over EUR's policy planning office. I hoped I might be chosen to lead EUR's office of NATO and regional security affairs, a far bigger and more prestigious organization than my PM shop. Instead Rick installed me one level higher, as his deputy responsible for directing the work of the NATO office, the element of the Soviet Affairs office handling security and arms control issues and the Office of Western European Affairs, where I had been a desk officer only four years earlier.

Overnight I moved from having ten subordinates to over fifty. My new position was one I might have reasonably aspired to in another decade. The issues were largely the same I had been working with in the PM, but the ability to influence outcomes was greatly increased. I had a much more experienced set of subordinates, EUR enjoyed much more leverage on European and East-West policy than the PM, and Rick Burt's star was clearly in the ascendance.

The European Bureau was stunned and apprehensive at this change. We in PM had been the insurgents in the hills who would occasionally swoop down to raid the peaceful EUR farmers and ride away with one or two of their issues. Now we had come to stay. What rapine and slaughter would ensue? On his arrival in PM a year earlier, Rick initiated a major purge, abruptly displacing most of that bureau's senior leadership, but he came to regret the scope and abruptness of these changes. Beyond importing Blackwill, Haass, and me, no other personnel moves ensued.

Rick's PM position had not required Senate confirmation, but the EUR job did. Rick was, therefore, installed on an acting basis while the Senate considered his nomination. This soon became a problem, as Senator Jesse Helms alleged Rick had divulged sensitive classified information while a reporter for the *New York Times* and put a hold on his confirmation.

One of the first issues we had to deal with was the conflict between the United Kingdom and Argentina over the Falkland Islands. Earlier that year the military junta governing Argentina had sent troops to seize this British colony located off the southern tip of South America. The resultant dispute, in addition to pitting Britain against Argentina, brought State and Defense into conflict and, within State, the European Bureau into conflict with the Latin American Bureau. To the intense discomfort of Margaret Thatcher and her government, Al Haig sought to mediate the dispute rather than support the British military effort to recover the islands. Across the river, Cap Weinberger unequivocally backed the United Kingdom, providing the British military with vital logistic, intelligence, and other forms of support. Within State the Latin American Bureau, under Tom Enders, encouraged Haig's ill-fated effort at shuttle diplomacy while Rick sought to discourage too great a tilt in the Argentine direction. Late one evening Enders sent out an instruction to several posts without clearing the telegram with EUR, explaining the next morning that no one had been left in EUR by the time the telegram was ready. For the duration of the crisis both bureaus would, henceforth, try to out-wait the other each evening to prevent a repetition of that incident, leading to many unnecessarily late nights. This sort of bureaucratic gamesmanship was not uncommon, particularly between two such highly competitive players as Burt and Enders.

Haig was an easily excited personality. He had entered Henry Kissinger's National Security Council as an Army colonel and exited the White House three years later as a four-star general, eventually returning to become Nixon's last chief of staff. Shortly after taking office as secretary, Haig appeared on the cover of *Time Magazine* over the caption "Taking Command." He described his role as "the vicar of foreign policy," which brought to mind the pope's role in the Catholic Church. On the day President Reagan was shot and undergoing surgery, Haig informed the cabinet and then the American public "I am in control," which was arguably true but constitutionally irregular.

Haig was convinced that Fidel Castro had been responsible for an attempt on his life. Concerned about leftist insurgencies in Central and South America, Haig talked about "going to the source," meaning Cuba. There had, indeed, been an effort to assassinate him only four days before he stepped down as supreme allied commander for Europe; a bomb blew up under the car in which he was traveling. But the more likely perpetrators were members of the Red Army Faction, a German terrorist cell then actively seeking American military targets.

Haig was keen to send back to Cuba the thousands of criminals and mental patients Castro had sent to the United States mixed in with a larger number of genuine refugees during the last year of the Carter administration. While we were still in PM Rick had been directed by Haig to put together a plan for their forcible return, which involved putting the Cubans aboard a fleet of surplus World War II landing craft, chaining them to the bulkheads, and sailing to Cuba. The American crews would abandon ship as these craft crossed into Cuban territorial waters, having headed the vessels toward nearby Cuban beaches. Haig took this plan to the White House and, according to Rick, returned crestfallen that it was not approved.

In late June 1982 Rick and I briefed Haig in preparation for a National Security Council meeting. He seemed particularly jumpy. At one point he shouted angrily at me and then relaxed and proceeded as if nothing had happened. Shortly thereafter, on arrival at the White House, he tendered his resignation, not with the intention of actually leaving but as a pressure tactic in his ongoing contest with Defense Secretary Weinberger and elements in the White House, including Chief of Staff Jim Baker, and his deputy, Mike Deaver.

A few days later I hosted a lunch for the foreign minister of Malta, following which I accompanied the minister to Under Secretary Eagleburger's office for a scheduled meeting. The new Maltese government had been misbehaving, flirting with the Soviet Union in an effort to extort more Western aid. This was the reason the minister was not being hosted at some more senior level. We sat outside the under secretary's office for almost an hour beyond the appointed time. Finally Eagleburger's secretary came to say, apologetically, that the under secretary would not be able to see the minister after all. No further explanation was offered, but later that afternoon we learned that Haig's resignation had been accepted. The following day I joined a long line of people saying farewell to the secretary and his wife. Not surprisingly they both looked stiff and exhausted.

Rick was in Europe when we learned of Haig's departure, and he immediately prepared to return. Eagleburger, anticipating such a move, had me tell Rick to continue with his full schedule of meetings in Europe. Larry wanted to avoid stirring up further anxiety among the Europeans. He also knew how vulnerable Rick felt, with his patron gone and still not confirmed in his new position. He instructed me to tell Rick not to worry on that score. This was mildly encouraging, although Eagleburger could not know what Haig's successor might choose to do.

George Shultz was soon nominated and quickly confirmed as secretary of state. Almost immediately he found himself in the midst of a major transatlantic row. Late the previous year the Polish regime had come under Soviet pressure to crack down on the Solidarity free labor movement. In response, the Polish leadership declared martial law. The Reagan administration reacted by applying economic sanctions on the Soviet Union. Among the activities sanctioned was a pipeline under construction to transport natural gas from Siberia to Western Europe. Our European allies were not prepared to forgo Siberian gas, so they issued regulations compelling their firms, including American subsidiaries in Europe, to ignore the American sanctions. *Time Magazine* characterized this confrontation as "one of the most emotional and dangerous disputes to rock the Western Alliance in the whole postwar period."

Haig had resisted the imposition of these extraterritorial American sanctions, knowing their likely reception in Europe. His failure to prevail against Weinberger on this issue was one of the reasons he had threatened to resign. Shultz spent much of his early months in office seeking to defuse the crisis, and his effort culminated in a multi-stop tour of Europe concluding with a meeting of NATO foreign ministers in Brussels. By the trip's end he had patched together a compromise in which the Europeans agreed, in rather unspecific terms, to restrict East-West trade in certain sectors and the United States agreed to drop the extraterritorial application of its sanctions on the pipeline's construction.

Shultz's approach to this trip was characteristic of his management of the department and the conduct of his responsibilities generally. He had brought no one with him when he came to State, and he made no major structural or personnel changes. He relied almost entirely on the career service and used the machinery of the department as it was designed to be used. As a personality, he was the opposite of the volatile Al Haig, just as self-assured but also self-contained and so low-key that he was typically characterized as inscrutable. His personal staff was small. Papers for him did not pass through any elaborate screening mechanisms. When briefed he asked incisive questions, and he seemed to take quiet satisfaction in uncovering areas of ignorance, a fate one did not want to experience twice. Shultz often brought his wife, O'Bie (for O'Brien, her maiden name) along on official trips. She was a pleasant, comfortable woman who gave an almost homelike ambiance to his modest entourage.

This management style gave a great deal of responsibility and put a great deal of pressure on the supporting bureaus and their leadership. For this December trip EUR positioned officers in each of the capitals to be visited, while Rick and I traveled with Shultz. We continuously updated and revised material for his meetings as we gradually put in place the final compromises that would conclude the dispute.

Throughout these months Rick remained unconfirmed. He betrayed little anxiety, behaved as if his position was secure, and continued to advance just the sort of moderate, pragmatic policies for which he was being criticized by Jesse Helms as insufficiently conservative. I admired Rick's constancy, his unwillingness to shape his advocacy to suit his difficult situation. So, eventually, did George Shultz. On the last evening of our European trip, when all the pieces of the pipeline compromise had fallen into place, Shultz finally assured Rick of his support. A week later the White House issued a statement urging the Senate to act positively on his nomination, and two months later Rick was confirmed.

Among the more satisfying aspects of my job was working to steer the newly elected Socialist government in Spain toward NATO membership. I made several visits to Madrid before and after the election that brought the Socialist leader Felipe Gonzalez to power. Spanish democracy was still young and the Spanish Socialists had only just recently broken from their Marxist past. I found the young party leaders and leftist intellectuals suspicious of the United States and hostile to NATO, but also open-minded and eager to learn. NATO, I argued, was where issues of European security were decided. If Spain wanted a seat at the table, it would have to join the club. In late 1982 Rick and I accompanied Schultz to Madrid. Over lunch I commented to the Socialist official on my right that his party would have the task of bringing Spain into the alliance. He almost choked on his soup. But four years later Gonzalez did just that.

Even in the administration's early days rumors circulated of Reagan's inattention and disinterest in foreign policy. Rick and I were enlisted to brief the president in preparation for his first G-7 summit meeting, and we were told to pretend that each of us was one of the other leaders, in my case Francois Mitterrand, and to present Reagan with arguments and queries he might receive from them. We were also sworn to secrecy lest it become known that playacting was an element of the president's rehearsal for his first G-7 summit. I found Reagan pleasant and alert, if not particularly fascinated with the material we were presenting. Jim Baker, then White House chief of staff, clearly thought we were pitching the president softballs. "What will you say," he interjected, "if Mitterrand raises the issue of fixed versus floating exchange rates?"

"I'll listen carefully to what Maggie says," replied Reagan with a smile, "and then I'll agree with her."

On a subsequent occasion I was again briefing the president when Baker came into the Cabinet Room wearing one white glove, which he waved over his head, saying, "It's time, Mr. President." Don Regan, then secretary of the treasury, looked mystified. The president explained that Michael Jackson had just arrived. "Who is Michael Jackson?" Regan asked. The president responded, "I used to have a cabinet secretary who didn't know who the Beach Boys were," referring to James Watt, who had canceled a Beach Boys July 4 concert on the mall in favor of Wayne Newton, a Las Vegas lounge act and personal friend. Though he later apologized when he discovered that Ron and Nancy were both Beach Boy fans, Watt was replaced a few months later. Don Regan was also eventually fired, presumably for more serious lapses than his failure to recognize the name of the world's then-biggest pop star.

Throughout Reagan's first term the dominant issue in transatlantic and East-West relations was what became known as the "dual track" effort to both deploy intermediate-range nuclear-armed missiles to Europe and to negotiate their elimination. Four hundred and sixty-four ground-launched cruise missiles (GLCMs) were to be based in the United Kingdom, Germany, Belgium, Italy, and the Netherlands and 108 Pershing II ballistic missiles would replace the shorter-range Pershing I missiles located in West

Germany.* These were all mobile systems, meant to spend some of the time traveling up and down the highways and byways of Western Europe in order to make them harder to target and, thus, more secure in the event of war. But the prospect of having missiles carrying live nuclear warheads driving through one's towns and villages was bound to raise anxiety.

Popular opposition mounted in all five of the basing countries. Hundreds of thousands marched to protest the deployments in Germany. The most tenacious resistance was mounted in Britain, where thousands of women converged on the intended GLCM base at Greenham Common, surrounded the facility, and set up an encampment, which they inhabited for almost a decade. Eventually a dozen such peace camps were set up throughout Europe.

NATO established a Special Consultative Group to manage the political and arms control aspects of the INF deployments. Every few weeks this group would meet to discuss the latest developments in talks with the Soviet Union and in the domestic politics of each of the basing countries. Rick chaired these meetings and, at their conclusion, held a press conference in which soothing messages were conveyed.

Moscow did its level best to stoke European opposition and had considerable success. The Soviets argued that the Pershing II missile was particularly destabilizing, as it could deliver a nuclear warhead on Moscow and, thus, their government leadership, with only a fifteen-minute flight time. The Russians argued, with some merit, that this would drastically reduce warning time, forcing their leaders to decide whether to launch an all-out nuclear attack on both the United States and Europe in the few moments before their capacity to make such a decision would be eliminated.

Paul Nitze headed negotiations with the Soviets. Already in his late seventies, Paul had been one of the major architects of America's Cold War strategy. In 1950 he had succeeded George Kennan as head of the State Department policy planning staff and subsequently served as deputy secretary of defense. His age and stature provided him a degree of independence, which became worrisome as the crucial deployment threshold approached.

U.S.-West European Relations During the Reagan Years: The Perception of West European Publics, Steven Smith and Douglas Wertman, Palgrave, 1992.

NATO's five-nation INF coalition was only as strong as its weakest link. If any one government faltered, the others would find it impossible to carry on. The Italians used the leverage this provided them to extort from us a promise never to set up another exclusive transatlantic consultative forum that excluded them as the Quad group had done. As our commitment grandfathered the existing mechanism, we agreed.

In the summer of 1982 Rick and I became aware that for several months Nitze had been meeting privately with his Soviet opposite number, Yuli Kvitsinski. In these discussions, the most significant of which took place during a walk in some nearby woods, Nitze had proposed an agreement outside the parameters of his negotiating mandate. Paul suggested both sides should deploy an equal number of INF missiles, but offered that the U.S. side would forgo deploying the Pershing II ballistic missiles and deploy only the slower and more vulnerable cruise missiles. This arrangement for equally limited deployments for both sides was exactly what we at State had been urging a year earlier, when Perle and Weinberger had pushed through the zero option. But Nitze's initiative now threatened to complicate the deployment process. Any adjustment in the U.S. negotiating position at this late date would lead one or more of the basing countries to postpone if not cancel its deployment, which would have a cascading effect on the others.

Fortunately Richard Perle persuaded Weinberger who persuaded Reagan to reject Nitze's proposal. Wider knowledge of this rejection might have had an even more negative effect, persuading many Europeans that Washington was not serious about securing negotiated limitations. Again fortunately, Kvitsinski never responded to Nitze's proposal. When the "walk in the woods" exchange became more widely known, as it quickly did, its failure could, thus, be blamed on Moscow.

East-West tensions peaked in early September, when the Soviet Union shot down a South Korean commercial airliner with 269 people on board. The plane had strayed into Soviet airspace on its way from the United States to Seoul. One week later we were in Madrid with George Shultz attending the concluding session of a two-year CSCE review conference. As with most such trips Rick and I, along with the rest of the EUR traveling team, were operating on little sleep and lots of caffeine. Our challenge was to balance several objectives. The first was to consolidate a tough Western reaction to the shoot-down. Our second objective was preserving, if possible, the modest but useful results of two years of East-West negotiation embodied in the text that the thirty-five foreign ministers had gathered to endorse. Third was preparing Shultz for an encounter with Soviet Foreign Minister Andre Gromyko that was bound to be confrontational.

At the last moment a key meeting was laid on for Shultz with the caucus of NATO ministers to discuss sanctions against Moscow. I hurriedly assembled the necessary briefing materials. Not finding Rick, I brought these directly to Shultz. Rick, on his return, became enraged that I had not waited until he could review the briefing package. I responded that Shultz had not much more than an hour to prepare for the meeting in question, and there was nothing in the package with which Rick was not already familiar. We were soon shouting at each other.

I went to bed assuming that our professional relationship was at an end. Early the next morning I was woken and told to take the first flight to Brussels. The previous evenings meeting among NATO foreign ministers had achieved an agreement in principal regarding further limits on trade with Russia. It was important that these measures be formally adopted by the NATO Council in Brussels later that very day to counterbalance the announcement of a positive conclusion to the Madrid CSCE meeting. My task, Rick explained, was to ensure that this occurred. I flew to Brussels, our blow-up of the previous evening forgotten, met with the assembled NATO ambassadors, and secured the necessary agreement.

In the summer of 1983, as the first INF deployments loomed, the need for handholding the European basing governments became intense. Rick decided to hold SCG meetings every two weeks, which he and I would alternate chairing. At each session he or I would first meet with the five basing country representatives, and then with the full NATO membership, where we would brief on recent developments in the Geneva negotiations, refine arguments in response to those of the anti-nuclear movement and the Soviet Union, issue a reassuring communiqué, and then hold a press conference.

In September the first GLCMs went into the Greenham Common base, which was still surrounded by the encamped women protesters, and in November the first Pershing II missiles arrived in Germany. The Soviets walked out of the INF negotiations and also the strategic arms talks, thereby terminating all efforts toward nuclear arms control between the two superpowers.

Later that year I had my first and last run-in with Lieutenant Colonel Oliver North. I was standing in for the secretary of state in a NATO exercise code named Able Archer. Meeting at the White House, we were simulating the decisions that would lead to a nuclear war with the Soviet Union. The meeting was chaired by an Air Force general on the NSC staff who was standing in for the president. We were scripted that day to decide to mobilize and deploy American reinforcement to Europe. Similar cells in other NATO capitals were going through similar scripted steps, which would culminate after several days just short of a decision to launch a nuclear strike against notionally advancing Soviet forces. There was really no leeway for originality in our role. We were simply to make an already scripted decision. The whole thing should not have taken more than half an hour. But the White House had recently installed some new computerized decision support technology and Ollie was keen to try this out. To do so he kept the rest of us playacting late into the evening. I left annoyed at the waste of time and the presumption of this inexperienced young tyro encroaching on my dinner hour. I instructed my staff to make sure I was never again scheduled to attend any meeting at which North would be present. Others were not so prescient.

Although we did not know it at the time, Able Archer had also disturbed the Soviet leadership, as the Soviet high command had taken our playacting quite seriously. Influenced by Reagan's tough rhetoric, they actually thought NATO was preparing for a preemptive nuclear attack. Subsequent analysis contained in a 1990 report to President Bush and declassified only in 2015 concluded: "In 1983 we may have inadvertently placed our relations with the Soviet Union on a hair trigger."

1984 was a very dark and dangerous year. One septuagenarian Soviet leader after another died. East-West relations were highly confrontational, and all U.S.-Soviet arms control remained suspended. Rick and I spent much of the year trying to persuade an apparently skeptical Shultz of the importance of getting these negotiations restarted. On one occasion we presented Shultz with a briefing, complete with Pentagon-style charts on large squares of pasteboard, showing the evolving U.S.-Soviet nuclear balance. My role was to flip the slides while Rick presented the case for renewed strategic arms talks, and Shultz listened impassively, asking a question or two. When we finished and the secretary had departed, his senior aide Ray Seitz provided a one-word reaction: "Boring!" But Ray was joking; he knew Shultz was biding his time until Weinberger could be sidetracked and Reagan was ready to reengage with Moscow.

Comic relief was provided by the behavior of three of our ambassadors, all accredited to small, prosperous, and friendly European countries. One envoy, a late-middle-age married man, was interrupted by the police while he was serenading a local young lady outside her home on a cold winter's night. His colleague in the adjoining country was observed on several occasions by the local police climbing out a second-story window of his residence on his way to a midnight tryst. The third American ambassador, assigned to a country that had recently relaxed its obscenity laws, took to showing pornographic movies in an adjoining room during large diplomatic receptions.

Ronald Reagan's reelection assured a degree of continuity in Washington, leading Rick to begin thinking about what he might like to do next. Over lunch one day he wondered aloud whether he should seek to succeed Arthur Burns, former head of the Federal Reserve Bank, who was then our ambassador to Germany. I thought this a capital idea, hastening to add that I would be happy to join him there.

In early 1985 Shultz and Gromyko agreed to resume both the INF and the strategic arms talks. Around the same time a Pershing II missile misfired in Germany killing three American soldiers. We had spent the last several years seeking to reassure the German public about the safety of these nuclear-armed missiles and now one had blown up. Happily, it was not armed, or even fully assembled. I traveled to the U.S. Army missile unit where the accident had occurred. The setting was pretty sobering. Whereas the cruise missiles under U.S. Air Force control spent most of the time stored in deep underground bunkers within hardened and closely guarded military bases, these Pershing missiles, along with all their associated equipment, were located in the open air with little in the way of visible security and no protection from the elements. Missiles, launchers, and command trailers were scattered around a football field-size area, and the soldiers walked from one to the other through the moist grass and muddy bare spots. In wartime this lack of fixed basing was designed to improve security by facilitating mobility and complicating hostile targeting. In peacetime, however, it seemed vulnerable both to accident and malign interference from anti-nuclear activists or even from the small but deadly terrorist cells still active throughout West Germany.

Rick had been replaced in the Bureau of Political-Military Affairs by Jon Howe, a young rear admiral on loan to State from the U.S. Navy.

Howe inherited the thankless task of trying to coordinate U.S. policy on arms control issues. Rick, ever competitive, waged bureaucratic warfare against PM with the same gusto as he had against EUR when the sides were reversed. Howe did his best to act as an honest broker between State and DOD, which tended to mean between EUR and DOD, since Howe did not seem to have strong views of his own. Richard Perle remained the principal protagonist on the other side. The U.S. military, represented by the joint staff, had tended to be more pragmatic and open to sensible arms control approaches until they were whipped into line by Perle. After one meeting in which the joint staff representative expressed cautious support for the State view, I overheard Perle threaten unspecified reprisals if this behavior was repeated.

I represented the European bureau in these invariably painful interagency encounters, doing my best at each meeting to fend off some new assault on the East-West arms control agenda. This was a lonely task, as Howe remained neutral, the National Security Council staffers supported Perle, and the joint staff had been beaten into line. Even the Arms Control and Disarmament Agency, under Ken Adelman, was an uncertain ally. Richard Perle was a skilled debater who came well-prepared and usually had a sympathetic audience. Perle's deputies, Frank Gaffney and Doug Feith, were even more difficult to deal with, rivaling their chief in rigid opposition to any positive movement in the arms control sphere while lacking Richard's eloquence and wit.

Not that Perle was always wrong. He insisted that the phased array radar under construction near the Soviet town of Krasnoyarsk was a violation of the Anti-Ballistic Missile Treaty, something we at State were reluctant to concede. His zero option for INF also prevailed in the end.

Rick and I were able to work cooperatively with Perle on an updating of NATO's military doctrine. West Germany had long resisted any strategy that contemplated prolonged conflict, whether conventional or nuclear, on its soil. Bonn, therefore, preferred that NATO threaten early escalation to strategic, that is intercontinental-range, nuclear weapons to discourage the Soviet Union from thinking that a European conflict could be confined either geographically or to only conventional weapons. The United States, for equally obvious reasons, preferred to envisage a slower, more drawn out process of escalation before arriving at intercontinental nuclear war. The longstanding NATO strategy of flexible response was an uneasy compromise between these preferences.

In conversation with a military officer on Chancellor Helmut Kohl's staff, I discovered some willingness to move the German position a bit closer to the American one. I alerted Rick to the opportunity, and he convinced Richard Perle to pursue the opening. Perle had a second home in the South of France, near Avignon, where he liked to spend the summer, and he and I met there with a German team headed by Kohl's national security adviser, Horst Teltschik. Over several leisurely meals at local restaurants we were able to hammer out a modest adjustment to NATO's strategy that was subsequently adopted by the membership as a whole.

During these years the nuclear freeze movement in the United States was at its height, and I often found myself defending administration policy before domestic as well as European audiences. Personally, I thought a nuclear war unlikely but hardly unimaginable, and I was well aware of its Armageddon-like consequences. It was for this reason that I thought the pursuit of arms control and détente with the Soviet Union to be a moral imperative, while also recognizing the need to maintain a stable nuclear balance and sustain deterrence. The apparent desire by Perle and other hardliners in the administration to actually win the arms race rather than seek mutual restraints struck me as deeply dangerous and highly irresponsible.

It was during this same period that I found myself drawn into doomsday planning. I was designated an essential personnel for "continuity of government." When a nuclear attack was deemed imminent, a small cadre of identified officials would take shelter far from Washington to govern the country were the capital to be destroyed. My experience with preparations for nuclear war had initially come at a much earlier age, in the early 1950s, as I was taught to take shelter under my schoolroom desk while air raid sirens sounded and thousands of people all over New York were hustled into makeshift shelters. There were then no Soviet bombers that could reach New York, and by the time there were, taking shelter anywhere near ground zero was recognized as futile.

It was with some skepticism, therefore, that I joined several dozen other officials at an underground facility well outside Washington to be briefed on our duties in the event of World War III. One of my State Department colleagues flatly refused to participate in the program, insisting that the last thing he would do in the event of an imminent nuclear attack would be to abandon his wife and children. I have always regretted not having taken a similar stand.

In the years since the demise of the Soviet Union, some have argued that the Reagan defense build-up, the president's harsh rhetorical stance (labeling the USSR the "evil empire"), and, above all, Reagan's infatuation with the vision of a space-based defense against a ballistic missile attack (known derisively as Star Wars) contributed to that collapse. If so, this was entirely fortuitous. It was certainly not what the advocate of these policies intended. Perle, Weinberger, and others pushed forever higher American defense spending because they genuinely believed that the Soviet Union was a growing threat. We now know that its defenses, like every other aspect of its society, were rapidly atrophying throughout the 1980s. Star War visionaries, most notably the president, genuinely believed that technologies were at hand that could protect the United States from a massive nuclear attack, something that remains as unfeasible today, more than thirty years later, as it was then.

Whatever impact Reagan's first-term tough guy approach may have had on Soviet decision-making, it certainly gave the president great cover from domestic criticism during his second term when he went further and faster than any predecessor toward nuclear disarmament. The early 1980s had seen the rise of a major anti-nuclear weapons movement in the United States and Western Europe, and these protests had been strongly stimulated by Reagan's harsh rhetoric and loose talk about nuclear war. The country was, therefore, much more receptive to the sweeping advances in détente and arms control that occurred in the late eighties than it would have been half a decade earlier.

Early in 1985 while I was on a visit to Brussels, Rick asked me drop what I was doing and fly to join him in Paris. On my arrival he confided that he would soon be named to succeed Arthur Burns in Bonn, and he asked me to join him as deputy chief of mission. I immediately accepted, believing this to be the best posting in the American Foreign Service. I was not to be disappointed.

TEN

A Small Town in Germany

WEST GERMANY WAS BOTH AMERICA'S most important ally and the principal prize over which the Cold War was being fought. It stood at the absolute center of the transatlantic and the East-West relationship. As ambassador to the federal republic, Rick would oversee not just the embassy in Bonn, but also the U.S. mission in West Berlin and five consulates, one of which, in Frankfurt, was itself the seventh largest Foreign Service post in the world. West Germany was also host to the largest concentration of American military strength outside the United States, hosting nearly 300,000 American soldiers and airmen overseen by three resident four-star generals. Cold War Germany contained the world's largest concentration of spies, American and otherwise. All this made U.S. Embassy Bonn and its six outposts probably the biggest and arguably the most important diplomatic mission in the world.

During the work week Bonn was a center of government, politics, diplomacy, and espionage. John le Carré memorialized this last feature in his novel *A Small Town in Germany*. But on the weekends Bonn was once again a small riverside university town, deserted by the politicians, most of whom returned to their constituencies. Official American visitors shunned Bonn on the weekends, as it had no night life, museums, or high-end shopping, preferring to spend their leisure time in London, Paris, or Rome.

When the West German capital was established here in the early 1950s, the United States built housing for its embassy staff. The American colony, as it was called by the Germans, was located on the banks of the Rhine. It was comprised of a hundred or so well-proportioned apartments, half a dozen large houses with riverside views, an elementary and a high school, a library, a movie theater, a supermarket, and a social club. Bonn was the only American embassy to have its own church, a lovely New England-style wooden chapel complete with belfry. This small community was not cut off from the city. There were no walls, the streets were maintained and policed by the German authorities, and the entire area was open to the German public. Indeed, a number of the embassy apartments were let to German families, while the community social club, with its pool, tennis courts, and restaurant also welcomed German members.

I arrived several weeks ahead of Rick, who was still going through the confirmation process. My predecessor, Bill Woessner, was returning to Washington to become the principal deputy to Rick's successor in the European Bureau. Bill was not looking forward to the posting. I had rather enjoyed the cut and thrust of Washington policymaking, even in the chaos of the early Reagan administration, but Bill expressed real distaste for this competitive, friction-filled environment.

An aversion to Washington among FSOs is not all that uncommon. Some people join the Foreign Service because they want to make policy, others because they want to live abroad. The former hope to influence in some small way the course of history; the latter want to experience, understand, and interpret foreign societies. There are, thus, Foreign Service officers who have little interest in meeting foreigners and others who have little interest in making foreign policy. Bill had clearly performed well in both capacities, else he would not be where he was and going where he was going. But his heart was not in the trench warfare that he knew awaited him as a foot soldier in the Shultz-Weinberger battles. Within a year he would retire to run a large German-American youth exchange program.

Bill had me to lunch on the terrace of his, soon-to-be my, house. It was a bright sunny day and the garden was in full bloom. We could hear the barges chugging up the nearby Rhine. His cook had prepared a light meal of fish and vegetables, which his butler served along with a dry white wine. Bill had somehow managed to extend his stay in Bonn to nearly seven years and would happily have remained longer, and I could see why. This was the most comfortable, attractive, interesting, and, arguably, most important post in the world. I could not believe my good fortune.

At thirty-eight, Rick would be the youngest American ever to serve as ambassador to Germany. He was replacing the oldest, Arthur Burns, who had been eighty-one when he departed Bonn a few weeks before my arrival. Although five years older than Rick, I was also younger and less advanced in the service than most of my peers in the diplomatic community and even my immediate subordinates in the embassy. Several of the old German hands on our staff were distressed to see the embassy headed by two tyros who spoke no German and had never served in the country before, and this led at least one to request a transfer.

I set to correcting the first of these deficiencies, scheduling two hours of German lessons each day. Eventually, I became proficient enough for most professional purposes, although informal conversation in a noisy, crowded room always remained a strain. Rick actually had a better facility for language and, although he worked less at it, became able to understand pretty much anything that was said and respond appropriately, if not at length. Nearly all German officials, journalists, academics, and business leaders spoke better English than we did German, yet many leading German politicians, beginning with Chancellor Helmut Kohl and the foreign minister, Hans-Dietrich Genscher, conversed exclusively in German.

Rick and his wife, Gahl, made a big splash on the German social scene. Both were young, poised, attractive, and photogenic. Gahl had been the White House social secretary under Nancy Reagan, and she and Rick met at a party hosted by the president and first lady aboard a yacht in the Potomac. In the government and diplomatic communities, Rick and Gahl had no competition. German politicians and high officials were notably frumpy, while Rick's colleagues in the diplomatic corps were all at least a generation older. The capital had no high society, but Rick and Gahl were quickly invited to gala balls and more intimate affairs in the cosmopolitan cities of Munich, Frankfurt, and Hamburg. Their every appearance was heavily covered by the German press and within a few months, they were, and remained throughout their tenure, celebrities of the first order.

I was happy to leave to them this aspect of our work. Early on, Toril and I had accepted an invitation to attend the annual ball given in Bremen in honor of German-American friendship. The city fathers turned out in remarkable numbers for this event, which was clearly a high point on the city's social calendar. But an evening dancing with matrons a decade or two my senior and attempting to converse over the music with my then-embryonic German was an experience I decided not to repeat.

Entertaining was, nevertheless, an important aspect of the job. On most weeks I would host one or two lunches with local officials or politicians. Senior American visitors would be put up either at Rick's house or mine and working dinners organized for them. Once or twice a year Toril and I held larger dinner dances, and Rick found a Rolling Stones cover band for these occasions. Earlier in his life Rick had been the vocalist in a rock band and could still be prevailed upon to perform a set, making him almost certainly the only member of the Bonn diplomatic corps to occasionally channel Mick Jagger.

Acting as an interface between the large American military presence and the national German authorities was an important aspect of our responsibilities. These relationships were generally positive and required only limited intervention on the embassy's part. Older Germans remembered and were grateful for the Marshall Plan, the Berlin airlift, and the continued American defense of their country. Younger Germans could be more skeptical, even critical, regarding American nuclear weapons deployments, but this was rarely manifested in discourtesy toward the hundreds of thousands of Americans residing in their country.

On one occasion, with Rick out of the country, I was invited to accompany Helmut Kohl to a joint U.S.-German military training exercise. On the flight back to Bonn Kohl asked me to join him at the front of the plane for coffee. The Luftwaffe steward poured us both a cup and I watched as the chancellor of Germany fished in his pocket, took out a small change purse, and handed the uniformed airman several deutsche marks coins in payment. Noticing my wonderment Kohl shrugged. "Nur in Deutschland," he said. I later discovered that Kohl also paid rent on his official residence.

Shortly before its release Rick organized a preview of the Tom Cruise film *Top Gun*. We rented a theater and invited several hundred guests, mostly senior German military officers. As the movie progressed I became increasingly apprehensive, imagining how this influential and conservative German audience was going to react to the film's over-the-top combination of machismo, nationalism, and aggression. For over forty years Germans' pride in their country and its military had been severely repressed as being too reminiscent of a Nazi past. I needn't have worried. As the crowd exited the theater it was apparent that these particular Germans had loved the picture in all its flag waving, testosterone fueled, jet propelled spectacle.

There were occasional irritants in the U.S.-German military relationship. One was the American Air Force commitment to low-level flying. The Air Force required its pilots train regularly in flying a few hundred feet above the ground, even through hilly and mountainous terrain, a technique which, in wartime, would allow them to attack an advancing enemy while evading radar detection. But having an F-16 zoom a few feet above one's house at near supersonic speed could be quite unnerving. Horst Teltschik, the chancellor's national security adviser, a hawk and ally on nearly all such matters, complained to me about being roused from a midday nap on his summer holiday. "Can't your Air Force take a lunch break?" he asked plaintively. Brokering accommodations of that sort was part of my job.

Sometimes the friction had a more serious, even tragic source. In 1988 three planes performing air acrobatics at a public airshow hosted by the America airbase at Ramstein, the headquarters of the U.S. Air Force in Europe, flew into one another. One of the three planes then plowed into a crowd of 300,000 people, killing sixty-seven and injuring hundreds more. Rick immediately rushed to the scene, having persuaded the German defense minister to accompany him. The public uproar lasted for weeks, and the fact that the German government had no role in authorizing or regulating such events became a source of controversy. The entirely innocent minister of defense paid the price and was soon forced to resign.

Late one evening I was alerted to a report of an imminent attack on American military personnel in Berlin. I immediately called the head of our mission there, who in turn contacted the commanding general. Military police were dispatched to every known gathering place of American servicemen in the city. One of these patrols arrived just a few minutes too late. A bomb went off at the La Belle Disco, killing two American soldiers and wounding sixty-seven others. Again Rick flew immediately to the scene and surveyed the wreckage. He was then faced with the difficult task of visiting with a wounded serviceman who had lost all his limbs and, shortly afterward, his life.

Press reports soon revealed that a telex had been intercepted from the Libyan government in Tripoli congratulating its embassy in East Berlin for the attack. The United States urged its allies to apply harsh sanctions against Libya in response, but the German government resisted. I suggested Rick give a press conference laying out the case for a united response. Unfortunately, Chancellor Kohl had called his own press conference for the same afternoon. In it he insisted that "sanctions never work." Rick was, naturally, asked to respond to the chancellor's statement, and he characterized Kohl's assertion as "pure theory." The German press found this terminological clash between the American ambassador and the German chancellor more interesting than the substance of their disagreement. Speaking on background, unnamed German officials stoked this controversy for several days, illustrating how hard it is for any outsider to best government leaders in their own domestic press.

Ten days after the La Belle bombing, having failed to secure united action on economic sanctions, the United States retaliated militarily. American aircraft, flying out of British bases and detouring around France, bombed Qaddafi's headquarters in Tripoli, killing his adopted daughter among more than two dozen other people. Ten years later, following the country's unification, the German authorities gained access to East German secret police files, allowing them to track down, try, and convict the four individuals directly responsible for the La Belle bombing. Eight years later still the Libyan government accepted responsibility for the attack and paid $35 million in compensation.

In late 1988 the embassy received another warning, this one of a planned attack on a transatlantic airline flight. I immediately directed that the German authorities and the relevant airlines be alerted. Several days later Pan Am Flight 103 took off from Frankfurt to London and New York. A bomb exploded as this plane transited Scotland, the debris falling on the town of Lockerbie. Two hundred and seventy passengers and crew were killed along with eleven victims on the ground. The next day an American security team found our warning about such an attack under a pile of papers on a desk at the Frankfurt airport. The Libyan leadership was again blamed, and eventually, years later, accepted responsibility for the attack.

West Germany had its own home-grown terrorist movement. Self-labeled the Red Army Faction (RAF) and better known as the Baader-Meinhof gang, this extreme leftist group was responsible for a number of deadly attacks beginning in the 1970s and continuing through the early

1990s. One occurred a few weeks after my arrival, when a car bomb exploded at an American airbase outside Frankfurt, killing two Americans and wounding twenty others. In preparation for that attack the perpetrators had kidnapped and killed an American airman to obtain his ID card, with which they gained access to the base.

On my way from Washington to Bonn to take up my new position, I stopped in Paris for a Quad political directors meeting. There I informed my German, French, and British colleagues that American counterterrorism authorities had information suggesting the Red Army Faction was beginning to collaborate with similar Italian and French extremist groups, the Red Brigades and Action Direct, raising the prospect of a transnational Euro-terrorist network. My European colleagues all scoffed at this notion and dismissed the warning.

A year later I was wakened around midnight to be told that Gerold von Braunmühl, the German political director, had been gunned down in front of his home an hour earlier, when returning from a dinner engagement. Von Braunmühl had been the German participant in that Paris meeting. Evidence subsequently indicated the Red Army Faction had, indeed, collaborated with the French group Action Direct in this attack. More ominous still, the killers, in their communiqué taking responsibility for the attack, stated that von Braunmühl had been targeted precisely because of his participation in the Quadripartite forum, which was labeled a counterrevolutionary conspiracy. This rattled the German authorities. The Quad forum was then still a closely guarded secret, so the communiqué suggested that the RAF might have a source of information from within the Foreign Office itself.

Rick's residence and mine were closely guarded and we both traveled in armored cars. Rick had a very professional German police security detail, which shifted to protecting me whenever Rick was out of the country. I did not find this entirely reassuring, as it struck me that suddenly acquiring a police detail probably made me a more visible target. I submitted, however, realizing that having established this detail, the German authorities needed to keep it busy. Fortunately, German terrorists did not target women or children. Toril and the boys were free to roam an otherwise very safe city.

Both American and German intelligence picked up occasional information about planned attacks on the embassy itself. Late one night the building took rifle fire from across the river. Bullets tore through the plasterboard walls, but the building was empty and no one was hurt. Security, nevertheless, remained a real preoccupation throughout our time in Bonn.

Germany, East and West, was also espionage central. On our side we worked closely with the relevant German authorities. Bob Gates, then the deputy director of central intelligence, and I represented the United States at a small and very quiet ceremony to mark the fiftieth anniversary of the West German external security service, the Bundesnachrichtendienst, or BND. This institution started life under American tutelage, and its original head was Reinhard Gehlen, who had previously overseen German Army intelligence on the Soviet Union during World War II. What was originally known as the Gehlen Organization was overseen by the American Army and then the CIA in the years leading up to the creation of the West German state. The relationship remained close thereafter.

Rick and I entertained a regular string of visitors from Langley, including Bill Casey, Reagan's CIA director, the swashbuckling Dewey Claridge, head of European operations for the agency, and his boss, Clair George. At a garden party for Casey, my children were spotted taking pot shots with their toy pistols at the director from our second-story window. All of these individuals later became enmeshed in the Iran-Contra controversy.

Another visitor in Bonn was John Kelly, then the U.S. ambassador in Lebanon. John had been my colleague in Sonnenfeldt's office, and later another deputy in Rick Burt's EUR. John was a bachelor at this time. On a couple of occasions he spent his leave in Bonn, staying with Rick and Gahl, and he regaled us with tales of his collaboration with Ollie North, still on the National Security Council staff, in efforts to free American hostages being held in Lebanon by the Iranian-backed Lebanese militant movement, Hezbollah. John said that, at Ollie's direction, he was keeping his superiors in the State Department in the dark regarding these activities. We warned John that this might not be prudent.

A few months later several American hostages held in Lebanon were released and brought initially to a U.S. Army hospital in Germany before being flown back to the United States. Rick drove to Frankfurt to welcome the hostages, and while waiting for them to disembark, spoke with Robert Oakley, Shultz's top adviser on terrorism issues. Rick congratulated him on securing their freedom. "You wouldn't be so pleased if you knew how this came about," Oakley responded. He explained that the release had been arranged by Iran in exchange for a shipment of American arms for use in that country's ongoing war with Iraq.

Only later did we, along with the rest of the world, learn the full extent of this three-way trade in which American arms went to Iran, American hostages were returned to the United States, and Iranian money went to the pro-Western Contra insurgents in Nicaragua.

Secretary Shultz subsequently testified to Congress that he had been unaware of the arms-for-hostages trade with Iran, and John Kelly was publicly branded as the "rogue ambassador." Given what Rick had been told by Oakley, Schultz's direct subordinate, the secretary's professed ignorance of the arms for hostages trade struck both of us as implausible. Years later documents surfaced that tended to confirm that Shultz had been aware at least of the Iranian angle if not the money transfer to the Contras.

One result of Iran-Contra was that instructions went out to all ambassadors directing that, henceforth, they should take direction exclusively from State, the only exception being orders that came from the president personally. Cap Weinberger, Bud McFarlane, Ollie North, Clair George, and Dewey Claridge were all charged with lying to Congress, only to be subsequently pardoned by President George H. W. Bush. Nor did John Kelly suffer any lasting damage. Quite the contrary; he was named by Bush to head the State's Middle Eastern Bureau.

Family life in Bonn was idyllic. Our sons could walk to school, return home for lunch, and roam further abroad as they wished. We had a big house with plenty of space, so my family and Toril's could visit regularly. We were able to visit Norway at least once a year. We also traveled extensively throughout Germany and beyond. The countryside around Bonn was dotted with ruined castles, lush farmland, vineyards, forested hills, and winding river valleys. Social life was active but not onerous, and our highly professional household staff made entertainment almost effortless. Weekends were uninterrupted.

Rick, Gahl, Toril, and I were together often. Rick and Gahl included us in all their entertainment, and we them. We visited Berlin together on a number of occasions; the ambassador had a second residence, complete with its own household staff, where we stayed even when traveling without Rick and Gahl.

Showing the flag in Berlin was an important part of our responsibilities. The U.S. Air Force flew us to and from Berlin whenever requested, requiring only a few hours' notice. Formally, the city was still occupied and, thus, under the ultimate control of the four victorious World War II powers, although in the West most responsibilities had long ago been ceded to the local German authorities. Soviet, American, British, and French representatives would meet periodically in the Kommandatura building to discuss issues related to Berlin security.

The American hierarchy in West Berlin had the ambassador at its top, under whom came the commandant of the Berlin Brigade, under whom, in turn, was the chief of the U.S. mission in Berlin, the top resident diplomat. The West German government funded official American expenses (and those of France and the United Kingdom) through what was still called the "occupation budget." The U.S. mission continued to run one of the city's most popular radio stations, Radio in the American Sector, or RIAS Berlin. Our mission also still held and controlled access to the Nazi Party archives.

I took my family to Berlin once via rail, on a train still operated by the American military. The train awaited us at a private siding close by the embassy. Overnight we ended our way slowly through East Germany. This was not an expeditious way to get to Berlin, but my sons would forever remember that they had once traveled on their own private train. Thirty years later Christian and Colin still recall the East German soldiers with AK 47s patrolling each of the small, rural stations we traversed that night. In Berlin I took them to the largest department store in the Eastern, or Soviet, sector. One look at the ill-stocked toy department—no Lego, no Star Wars figures—was enough to convince my sons of the superior merits of capitalism.

The periodic Berlin crises of the 1940s, fifties, and sixties had been brought to a conclusion in a 1972 agreement between the four occupying powers regulating access to the city. Throughout our time in Germany the city remained quiet and there was no need to exercise the sweeping authority the occupying powers retained. Diplomats, military personnel, and most foreigners could travel freely to and from East Berlin. West Berliners and other West Germans had more difficulty crossing the wall, while East Germans were shot for trying.

The East Berlin opera was a great favorite among allied personnel. It occupied its lovely old prewar house on the Unter den Linden. Comparable in quality to Western opera companies, it was much less expensive, and during the intervals the lobby was often filled with allied soldiers in full dress uniforms of every shade of blue, green, khaki, and even the tartan of an occasional Scot regimental kilt.

The wall, Checkpoint Charlie, and a host of other Cold War artifacts were reminders of an earlier, tenser era. These structures and the elaborate, often arcane procedures through which occupation and division of the city were maintained had been preserved for decades as if in amber. In late 1986 we participated in yet another Berlin ritual when we negotiated the last of the classic Cold War spies swaps.

Like so much else about Berlin in the late 1980s, this swap followed a time-honored choreography. Olaf Grobel, the head of our political section, traveled to Berlin to meet with Wolfgang Vogel, the same East German lawyer who, twenty-four years earlier, had brokered the first such exchange, the one that brought the captured U-2 pilot Francis Gary Powers back to the United States in exchange for the convicted Soviet spy Rudolf Abel. Our trade involved several real Soviet and Western secret agents and also the well-known Soviet dissident Natan Sharansky. The exchange took place at midnight on "the bridge of spies," the Glienicke bridge, which spans the River Havel, connecting West Berlin to Potsdam in East Germany. Rick was waiting on the Berlin side to welcome Sharansky and the others to freedom.

Air traffic to West Berlin was monopolized by three non-German carriers: Air France, British Air, and Pan Am. All three had to fly through narrow air corridors that had been established in 1945. The free market-oriented Reagan administration decided to introduce the "open skies" concept to the rigidly apportioned Berlin market, thereby freeing a wider range of American carriers to compete to provide more traffic on this route. The British and French resisted, leading to weeks of increasingly tense negotiations. The standoff among the three allied governments eventually threatened to interrupt air service into West Berlin, something even the Soviet Union had shrunk from doing. Leading these talks for the U.S. side, I discovered that commercial negotiations among nominally friendly governments could become at least as acrimonious as the East-West bargaining with which I was more familiar. Eventually, after several late-night sessions, we secured an agreement to liberalize the Berlin air travel market.

West Germany's long-serving Foreign Minister Hans-Dietrich Genscher was the leading proponent of dialogue with both Moscow and East Berlin. This often put him at odds with the harder-line Reagan administration. Rick and I spent much of our four years in Bonn seeking to persuade Chancellor Kohl and his more conservative advisers to rein in his foreign minister but our efforts were seldom successful. Genscher was too skillful and too much in touch with mainstream German opinion to be circumvented. At one point Rick was quoted by the German press referring to Genscher as a "slippery man." Like the "pure theory" reference to Kohl's dismissal of sanctions, the "slippery man" characterization was seized on by the German media, fed by protestations from unnamed Foreign Office officials who complained about such a shocking transgression. Despite, or more likely because of, these protestations, this description stuck. Henceforth German and American media commentary would routinely characterize Genscher as "slippery." Even forty years later, when Genscher passed away in 2016, Rick's phrase found its way into both the *New York Times* and the *Washington Post* obituaries.

Genscher's Ostpolitik (Eastern policy) was making only limited progress in overcoming his country's division, but there were big changes underway in the larger East-West relationship. These were only intermittently apparent to us in Bonn. Late one evening in 1986, I received a call from Roz Ridgway, Rick's successor in EUR. She called from Reykjavik, Iceland, where she was with President Reagan and Mikhail Gorbachev and asked me to urgently inform the German government that Gorbachev had agreed to the zero option of INF missiles. Roz also referred elliptically to even more startling developments that "you will not believe." We soon learned that Gorbachev had proposed abolishing all nuclear weapons and Reagan had come close to accepting, balking only at Gorbachev's demand that he give up his cherished dream of a space-based shield against nuclear attack. This was pretty breathtaking stuff.

Eight months later Ronald Reagan was scheduled to visit Germany and I flew to Berlin to scout locations for a speech. The head of our mission there, John Kornblum, drove me around to four possible sites. I liked the one directly in front of the Brandenburg Gate, where the Berlin Wall divided the city at its most monumental spot. John accurately cautioned that this location would be perceived as provocative, certainly by the Soviets and East Germans, but also by some Berliners and West Germans. I, nevertheless, was struck by the visual and symbolic appeal of the spot that stood directly before the Soviet Union's World War II memorial, faced the location of the pre–World War II American embassy, and looked out upon the arch through which the Kaiser's armies had once marched. On returning to Bonn, I sold Rick and then the White House advance team on this site. As John had predicted, the West Berlin authorities resisted, but backed by ultimate allied authority over Berlin, he was able to ensure that the event took place at this historic location.

"Mr. Gorbachev, tear down this wall" may be the single most repeated sentence Reagan ever uttered. Certainly it ranks with Kennedy's "Ich bin ein Berliner" among high points in American Cold War rhetoric. Yet none of us who heard it actually thought Gorbachev would do as he was asked.

A few months later Ken Dam, Shultz's top deputy, visited Bonn on his way back from Moscow, and told us that Gorbachev had agreed to withdraw all Soviet forces from Afghanistan. This seemed almost as improbable as his tearing down the wall.

During what was to be our last year in Bonn, Rick was working to persuade Washington of the need to replace the then-obsolete Lance missiles, many of which were based in Germany, with a new generation of short-range nuclear armed missiles. By now intermediate-range missiles had been banned and all the Pershing II and nuclear-armed cruise missiles were in the process of being withdrawn from Europe. Still permitted, however, were shorter-range weapons. Earlier in the decade, Germany, along with other NATO allies, had agreed that when the Lance system became obsolete a new nuclear-armed missile should be fielded as a replacement. In the succeeding years, as had been the case with INF, popular opposition to short-range nuclear force (SNF) modernization gained ground. "The shorter the range, the deader the Germans" was the opposition's rather apt rallying cry. The German government was divided, with some favoring Lance modernization. A few German officials even opposed a new zero option offer to the Soviet Union, fearing the absence of such weapons would leave Germany open to conventional attack.

I drafted a message, which Rick sent, arguing the importance of replacing Lance with a new missile system and opposing any effort to bargain this possibility away in negotiation with the Soviet Union. Our telegram employed the same arguments that had been used in promoting INF deployments a decade earlier. This time, though, my heart wasn't in the effort. Predictable German resistance and the dovish mood that had swept late-Reagan Washington made ours a hard sell and we eventually received a signal from Shultz to stop agitating the issue.

One of the first nominations put forward by newly elected President George H. W. Bush was for Vernon Walters to become ambassador to

West Germany. Rick was to move to Geneva, where he would head negotiations to complete a new strategic nuclear arms treaty with the Soviet Union, and I would stay and overlap with Walters for several months before I returned to Washington to become principal deputy to Ridgway's successor at the head of the European Bureau.

Toril and I threw a big going away bash for Rick and Gahl. The theme was *Casablanca*, Rick's favorite movie, and embassy carpenters converted the library in our residence into a fair imitation of Rick's Café, complete with our butler in the guise of a tarbooshed bartender. Rick donned a white dinner jacket, fronted the band, and channeled Mick Jagger for one last time.

While in Washington awaiting confirmation for his new post, Rick sought to interest the Bush administration in Lance replacement. As a result he was asked to return and pitch Chancellor Kohl on the topic. We both went to see Kohl in a small town in Austria where he was vacationing, and the chancellor met us alone in the back room of a rustic bierstube. He listened politely but made no commitment.

I first encountered Vernon (Dick) Walters twenty years earlier, when we were both serving in Paris. He was the embassy's top military attaché, and later, it was he who arranged Kissinger's clandestine meetings with the North Vietnamese negotiators. Walters continued to conduct clandestine missions for successive administrations, eventually rising to become the deputy director of the CIA. In that capacity he rebuffed pressure from the Nixon White House to involve the agency in the Watergate cover-up. Subsequently he became Reagan's ambassador to the United Nations.

While awaiting confirmation Walters was quoted in the press predicting that German unification could occur within the next decade. This left everyone in Bonn, Americans as well as Germans, scratching their heads and wondering what on Earth gave him such an implausible notion.

On his arrival in Bonn, Walters treated me with great kindness. He was a garrulous fellow with an incredible facility for languages and a seemingly inexhaustible fund of anecdotes. (Rick, who once sat next to Walters on flights to and then back from a funeral in New Delhi, maintained that Walter's store of anecdotes was not, in fact, inexhaustible, but rather were recycled several times in the course of this trip.) Be that as it may, I found Walters an amusing companion and a very gracious boss.

Shortly after Walter's arrival Bush made his first presidential visit to Europe. Stepping down from *Air Force One*, the president walked along the usual receiving line. Seeing me toward its end, he suddenly reached over several intervening people with a handshake and a "great to see a familiar face" greeting. This was typical of his warmth and courtesy, even to someone he could only barely have remembered from various meetings while vice president. As Walters was a lifelong bachelor, Toril had the pleasure of escorting Barbara Bush through her program over the next several days.

Bush gave his major address of the trip in Mainz. There he called for "Europe whole and free," his first use of that phrase. He also spoke of "partnership in leadership" with Germany, a concept Rick had long pushed. Rick and I had recommended that he also use this occasion to explicitly endorse the goal of German reunification. Bush did not go that far, perhaps because he had already said something to that effect in a newspaper interview a few weeks earlier.

On his way to Germany Bush stopped first in Brussels for a NATO summit, where it was agreed to postpone any decision on Lance modernization until the following year. This delay was intended to keep that issue out of the upcoming German national elections, but a year later the world had changed so dramatically that the matter was dropped forever.

Even from the relatively placid backwater of Bonn it was becoming clear that things elsewhere in Europe were beginning to move. In preparation for my upcoming assignment I made short visits to Warsaw, Budapest, and Moscow. In all three capitals I felt the ice of half a century beginning to crack, yet I still had no sense how far and how fast this was to go. I also visited East Berlin, where I met with Lothar de Maizière, leader of the tame "opposition" party long tolerated by the Communist regime. We lunched on the terrace of a newly opened Western-style hotel, and neither of us could imagine that in less than a year this pleasant and apparently inconsequential man would become East Germany's first non-Communist leader and its last head of state.

Ray Seitz was Jim Baker's pick to head EUR. Ray was the junior Africanist Kingman Brewster had made deputy head of his political section ten years earlier. He had gone on to become George Shultz's executive assistant, and then returned to London as deputy chief of mission. I was to arrive in Washington early that summer to run the bureau while Ray awaited confirmation by the Senate.

Toril, the boys, and I left Bonn with some reluctance. Nowhere else was the work, play, and family time in such positive balance. Helping run

America's largest diplomatic mission and represent the United States to its most important ally was endlessly fascinating, and living in a bucolic small town on the banks of the Rhine, facing hillsides sprinkled with vineyards and topped with ruined castles was idyllic. Little did we imagine that the city we were leaving was about to fade back into obscurity, the country to reemerge as a once-again unified nation.

ELEVEN

A World Reordered

ON THE DAY I ARRIVED at the department, I was asked whether I wanted to officially begin signing memos as the acting assistant secretary, even though the paperwork relating to my own appointment was still incomplete. "What's the alternative?" I asked. I was told that Felix Bloch, then the most senior of the bureau's office directors, would become acting if I declined. I was pretty sure neither Baker nor any of his lieutenants would know who Bloch was, so to avoid confusion, I said to put my name on papers going out of the bureau. The next day, the FBI informed me that Bloch was under investigation for espionage; he had been under surveillance and was observed passing what was thought to be secret information to a contact in the Soviet embassy. This soon became public but, happily, when it did so, Bloch was not identified as the head of State's largest geographic bureau, the one responsible for relations with the country for which he was allegedly spying.*

---

*Bloch was fired, but never charged.

A few days later I was on my way back to Europe, accompanying President Bush on a visit to Poland and Hungary. Both countries were liberalizing fast. Since my brief visit only a few weeks earlier Solidarity, the formerly illegal Polish trade union, had won a sweeping electoral victory and been asked to form a government, and Hungary had begun to dismantle barriers to free movement with the West, opening its border with Austria. This move would generate the largest outflow from the German Democratic Republic (GDR) since the wall went up in 1961, as East Germans seized the opportunity to immigrate to West Germany via Hungary and then Austria.

We traveled to Gdansk, where Bush met with Solidarity leader Lech Walesa, and in Budapest Bush spoke to a huge outdoor gathering. As Eastern Europe liberalized, the once unthinkable idea of Western aid to these countries became attractive. Several weeks later I joined the Sherpas preparing for that summer's G-7 summit and urged a major Western program of aid to what were still Warsaw Pact member states. This proposal was accepted, the only disagreement being whether such assistance should be overseen by foreign or finance ministers. Shortly thereafter the G-7 leaders, meeting in Paris, agreed to initiate such assistance to be overseen in the U.S. case by the State Department.

Seitz was confirmed and took over the bureau leadership shortly thereafter, and we began to put together the rest of our leadership team, selecting three other deputies. The slate we submitted were all white males, like every EUR front office before it, but the rules had changed. We were told by the Seventh Floor that one of these deputies would have to go to a woman. Accordingly, we reversed the order of two intended promotions. The woman we had chosen to take over the office of NATO and political-military affairs, perhaps the largest and most prestigious such unit in the department, instead received a double step up to become the deputy responsible for overseeing both that office and the one responsible for Western Europe. The officer we had intended to appoint as deputy was, instead, confirmed as the head of the NATO office, which he had been running on an acting basis.

The woman in question went on to a successful career, becoming both an ambassador and an assistant secretary. This she probably would have achieved in any event, as she was already marked as a high flyer, but the man never advanced further. He continued to serve loyally and professionally, but the fire was out, the intensity gone. I believe these personnel actions did the woman little good and the man a disservice. Yet the policy of requiring each bureau to appoint at least one woman deputy (which was never written down and was quite possibly illegal) would significantly accelerate the emergence of a cadre of senior women in positions of responsibility where they could serve as mentors for younger officers and role models for new entrants.

The division of labor between an assistant secretary and principal deputy tended to be similar to that between an ambassador and a deputy chief of mission, the former mostly looking outward, the latter inward. Seitz's efforts were largely directed toward the Seventh Floor, other agencies, and other governments, while mine focused on the operation of the bureau and its relations with other elements of the department.

Within the new administration there were three levels of officials dealing with the fast-changing European landscape. At the center were Bush, Baker, and Scowcroft. Directly supporting Scowcroft and the president were Bob Gates, then deputy national security adviser, and Bob Blackwill, the NSC senior director for Europe. Directly supporting Baker were Bob Zoellick, then counselor of the department, and Dennis Ross, head of the policy planning staff. A third tier in the White House included Condi Rice and Philip Zelikow, both of whom worked under Blackwill. Rice was a young academic Soviet expert and Zelikow a junior Foreign Service officer. At State, supporting Baker and his inner circle, were Seitz, me, and the rest of the bureau.

Zelikow and Rice later collaborated on a history of German unification, *Germany Unified and Europe Transformed: A Study in Statecraft*. In it they describe Seitz as a "diplomat's diplomat, a man in whom grace and wit were joined to a keen, careful mind." Turning to me, they wrote that Dobbins "knew Germany well and, though more acerbic than Seitz, had one of the quickest analytical minds in the Foreign Service."

In my defense, I can only note that almost everybody was more acerbic than Seitz, whose wit was sharp but never unkind. Ray was, in fact, the most consistently amusing person I have known, combining a rare degree of polish with a warm, easy manner. I was fortunately placed as the only person within these several concentric White House and State Department circles with direct experience of Germany. There were others in the service more knowledgeable than I, but they were in the field. I was in the right place at the right time.

Baker, who had been White House chief of staff and later secretary of the treasury under Reagan, and had then run Bush's presidential campaign, was clearly second only to the president, and he was usually very careful to keep Scowcroft and, thus, the president informed about his every move. In fact, Baker seemed to spend almost as much time in the White House as at State. Relations with the Defense Department, under Dick Cheney, were cordial, with no disagreement on the big issues and only limited DOD involvement in most American diplomacy over the upcoming year.

Blackwill, Seitz, and I were all veterans both of Kissinger's Seventh Floor and Brewster's London Embassy. Zelikow and Rice were new to government service, razor sharp and eager to collaborate; penetrating Baker's inner circle was our greatest challenge. Unlike Shultz, and like Kissinger, Baker erected a wall of separation between himself and the bureaucracy he headed. But whereas Kissinger relied almost exclusively on Foreign Service officers to provide this barrier, Baker brought his buffer with him. Margaret Tutwiler, nominally the assistant secretary for public affairs, served as his chief of staff. Bob Zoellick was his top policy adviser, with Dennis Ross as his able lieutenant. Bob Kimmitt, the under secretary for political affairs, handled the wide range of issues that did not require Baker's regular attention. Larry Eagleburger, as deputy secretary, ran the department, but did not play a prominent role in European issues in these early years. All these individuals except Eagleburger had come with Baker from Treasury.

Baker also brought with him a couple of schedulers. These ladies controlled not just access to the secretary but places in his motorcades, seats on his plane, and placement at official meals. They could make your life easy, or miserable. All of Baker's people were fiercely loyal and initially somewhat suspicious of the career establishment, and even of those few political appointees left over from the Reagan administration. Baker himself once commented to me how much more difficult was a friendly takeover than a hostile one. When one party succeeds another in the White House, all political appointees expect to be replaced. When a new president of the same party takes office, these same appointees assume they can stay. Baker and Bush had to disappoint a number of incumbent ambassadors and a few senior department officials in this regard. Eventually Zoellick himself moved up to become under secretary for economic affairs as a result of one such departure, while also retaining the counselor title and his hold on European issues.

As East Germany's Warsaw Pact neighbors began to liberalize, an increasing number of East Germans began traveling to Hungary and Czechoslovakia in the hope of being able to go on to the West. Initially they were not allowed to proceed westward, but neither were they forcefully returned to East Germany. A large number of fleeing East Germans ended up seeking refuge in West German embassies in Budapest and Prague. At one point nearly 5,000 East Germans crowded into Bonn's Prague Embassy compound. With Baker's assistance, Genscher secured the agreement of both the Czech and East German authorities to have these people transported in a sealed train back through the GDR and on to West Germany. The East Germans then closed the border with Czechoslovakia. But Hungary began allowing East Germans to transit to the West via its border with Austria, from whence they could travel freely to West Germany, where they were immediately welcomed and treated as full citizens. Soon tens of thousands of East Germans were making this journey.

Early in October, eighteen East Germans entered the American embassy in East Berlin seeking asylum. I was asked to join Baker in his private dining room on the eighth floor of the department, where he was lunching with his inner circle. I was served some soup and asked for my advice on how to handle the situation. I urged that the asylum seekers be turned out of the embassy provided we could receive assurances from the East German authorities that they would suffer no consequences. I recalled for Baker the American experience with Cardinal Mindszenty, the leader of the Catholic Church in Hungary, who had sought refuge in our Budapest Embassy in 1956 and did not leave until 1971. Eagleburger agreed that our small embassy in East Berlin could not easily house eighteen people, let alone the larger number who might follow.

This was not the answer Baker wanted. "I'll call Shevardnadze," he said. And he did, working out an arrangement under which the eighteen were allowed to go west, provided the embassy closed its doors to future such attempts. I, thus, learned that Baker, who had already established a relationship with the Soviet foreign minister, had a clearer idea than I regarding what might be possible in these fast-evolving circumstances. He also had an almost infallible sense of the American domestic ramifications of foreign policy choices.

During my years in Bonn I often addressed the question of German unification. Rhetorically, the American position was unassailable; we were

for a unified Germany, the achievement of which was blocked by the Soviet Union. As long as the Soviets maintained their veto there was no need
for American officials to elaborate further. I spoke on the topic at a Social
Democratic Party conference chaired by Willy Brandt, the former mayor
of West Berlin and, later, chancellor. In response to my remarks several
participants alleged that the continued American military presence in
Berlin was an obstacle to improved relations between the two German
states. I responded that the United States was under the impression that it
was preserving a free Berlin as the ultimate capital of a reunified Germany,
but that if the West Germans wanted us to go, all they had to do was ask.
Brandt, who had been mayor when the wall went up, nodded his assent
and this line of questioning subsided.

Conservatives were sometimes critical from the other side, fearing too
much was being done via Genscher's Ostpolitik to consolidate the current
divisions between the two German states. These audiences, too, generally
found the simple American message reassuring.

Privately I wondered whether Germans should devote so much attention to and feel so much frustration regarding what I thought to be an
unattainable goal. Would they not be happier and better off taking satisfaction in the remarkable democratic and economic achievements of the
West German state?

Shortly before my arrival in Washington the new administration had
conducted a review of European policy. The final paper reflected the views
of Seitz's predecessor, Rozanne Ridgway, who once served as ambassador
to East Germany. She advised staying away from the issue of German unification. "There is no more inflammatory and divisive issue and it serves
no U.S. interest for us to take the initiative to raise it," this document concluded. In early October I drafted a new memo to Baker on the subject in
which I took a rather different line, advising that, while the unification had
not yet become an operational policy objective for the West German government, "popular forces in the East could push events more rapidly than
now foreseen toward new arrangements for Germany." I advised against
seriously engaging the East German regime and urged that the United
States follow the West German lead in advocating unification without
prescribing when and how it might be achieved. The policy planning staff
attached a dissent to this memo. Dennis Ross also sent a personal note to
Baker urging that the United States dampen speculation about unification
in favor of supporting reform in the GDR, pretty much the opposite of my

recommendation. Dennis did advise Baker to consult with German officials on the issue and consider the need for U.S. initiatives.

These missives illustrate the disadvantage under which Ray and I suffered in competing with the policy planning staff for Baker's attention. Ross could comment on anything we sent to the secretary before it reached Baker, whereas we never saw what Ross sent before or even after its receipt. I learned about this particular note to Baker only years later, when the Zelikow-Rice history was published. That I myself had enjoyed similarly privileged access to the secretary fourteen years earlier as part of Sonnenfeldt's staff made this disadvantage no easier to bear.

On the night of November 9 the Berlin Wall was opened and thousands of Berliners crossed freely back and forth for the first time in decades. The East German regime had intended to liberalize travel for its citizens, but a premature and insufficiently qualified announcement to that effect had precipitated a much more dramatic and irreversible breach than intended.

November 10 was a holiday in Washington, but I was in my office when my secretary entered to say, "President Bush is on the phone. He wants to speak to you." Baker was with Bush in the White House. Both of them wanted to know whether we had been able to reach Genscher regarding a Gorbachev proposal to convene a four power ambassador's meeting in Berlin. I said we had. With German, French, and British agreement the Soviet request for a four power meeting was declined, at least for the time being.

Later that day I went for a walk in Rock Creek Park, during which I mulled over the implications of the previous night's events. On reaching home I jotted down a few notes and, the next morning, sent Baker a brief memo. In it I recommended we avoid any suggestion of a "superpower condominium," tie any aid to the GDR to free elections, resist setting out our own blueprint for change in Europe, keep the emphasis on German self-determination, stay away from four power intervention, and begin to work with Bonn, Paris, and London on guidelines for channeling movement toward German unification. "We need now to begin considering how Germany's Western ties can in practice be assured in a transformed European context," I wrote. Baker annotated the memo to indicate his agreement on all these points.

On November 28 I joined Scowcroft, Blackwill, and John McLaughlin, then head of the CIA's European analysis division, to brief President

Bush for a meeting with Gorbachev that was to be held several days later in Malta. Kohl had made a major address the previous day in which he laid out a ten-step process that could lead to German unification. I said that this speech transformed the issue of unification from the aspirational to the operational. We now needed to think of it as a real possibility, and McLaughlin agreed.

The British and French were as eager as the Soviets to slow Kohl down. London and Paris joined Moscow in pressing for a meeting of the four power ambassadors. After getting Genscher's reluctant agreement and carefully limiting the agenda for the meeting, we concurred. On December 10 Ambassador Walters joined his British, French, and Soviet opposite numbers for the first four power gathering at the ambassadorial level in several decades. It took place at the Kommandatura building from which the four powers had once ruled Berlin. Walter's instructions were to keep the whole thing low-key. Unfortunately, he and his three colleagues allowed themselves to be photographed standing in front of this iconic site. This upset the Germans and also annoyed Baker, who arrived in Berlin the following day.

We had dinner that evening with Helmut Kohl, who was also visiting Berlin. After Kohl departed Baker summoned Walters and me to a session with Zoellick and Dick Barkley, our ambassador to the German Democratic Republic. Baker said he was considering going to East Berlin to meet with the GDR leadership the following day, and he asked our opinion. Walters and I argued against the idea. The GDR was on its third leader in seven weeks. Erich Honecker had resigned on October 18 in favor of Egon Krenz, who lasted exactly one month, to be replaced by Hans Modrow, yet another Communist, but reputed to be more reform-minded. I argued that the first ever visit to East Berlin by an American secretary of state would enhance the stature of a regime that was on its last legs while also inserting the United States into the dialogue on unification that we wanted to see led by the Germans. Barkley argued for the meeting. Baker listened to us all and decided to go ahead with the visit.

This was, as far as I know, the last substantive discussion between Baker and Walters, despite the administration's intense focus on Germany over the ensuing months. Baker's mind was quick and analytical; Walters' the polar opposite: ruminative, loquacious, and anecdotal. Walters had remarkably sharp insights but no capacity to explain how he had arrived at them. Asked to expand on some conclusion, he would respond with one of his endless stock of stories. It was probably inevitable that Baker's team would exclude our embassy in Bonn from any meaningful role in the unification process, but this incompatibility in temperament made it more certain. Walters was disappointed at my failure to keep him apprised of Washington developments. Given how well he had treated me during our few months together in Bonn, I also felt bad about it, while recognizing that my own access depended on not extending the circle further.

The following evening our motorcade traveled via the Glienicke Bridge to Potsdam, where we met with Hans Modrow and several of his associates. A few minutes into the meeting my heart nearly stopped as a gentleman entered the room who bore a striking resemblance to Egon Krenz, the recently displaced successor to Honecker. Fortunately, this turned out to be the waiter.

Discussion followed the expected lines. Baker conditioned American assistance on free elections, and Modrow promised reforms. We next visited a nearby church where we met with Lutheran church leaders, who told us that popular sentiment in favor of unification was growing quickly.

Baker's visit to the GDR did no harm, and perhaps a little good. He liked to make a splash and the opportunity to be the first American secretary of state to visit East Germany was too attractive to resist. He was also largely free of the forty years of accumulated Cold War baggage that, for others, including myself, obscured the scope and speed of the changes underway. Thanks to his frequent contact with Gorbachev and Eduard Shevardnadze, Baker was also more keenly aware of the changes underway in the Kremlin and the opportunities these offered.

Baker remembered and later rewarded Dick Barkley, despite the fact that his embassy was to prove consistently wrong in gauging East German opinion. The embassy's contacts were generally with officials, intellectuals, and dissidents, and these groups tended to share the regime's social aspirations even while seeking greater freedom and openness in their pursuit. My view was that the population as a whole would be a lot more interested in securing West German level of wages, unemployment benefits, and pensions than preserving the East German social welfare system. Our conversation with the East German Lutheran pastors supported this view. Once Kohl promised to trade ostmarks for deutsche marks on a one-for-one basis, which he did four months later, the German Democratic Republic was finished.

All our ambassadors from East as well as West Europe, including the USSR, were assembled in Berlin that weekend to meet the secretary. Baker spoke briefly about the shifting European scene without much detail on Germany. He then departed for other appointments, leaving me to run the meeting. In response to questions raised by Baker's presentation, I was more precise in specifying that the reunification of Germany was now our objective, and that the administration was determined that this unified Germany should remain firmly in the Western camp. This led to a number of incredulous responses on the part of the thirty-five assembled ambassadors, and a particularly sharp reaction from Jack Matlock, our man in Moscow. They, nevertheless, all left with a clear sense of where Washington was heading.

Over the next several months there were intense bilateral contacts among all the main capitals during which time the East German regime steadily lost control and legitimacy. Bush and Baker were able to secure firm commitments from both Kohl and Genscher to a unified Germany remaining in NATO, albeit with some reservations about NATO troops moving into East Germany. Baker also began to socialize this unwelcome idea with Gorbachev and Shevardnadze. The major move during this period was agreement to establish a six-power forum including both German states along with the four World War II victors to deal with the external issues of unification.

Various people have been credited with originating the idea for what became known as the Two-Plus-Four forum; that is, the two German states plus the four World War II victors. The first mention of such an arrangement, according to the Zelikow-Rice book, was in a memo from Rice to Scowcroft. The second was in a conversation between Gorbachev and one of his advisers. Early in January I had sent a note to Dennis Ross proposing the creation of such a group, but Dennis replied cautiously, suggesting the time was not yet ripe. A few weeks later Zoellick and Ross presented the idea to the secretary, only subsequently asking Ray and me for our opinion. We responded negatively, arguing that, as described by Zoellick and Ross, the proposal accorded the Soviet Union too much influence over a process in which the two German states should be taking the lead. Scowcroft and Blackwill were also opposed. Nevertheless, over the next few days Baker began to discuss the idea, first with Genscher, then Gorbachev, and then with the rest of the intended participants. Within ten days from when the idea was presented to him, Baker had secured the agreement of all other five participants. This accord was announced during a NATO-Warsaw Pact ministerial meeting that all six foreign ministers were attending in Ottawa.

Scowcroft felt Baker had acted without adequate consultation, although Bush had agreed to his putting this idea to Kohl and Gorbachev. The NSC staff and EUR collaborated in narrowing the mandate for the group. We both wanted to ensure that this forum dealt only with the eventual disposition of four power rights, leaving other aspects of unification to be dealt with elsewhere. Zoellick and Ross had begun with a more expansive concept, suggesting that the Two-Plus-Four might deal with all external aspects of reunification, which could include borders, alliance relationships, and foreign troop presence among other things. Eventually everyone in Washington acknowledged that, while no one would be able to prevent the participants from discussing anything they wished, the United States (and undoubtedly the Germans) should insist that the forum could only decide on four power-related issues. Other issues might be discussed but then referred to other venues for decision.

I did not feel that Zoellick and Ross had taken my idea and presented it to the secretary as their own. The six-power configuration was, after all, an obvious and even necessary mechanism to manage an orderly reunification process, and many people arrived at that conclusion independently. I was irritated that Ross discouraged me from developing the idea, and then a few weeks later presented it to Baker, only afterward asking Ray and me for our input. Scowcroft was also upset at what seems to have been the only serious lapse in White House-State coordination over the entirety of this year-long effort. For his part, Baker was doing what he did best, turning a proposal into an agreement, in this case with breathtaking speed.

The Two-Plus-Four forum, thus, became the clearinghouse for handling issues related to German unification. Three wider processes proceeded in parallel with the Two-Plus-Four, each designed to embed a larger, more powerful Germany in a broader set of relationships. Pan-European arms control negotiations worked toward substantial reductions in non-nuclear forces throughout the continent, and pan-European political consultations sought to convert the periodically convened Conference on Security and Cooperation in Europe into a standing organization, with an executive and parliamentary body of its own, to give concrete meaning to the concept of a Europe whole and free. Finally there were negotiations aiming at deepened integration within the European

Community. The arms control talks were designed to ally the security concerns of Germany's neighbors. The conversion of CSCE to OSCE was intended to provide Moscow a pan-European club to which it could belong, and the deepening of ties within the European Community was intended to embed a united Germany in this larger whole. Baker gave impetus to this latter move in a speech delivered in December in Berlin. There he set out the broad framework for American policy toward European unification. The speech explicitly endorsed further European integration and put forward several initiatives, including a proposal for the establishment of formal links between the European Community and the United States.

With Dennis Ross on leave, Zoellick asked me to prepare Baker's remarks. I wrote an initial draft, which we then worked on together. Riding in the staff bus back from the site where Baker had delivered this speech, Margaret Tutwiler, Baker's press spokesperson, asked whether she should let the press know that, as usual, Dennis Ross had written the speech. After a pause, Zoellick advised against any attribution of the authorship.

The first Two-Plus-Four foreign ministers meeting took place in May. A subordinate grouping of the six political directors was established to prepare and follow up on these discussions. The four Western political directors also met regularly to coordinate the allied position in advance of the six-power meetings. Since Sonnenfeldt's departure fifteen years earlier, the American participant in political director level meetings had been the assistant secretary for Europe. In this case, Baker designated Zoellick to lead for the United States, accompanied by Seitz and, often, Blackwill. Given the importance of these meetings at this critical point in time, reinforcing the American side in this manner was a sensible move; it was also reflective, however, of Baker's reluctance to delegate beyond his inner circle.

As we moved into the summer of 1990 German unification became almost inevitable. The only remaining question was whether all the many interrelated strands—the renunciation of four power rights, the conclusion of a conventional arms control treaty, the deepening of European integration, the conversion of the Conference on European Security and Cooperation into a standing East-West organization, and a revision of NATO strategy to take account of the new more benign environment—could all be brought to a more or less simultaneous conclusion.

In July Baker took a brief vacation, and his entire entourage took advantage of his absence to do the same. So did Seitz. No sooner were they all gone than I received a call from Dieter Kastrup, the German political director, insisting on holding a Quad meeting to settle several remaining differences among the four Western parties. In this pre–cell phone era, Zoellick and Seitz were unreachable. Eventually, I agreed to join the other three political directors for a meeting in Bonn. The still-open issues all concerned aspects of four power rights the British and French wanted to preserve. The Germans were more than willing to continue the arrangements in question, but they did not want to be required to do so. I pressed the U.S. view that Germany should emerge from the Two-Plus-Four process entirely sovereign and that we should all trust the resultant unified government to do the right thing. This argument, the core of the American approach over these months, prevailed. As a result the Western side was able to go into the conclusive round of Two-Plus-Four Talks unified on every point.

On his return Zoellick was annoyed to find I had participated in these talks without his consent. I responded that he had left no contact information and that events in Europe were not standing still. After having had a chance to review the results of the political directors meeting, Bob relented, expressing satisfaction with the outcome.

On the evening of August 2, I was home, about to sit down to dinner, when Bob Kimmitt telephoned with the news that Saddam Hussein had invaded Kuwait. He asked that I return to the department. Along with half a dozen others, we spent that night in a prolonged interagency meeting conducted via a secure video connection linking us to similar groups at Defense, the CIA, Treasury, and the White House. By early morning we had frozen Iraqi financial assets in the United States and the United Kingdom, the major European financial hub, launched a diplomatic campaign to isolate Saddam, brand him as the aggressor, and secure United Nations Security Council authorization for an international response. Over the succeeding six months we in the European Bureau mobilized allied political and financial support and European participation in a military campaign to defend Saudi Arabia and liberate Kuwait. Even the Soviet Union voted to authorize the American-led operation. Gorbachev was invited to also send troops but, on reflection, demurred.

On September 12 the Two-Plus-Four Treaty was signed. The four World War II victors renounced all rights with respect to Germany. Flying back from this historic session, Baker mentioned that he needed to find a replacement for the departing American ambassador in London. Ray volunteered that he had an excellent command of English. Two months later Ray was, indeed, nominated by President Bush to become the American representative to the Court of St. James's, thereby becoming the first, and so far the last, Foreign Service officer to hold this post.

Through the late summer and fall of 1990 all the other strands of European transformation were brought together in a series of summits and ministerial meetings. On October 3, less than a year after the fall of the Berlin Wall, Germany was unified, an outcome endorsed by the entire continent.

Some months later Zoellick asked me whether I thought the enlarged Germany would continue to behave in the international sphere largely as had the West Germany of old. Behind his question was a natural concern that the addition of seventeen million new citizens who had been raised on an unrelenting diet of anti-American, anti-capitalist, and anti-NATO propaganda would make some difference to Germany's foreign and security policies. I replied that the top priorities of East German voters would be economic and social, that they would be content to leave foreign and security policies in the hands of the West German elites in exchange for the resource transfers that would raise them to a comparable living standard. By the time that had been achieved, East German political leaders would have become thoroughly Westernized. This has largely proved to be the case, as is perhaps best evidenced by the record of Angela Merkel, a Lutheran pastor's daughter born and raised in East Germany, the spokesperson for the last East German government, and, since 2005, the chancellor of a united Germany. Merkel has continued to champion a liberal, democratic, and open international order against the wave of populism and narrow nationalism currently sweeping the Western world.

TWELVE

And Disordered Anew

EARLY IN 1991 RAY STEPPED down as assistant secretary, leaving me to run the bureau until a successor could be named and confirmed. Rather to my surprise Blackwill returned to Harvard, to be replaced by David Gompert, another veteran of Henry Kissinger's Seventh Floor.

Soon after Ray's departure I sent Baker a memo urging greater support for reform in the Soviet Union. I modeled it on the brief paper I had sent him the day after the Berlin Wall came down. I urged a major effort to help Gorbachev effect the changes he was trying to make, as I felt there was not an adequate sense of urgency within the U.S. administration, nor full realization of the opportunity before us. Gorbachev clearly was sincere; the changes he sought were sweeping and the outcome, if successful, of considerable advantage to the United States. This time there was no reaction, and I doubt the memo had any impact.

At my urging Eagleburger had taken charge of a growing program of economic assistance to the reforming countries of Eastern Europe. Zoellick launched a similar but more modest program of help to the Soviet Union, having successfully wrestled with Treasury for leadership. I found this latter effort cautious and inadequate, and I feared Gorbachev's failure would lead to a reversion to the old Soviet regime, as, indeed, almost happened. In retrospect I have to admit that the United States probably could not have provided economic assistance on a scale necessary to affect developments in a country the size of the Soviet Union, particularly given the cluelessness of the Soviet leadership regarding the needed reforms. But it seemed worth a larger investment at the time.

One consequence of German reunification had been to accelerate movement toward European integration. This took several forms, the principal of which was the Treaty of Maastricht, concluded at the end of 1991. This agreement rebranded the European Community as the European Union (EU) and mandated the creation of a common currency, what became the euro. Another provision of this treaty was to launch the Common Foreign and Security Policy (CFSP), as one of the main pillars of the new union, which initiated a major transatlantic debate. Paris in particular was eager to see European institutions take on greater responsibilities for security, believing France would carry more weight in a forum without the United States than it did in NATO.

At this point the Soviet Union was still in existence, and its future course was anything but certain. The thought of two competing organizations, NATO and the EU, somehow sharing responsibility for European security in the face of a potentially hostile superpower made me nervous. In March I sent a telegram to our embassies in all the NATO capitals laying out the administration's concerns and proposing guidelines to de-conflict the work of the two organizations in the field of security. Although intended to be delivered orally, these points eventually found their way in writing to the desk of French President Mitterrand, who took strong exception to their tone and content. What became known as the Dobbins's démarche enjoyed a brief notoriety as a result. This left me with the reputation as an opponent of European unity. In fact I was among its strongest proponents in official Washington, and became even more so once the Soviet Union disappeared, at which point the United States no longer had to fear being maneuvered into a superpower confrontation as a result of decisions made in an organization to which we did not belong.

Through the early months of 1991 the states of Eastern Europe continued to progress toward democratic rule. This occurred peacefully in all but Romania, where President Ceausescu had been overthrown and executed the previous December. I visited Sofia, which was calm, and Bucharest, which was infested by packs of wild, reputedly rabid dogs. Our main pre-occupation during these months was the fate of Yugoslavia, which had survived intact for a decade after Tito's death but now appeared on the brink of collapse. Cold War pressures had helped stabilize this ethnically, linguistically, and religiously divided country, but now, as the other nations of Eastern Europe broke free of Soviet hegemony, a couple of Yugoslavia's constituent republics sought to go their own way as well.

Slovenia, the smallest, most economically advanced, and most homogeneous of these republics was the most insistent, and Croatia was determined to follow Slovenia out the door. Bosnia was unwilling to remain in a much-diminished Yugoslav state that would be even more dominated by its largest component part, Serbia. Slobodan Milosevic, then president of Serbia, was unlikely to long resist Slovenia's departure, but seemed certain to react more forcefully to that of Croatia or Bosnia, both of which had large Serb minorities. It was evident that the breakup of Yugoslavia was not going to proceed peacefully.

The crisis came to a head in late June just as Baker was scheduled to attend a Europe-wide Organization for Security and Cooperation in Europe (OSCE) ministerial meeting in neighboring Austria. Baker wanted to be the first senior American ever to visit Albania. I argued that he should not literally fly over Yugoslavia just as that country was about to descend into civil war and urged that he at least make an attempt to dissuade its leaders from such a course. Somewhat reluctantly Baker agreed, and we arranged to stop in Belgrade for a day on our way to Tirana.

In Vienna we succeeded in getting a statement from the thirty-five-nation gathering warning all the Yugoslav parties against a breakup. In Belgrade we met with the by then largely powerless Yugoslav prime minister, Ante Markovic, and then individually with each of the Republic leaders, including Slobodan Milosevic of Serbia, Franjo Tudjman of Croatia, Alija Izetbegovic of Bosnia, and Milan Kuchan of Slovenia. Baker also met for a few moments in the basement of our hotel with Ibrahim Rugova, representing the Muslim Albanian population of Kosovo, a nominally autonomous province of Serbia.

Kuchan insisted that Slovenia would declare its independence four days hence. Tudjman said he would wait if Kuchan did, but Croatia would have to leave as soon as Slovenia made its move. Izetbegovic agreed entirely with Baker's effort to stem the collapse, noting that it was his republic, divided as it was between Catholic Croats, Orthodox Serbs, and Muslim Bosniaks, that would pay the price for the other republic's rash action. Milosevic agreed with Baker that there should be no unilateral declarations of independence, but listened impassively to the secretary's warnings against the use of force.

Baker, the consummate dealmaker, spent the day searching for some agreement, however slight, that might be reached and announced. I advised that there was probably no deal to be had among this group, and suggested the best we could do was leave behind a clear warning that unilateral steps toward independence would be not recognized by the rest of the world. Baker agreed, and Ross and I quickly drafted such a statement, which Baker issued at the day's close.

The next morning we flew on to Tirana, the capital of Albania. Coming in low over the city, we were struck by what appeared to be dozens of concrete mushrooms planted on all the hillsides. These, we learned, were among thousands of tiny pillboxes that the former dictator, Enver Hoxha, had sprinkled throughout the country to defend it from foreign invaders. Until Hoxha's death in 1985 Albania had been the world's last Stalinist dictatorship. Hoxha had broken with Moscow over Khrushchev's denunciation of Stalinist excesses, turning, instead, to Mao's China for support. Albania protested the Soviet invasion of Czechoslovakia in 1968 and left the Warsaw Pact as a result. Hoxha then distanced his country from China following that country's warming relations with Washington. In consequence, Albania had remained the poorest, most repressive, and most isolated country in Europe; it was North Korea on the Adriatic. Albania was the last Eastern European country to start down the democratic path, installing a coalition government including non-Communists only two weeks prior to our arrival.

We were met at the airport by our man in Tirana, William Ryerson, a mid-level consular officer who had been sent in a few weeks earlier to begin setting up an American embassy. Driving into town from the airport, we found ourselves surrounded by tens of thousands of people walking in the same direction. Recognizing who we were, they crowded in upon our small motorcade, to the point that it seemed they were going to bodily lift our cars and carry them into the city. The *New York Times* reported that "hands reached out from every direction to touch the secretary of state or to pound on the windows of his car. Albanians kissed the hood and windows and showered the car with flower petals, and one man threw himself in front of the limousine and kissed the road—anything to make a link with the representative of America."

Somehow we kept moving, very slowly, and no one was injured. On reaching the city center Baker was shown to a temporary stage on wooden scaffolding overlooking the main square. Below us was a crowd of several hundred thousand people. The *Times* reported that, "There were children on their fathers' shoulders and old people flashing V for victory signs. There were people on rooftops, on balconies and hanging from trees. One woman held her baby out of a fourth-floor window."

As Baker moved forward to speak, the crowd began to surge toward him in the throes of an almost religious rapture. I became seriously concerned about the stability of the platform on which we were standing, fearing injury for those on top and those below if the crowd pressed too hard on the supports. Sensing that we might be overwhelmed, Sali Berisha, the most prominent spokesperson for the non-Communist reform movement, stepped to the microphone and calmed the awaiting multitude. "Welcome to the company of free men and women everywhere," Baker began.

Following his speech we adjourned to a nearby café where Berisha introduced us to a small group of dissident leaders. The six men he had assembled counted between them more than 150 years in jail. One of these introduced himself thus: "This is a big day for me, Mr. Secretary! This morning, after twenty-seven years in prison, I was released. Today at noon I was married. And now I am meeting with the American secretary of state."

We ended the visit with a call on Enver Hoxha's successor, President Ramiz Alia. At the conclusion of their meeting, Alia asked Baker if there was anything he could do to help establish the new American embassy. Baker turned to Ryerson, who said he could use a telephone. On returning to his hotel that evening, Ryerson was greeted by disgruntled fellow guests to be shown the spot in the lobby where the hotel's only telephone had been ripped out to be installed in his room.

By this time we were halfway back to Washington, having experienced the warmest most emotional welcome any American delegation to any country may have ever received.

Undeterred by Baker's warning, the Slovenes moved their declaration of independence forward a day. On June 25 they seized border posts and other Yugoslav federal facilities. Press reporting of the ensuing Ten-Day

War was grossly one-sided. Austrian journalists, the only ones present, portrayed the Yugoslav Army as the aggressor, and American television replayed video of civilians in downtown Ljubljana running for cover as air raid sirens sounded. In fact there were no air raids, no bombing, and no civilian casualties. The fighting had been initiated by Slovenian Territorial Defense Forces, and most of the casualties were young Yugoslav Army conscripts.

These events led to a brief furor in Washington, where Jim Baker was accused of having given a green light to this alleged Yugoslav Army offensive when he had urged the Slovenes not to secede. It was even suggested that his attempt to hold Yugoslavia together was undertaken in deference to Mikhail Gorbachev, in order not to encourage similar separatist tendencies in the Soviet Union. In fact, this particular rationale had never even occurred to me and I had been the only advocate of Baker's visit to Belgrade.

Senior members of Congress wanted Baker or Eagleburger to come up and explain our policy. They sent me, instead, an early indication of their desire not to become too enmeshed in this issue.

I met with a dozen senators who were initially skeptical, but eventually seemed convinced that our only objective in counseling against the unilateral Slovenian (and Croatian) moves was to save lives, certain as we were that the breakup of Yugoslavia was not going to go peacefully. A day or two later Baker called on Bob Dole, then the senate majority leader. Criticism died down, but so did any remaining enthusiasm Baker may have had for personal involvement in this mounting crisis.

To be fair, Baker had a lot else on his plate. The Gulf War had only just been brought to a successful conclusion. The Soviet Union was tottering. Baker and his team were promoting a new Middle East peace initiative, preparing to launch negotiations on a North American Free Trade Agreement, and trying to conclude the Uruguay Round global trade talks. Zoellick was heavily engaged in the latter two initiatives. Eagleburger might have been expected to pick up the ball on Yugoslavia, where he had once been our ambassador, but he proved quite unwilling to do that.

The Ten-Day War in Slovenia ended with an agreement brokered by the European Community under which Yugoslav forces withdrew from both Slovenia and Croatia in exchange for which the two republics agreed to postpone independence for three months. The effect was to allow Slovenia to get away scot-free, while Croats and Serbs began preparing for an extended conflict.

Most mornings when he was in Washington, Baker would meet with his inner circle and the five regional assistant secretaries. I would regularly have some piece of bad news from Yugoslavia to impart. Occasionally, several of us would adjourn to Baker's inner office to continue the conversation. Everyone would then look to Eagleburger, who had served twice in Yugoslavia, for counsel. Larry invariably said he agreed with the course of action I was advocating, but then added that, in his opinion, it wouldn't work. After one such exchange Zoellick rounded on him saying, "Larry, you can't keep saying you agree with a policy that won't work. You need to provide us recommendations that will." Eagleburger just shrugged.

Scowcroft, who had also spent time in Yugoslavia as a military attaché, took the same fatalistic view of the brewing conflict. Both he and Larry agreed with my predictions of impending disaster, but thought there was little the United States could do to prevent it. They were, therefore, disinclined to expend much effort trying.

The disintegration of Yugoslavia was the first European crisis since the end of the Cold War. Europe's leaders were eager to see the European Community play a larger political role in the continent, and they seized on this opportunity to do so. The Bush administration was more than happy to leave the problem to them. The presidency of the European Community rotated every six months, and during the first half of 1991 Luxembourg held the presidency. They were not the most powerful of its members, but were eager to take up the challenge and willing to spend pretty much full time on it. Jacques Poos, their foreign minister, went so far as to call this "the hour of Europe." I traveled to Luxembourg to meet with Poos and remained in daily contact with his political director through the duration of their EC presidency.

The European Community had initially been successful in brokering an end to the fighting in Slovenia and heading off conflict in Croatia, and for a while they maintained a united front in opposing recognition of any breakaway republic. This determination began to fade after Slovenia's so-called Ten-Day War, which Austrian journalists had so misrepresented to the global audience. Germany, which had just gone through its own experience of self-determination by incorporating East Germany, was more inclined than others to sympathize with Slovenian and, particularly, Croatian aspirations.

At one morning staff meeting I warned Baker that Genscher was about to reverse position and come out publicly in favor of recognition of Croatian independence. This led to another huddle in Baker's inner office, where I argued that recognition of Croatia would spark renewed and this time larger-scale fighting. It would also turn a brewing civil war into an international conflict in which the United States would ultimately find itself embroiled. Baker said I was exaggerating. When I insisted he told me to call my German opposite number and dissuade them from any such move. "This would be a lot more convincing coming from you," I said. "No," he demurred. "You do it."

Accordingly, I called Jürgen Chrobog, Kastrup's successor as political director, and said I had been directed by Baker to urge that his government not recognize Croatia. Such a step would, I insisted, pave the way for a widened conflict. Chrobog said I was exaggerating, to which I replied heatedly, "It is ironic that the European power least likely to step in to stop this war is the one that is going to precipitate it."

By late summer the Serb majority regions within Croatia were declaring their own secession from Croatia in favor of union with Serbia. Croat and Serb forces (which included, in the Serb case, the Yugoslav Army), were preparing for battle. Tudjman, the Croat president, appealed for an international peacekeeping force, and France proposed that the Western European Union should organize one. Germany supported this proposal. On a quiet Saturday in August, when everyone of importance was away from Washington, David Gompert and I put together a telegram instructing our embassies in Europe to support the French proposal. David reached Scowcroft and I contacted Eagleburger at his weekend home in Charlottesville, and we persuaded both to approve the instruction.

By Monday morning the British were desperately contacting every relevant official in Washington trying to get this policy reversed. London argued that the French were using the excuse of conflict in Yugoslavia to resurrect an organization that had been moribund since the creation of NATO in 1949. The British alleged that the French intention was to thereby weaken that Atlantic institution in favor of the European. The British succeeded in alarming our Defense Department to the point where we were forced to back off our support for the French proposal. The result was that the Bush administration, which was itself determined not to engage in any peacekeeping effort and, therefore, not to allow NATO to do so, joined the United Kingdom in suppressing the only alternative then on the table. An opportunity was lost to deploy international peacekeepers into Croatia before fighting broke out and before Bosnia followed Slovenia and Croatia down the road to independence.

The British government at that time bears a heavy responsibility for putting some rather arcane issues of European construction ahead of effective action to forestall the most violent European conflict since World War II. Britain was understandably loath to take on a military commitment that the United States was shirking, yet six months later this is exactly what occurred. A United Nations' peacekeeping force composed heavily of British and French troops was dispatched into Croatia and Bosnia, but the opportunity to head off the conflict had been lost. War had already begun in Croatia and spread to Bosnia. Britain, thus, found itself embroiled militarily in a disintegrating Yugoslavia without American support under far worse conditions than had they supported the French initiative half a year earlier.

One of the more sympathetic visitors I received during these months was Lennart Meri, the foreign minister of Estonia, then still part of the Soviet Union. This dignified elderly gentleman represented a nation that had been carved out of Russia by Germany in World War I, established as an independent state in the postwar settlement, incorporated back into the Soviet Union in 1940, taken over by Germany again in 1941, and taken back by the Soviet Union in 1944. Like several other Soviet republics, the Estonians were beginning to agitate for independence. I hosted a lunch for Meri, listened sympathetically but noncommittally to his requests for American support, and urged patience. Bush and Baker had been pressing Gorbachev to avoid using force against those in the Baltic states who were demonstrating for independence. The fact that Meri could travel and present himself in Washington as that country's foreign minister was itself evidence of Gorbachev's forbearance.

Following our meal, I walked Meri out through the State Department's ceremonial lobby. Above us hung the flags of all the world's nations. Meri proudly pointed out to me the flag of Estonia, displayed here as it had been since the building opened in 1961 as a visible reminder that the United States had never recognized the incorporation of his country into the USSR. In less than a year Estonia was again free, and Meri became its second president.

As summer approached I was offered the choice of two ambassadorships, to Turkey or to the European Community, headquartered in Brussels.

I chose the latter, and Baker sent the recommendation to the White House.

At the end of July I traveled with Secretary Baker to Moscow. Dennis Ross, Jack Matlock, our ambassador, and I accompanied Baker into the inner reaches of the Kremlin for a meeting with Gorbachev. We walked through a series of incredibly ornate, beautifully kept rooms. Baker took only Ross into the session with the Russian leader, leaving Matlock and me sitting for several hours in an adjoining anteroom. I was annoyed and disappointed, although not surprised. I could only imagine how painful it was to Matlock, who was, after all, the president's personal representative.

That evening we all dined at Spaso House, Matlock's residence, with a number of dissident and opposition figures, including representatives from several aspiring breakaway republics. Following dinner we had a private meeting with Nursultan Nazarbayev, the soon-to-be president for life of an independent Kazakhstan.

A couple of weeks later the world was again turned upside when a group of hardline Communists staged a coup and took Gorbachev prisoner. President Bush immediately brought together his senior advisers. Baker and his inner circle were all on vacation, so Eagleburger and I represented State. Other participants included Secretary of Defense Cheney, Chair of the Joint Chiefs Colin Powell, and Brent Scowcroft. The mood was somber, pessimistic, and passive. Everyone seemed convinced that the era of glasnost and perestroika was over, and that we soon would be back to business as usual with the old Soviet Union. No one suggested there was anything we might do to affect the course of events.

Riding back to State with Eagleburger, I remarked that the coup was not necessarily destined to succeed.

"Why not?" Larry asked.

"Because they aren't shooting anyone," I responded.

Indeed those behind the overthrow proved singularly inept. Gorbachev was confined to a dacha in the Crimea but retained access to an open telephone line to Moscow. The newly elected president of Russia, Boris Yeltsin, was left at liberty. He immediately moved to the Russian parliament building, known as the White House, which became the center of resistance. Muscovites began joking, "You know the Soviet Union is finished when the Bolsheviks don't know how to organize a coup."

Later that same day Bob Gates convened a deputies meeting to discuss the situation. By this time Yeltsin was standing on top of a tank in front of the Russian parliament haranguing a crowd of protesters. Still no one in Washington seemed to think we might do or say anything to affect the situation. I ventured that Yeltsin seemed to be taking phone calls, but this suggestion was only taken up a day later; the tide had clearly turned by the time President Bush called Yeltsin with a message of support.

Manfred Woerner, NATO's secretary general, called an emergency ministerial meeting of the NATO Council, and Baker returned from leave to attend. As soon as the sixteen foreign ministers were seated Woerner called the session to order. No sooner had he begun to speak, however, than an aide handed him a note. "Excuse me," he said, "I have to take a phone call."

What on Earth? In the organization's forty-two years, the secretary general had never kept a ministerial council waiting to answer the telephone.

For ten minutes or so we all sat in wonder. Then Woerner returned. "I have just spoken to Boris Yeltsin," he reported. "He has informed me that the coup is over. Gorbachev has been released."

The first person Yeltsin had thought to call with this news was the secretary general of NATO. The world was, indeed, spinning fast.

The rest of the session was anticlimactic. Each minister spoke briefly, but most of their remarks had been overtaken by events. There then followed a rush to the television cameras.

In 1991 there was only one twenty-four-hour news channel, CNN. By longstanding custom, the secretary general briefed the press first, followed by the American secretary of state, and then by such others who wished to speak. On this occasion, however, there were even more important personages already in line. First, Boris Yeltsin went before the CNN cameras in Moscow. Next came President Bush in Washington. Bush was asked if he had spoken to Secretary Baker. "No," he replied. "I have been trying to call him but have been unable to get through." Baker, who was at that moment on the line to Moscow with one of Gorbachev's advisers, immediately rang off and called the president.

The most remarkable part of the day was yet to come. Baker and I drove to the home of our NATO ambassador, a house set in several acres of parkland on which grazed a small herd of cows. Baker strolled out to look over the livestock and I made some remark betraying complete ignorance of animal husbandry. Baker corrected me with a wry shake of the head.

Back in the house, our visitor was shown in. It was Andrei Kozyrev, a young Soviet diplomat who until recently had headed the foreign ministry office responsible for United Nations' affairs. Today, however, he represented not the Soviet Union but Russia. He was, as he would remain for several years, Russia's first post-Soviet foreign minister. Kozyrev told us Yeltsin could be erratic and difficult to work for but was committed to cooperation with the West.

So the day that began with NATO ministers meeting to insist Gorbachev be returned to power ended with an exchange between the American secretary of state and his Russian, not his Soviet, counterpart. By that year's end, the Soviet Union had dissolved into fifteen separate states, and young Mr. Kozyrev had succeeded Maxim Litvinov, Vyacheslav Molotov, Andre Gromyko, and Eduard Shevardnadze as Moscow's top diplomat.

Baker returned to his vacation, and it fell to me to accompany President Bush on a long-planned visit to Greece and Turkey. We intended to use the trip to mediate longstanding Greek-Turkish differences over Cyprus. Unfortunately, in the days immediately preceding our departure, both Greek prime minister Mitsotakis and Turkish president Ozal lost control of their domestic political constituencies. As a result neither leader had sufficient authority to engage on this controversial matter. The trip was, consequently, almost entirely touristic.

And it was tourism in the grand style. A brand new Boeing 747 had just been delivered, the first jumbo jet to serve as *Air Force One*, and this was its maiden voyage. In Athens the prime minister walked with us up to the Parthenon, closed to the public for the occasion. The next day we flew to his personal home in Crete, where we dined on a terrace looking out over the Mediterranean. We were entertained at a state dinner in Ankara, at which all the flatware was of solid gold. I wondered that we were not made to walk through metal detectors on our way out. The high point of the trip came in Istanbul, where President Ozal gave us a personal tour of Topkapi, the former Sultan's palace. This was followed by a cruise along the Bosporus, which was closed to sea traffic for the occasion. Driving in from the airport Gompert and I had noticed dozens of ships riding at anchor offshore and wondered why. Now we knew.

There was one hiccup. On our arrival in Athens I received a message from Washington warning that a terrorist attack was likely to coincide with the president's visit to Turkey. Since the downing of Pan Am Flight 103 over Scotland, the practice had developed of issuing public alerts when intelligence of this sort was in hand. The State Department was seeking my approval to make an announcement alerting the public to the possibility of such an attack. Recognizing that the Turks would be very unhappy with any country-specific mention, I changed the announcement to warn of a possible attack "somewhere in the eastern Mediterranean region." I went over the announcement with David Gompert and we both informed Brent Scowcroft, following which I authorized the announcement.

Later that morning we were seated around a conference table in the Greek prime minister's office. A member of his staff handed Mitsotakis a copy of the announcement and the prime minister became agitated. He protested that this warning would have a negative impact on tourist travel to Greece and asked Bush to rescind the announcement. The president was totally blind-sided and turned to ask us what was going on. The U.S. side huddled in an adjoining room, where I explained what had happened and Gompert stepped forward to share the blame. Scowcroft said nothing, just looked on censoriously as we explained ourselves. The president was visibly upset but held his temper, and the following day, as we flew from Greece to Turkey, he signed off on my nomination to become ambassador to the European Community.

THIRTEEN

From Community to Union

AMONG THE BYPRODUCTS OF GERMAN unification was the Treaty of Maastricht, still being negotiated as I got ready to leave for Brussels. It was intended to set the European Community on the path to union. The transformation was to involve more than a name change. It included the creation of a common European currency and a common European foreign and security policy. The United States had supported further steps toward European unity as one element of its overall approach to German unification. How the specifics of these new integrative steps would affect American interests was less clear, and these were issues I began to explore as I prepared to take up my new post.

Before leaving Washington I called on Treasury Secretary Nicholas Brady and on Federal Reserve President Alan Greenspan. In both cases I asked their views on the move toward a single European currency. Brady replied that he and his colleagues at Treasury had never really discussed the issue. He also said the question had not come up in his regular meetings with European counterparts in the G-7 forum. One of Brady's senior advisers expressed concern that a single currency was likely to slow

European economic growth. Greenspan, in contrast to Brady, said that the single currency was regularly discussed in his meetings with European central bankers. Neither Treasury nor the Fed suggested the United States should oppose this project.

Washington was more concerned about the move toward common European security policies. Several problems were apparent. Was the European Union going to form a caucus within NATO, facing the United States with coordinated views on issues before the alliance? This could diminish American influence and slow the decision process. Would the EU adopt positions on issues of European security at variance with those of the United States? If and when non-NATO states on the Russian periphery joined the EU, something already in prospect in 1991, would they fall within an EU but not NATO security perimeter, and how could that possibly work?

The treaty was concluded in December 1991, a few months after my arrival in Brussels, but ratification turned out to be time consuming and uncertain. Denmark held a referendum in which voters rejected the treaty. Minor changes were made to the agreement and it was again put to a vote, this time securing Danish approval. France also held a referendum on the issue, which very narrowly passed. The process kept European leaders, and observers like myself, on tenterhooks for the next eighteen months.

It was frustrating being the American representative to an organization to which the United States did not belong. The inner circle of diplomatic missions in Brussels included EC member governments, and these envoys were engaged in constant high-stakes negotiations while the rest of us had our noses pressed to the glass, seeking to determine what was happening and influence it to our national advantage. My job was, thus, a somewhat more prestigious but less remunerative form of lobbying.

The city itself was cosmopolitan and comfortable. Toril and I occupied a lovely nineteenth-century brick and stone house, almost but not quite a chateau. It was situated on several acres of landscaped grounds that included a gatehouse and a stable, some of which had been converted to a guesthouse, although the horse stalls remained. Downtown Brussels, on the far side of a large park, had been heavily redeveloped soon after World War II and, consequently, possessed all the charm of K Street in Washington D.C. It was also filled with much the same sort of people: bureaucrats, lawyers, and lobbyists from all over Europe and beyond. The city was surrounded by woodland but lacked the museums and historic cityscapes of London or Paris. When it rained, which was often, there was little to do indoors other than eat. Fortunately the quality and profusion of Brussels' restaurants rivaled those of the other major European capitals.

Common monetary and security policies were still in Europe's future, but trade had long been a Community responsibility. The EC was the world's second largest economy and the United States' largest trade partner. The European Commission, the operational arm of the Community, represented all twelve member countries in all trade negotiations. The Commission was, thus, Washington's most important interlocutor in the Bush administration's efforts to conclude a global trade accord.

Begun five years earlier in Uruguay, these negotiations were already in their second year of overtime. The main blockage was differences between the United States and Europe over trade in agriculture. The United States, a relatively low-cost food producer, wanted greater access to the European market and limits on subsidized European farm exports. The American position represented a challenge to one of the cornerstones of European integration, the Common Agricultural Policy, under which the Community paid generous subsidies to European farmers and erected high barriers to imports.

On the American side responsibility for this aspect of the negotiations was shared between U.S. Trade Representative (USTR) Carla Hills and Secretary of Agriculture Ed Madigan, and there was little trust between the two. Bob Zoellick, now the under secretary of state for economic affairs, was doing his best to bridge these differences. Responsibility on the European side was similarly split between the commissioner handling trade and a colleague responsible for agriculture. These two did not get on particularly well either.

Both these commissioners and their advisers were accessible and willing to talk reasonably freely about the negotiations. My American colleagues, in contrast, did their level best to exclude our mission from these matters except when negotiations broke down entirely, as they too often did. At this point, Carla Hills would call and ask me to intervene with the commission to get the dialogue back on track. Once I had done so, her staff would again seek to shut us out until the next crisis.

Leaders on both sides of the Atlantic were eager to bring the Uruguay Round to a conclusion. Not only were deep cuts in trade barriers at stake, so was the creation of the World Trade Organization, intended to be a more powerful successor to the General Agreement on Trade and Tariffs.

Shortly after my arrival in Brussels I joined President Bush in the Hague for a meeting with Dutch prime minister Ruud Lubbers, who then held the rotating European Council presidency, and Jacque Delors, president of the Commission. Baker, Hills, and Madigan all participated, and Bush sought to advance agreement on the outstanding agricultural issues, gently encouraging Madigan in this regard, but to little effect.

Some months later Baker came to Brussels for a meeting with Delors. In preparation for this session Madigan and I spent a long night negotiating with Ray MacSharry, the European commissioner for agriculture. Dutch prime minister Lubbers, then president of the European Council, also participated in this late-night session; his presence was unusual, as trade negotiations were a commission, not a council, responsibility. The four of us talked for several hours. Lubbers and I suggested several bridging formulas, which both MacSharry and Madigan resisted.

The following day Baker and Delors chaired a meeting of the two sides, and I called Lubbers and urged him to join the meeting, which he did. Again MacSharry and Madigan refused to budge.

My efforts to bridge these differences earned me an angry reproach from Madigan, but Lubbers paid a higher price. Helmut Kohl is said to have vetoed Lubbers' candidacy to succeed Delors at the head of the European Commission out of pique over the prime minister's interference in these very talks.

Pressure was mounting on both sides. Bush hoped that Kohl, in gratitude for the pivotal American role in German unification, might help push these talks across the finish line, and wanted him to do so prior to the 1992 American presidential election. Kohl proved unresponsive.

Following Baker's visit Bob Zoellick arrived with Carla Hill's deputy and Madigan's principal trade adviser for another round of talks. True to form, the USTR representative insisted I was not to participate in these discussions, and he was visibly upset when I forced the issue the next morning.

A few months later, after the American elections, the two sides met in Blair House, the American president's official guesthouse. Bob Zoellick had moved with Baker to the White House to become deputy chief of staff. From this position Zoellick was better able to mediate between Hills and Madigan and, as a result, the United States and the EU reached an agreement in principle curbing subsidies for agriculture and expanding access to the European market. The French government balked at the Blair

House agreement, so it took another year to conclude what remains to this day the most substantial round of global trade liberalization ever.

Throughout these talks I was continually amazed how much more tense and confrontational trade talks were than U.S.-Soviet negotiations on nuclear arms reductions or German unification. In those security and geopolitical forums, where the stakes had sometimes been literally existential, the negotiators sought to establish a cordial relationship of at least limited trust and work together toward an accord that would satisfy each of their governments. Trade talks seemed to be conducted in a much more hostile and suspicious atmosphere, with periodic blow-ups, following which one side or the other would have to be coaxed back to the table. This may have had something to do with the particular personalities involved, but also with the number and variety of domestic constituencies to which trade negotiators had to answer and the cold hard cash into which the results of any agreement would be translated. Still, it seemed discordant to me that negotiations between bitter adversaries affecting the fates of nations and the survival of the human race could be conducted with greater civility than those between close allies over the price of vegetables.

As ambassador to the European Community I was accredited to all twelve member governments. This gave me license to range pretty freely across Europe and express myself broadly on European policy. Transatlantic and intra-European relations were in flux as both Washington and European capitals devised policies to deal with a liberated Eastern Europe and the fifteen new states carved out of the former Soviet Union. In a series of speeches and less formal remarks, I waded into these debates.

Despite the intense public debate in Europe over the Treaty of Maastricht and the deepened integration it was intended to introduce, I assured Washington that this agreement would ultimately be ratified by all parties. I assured the Europeans that Washington fully backed the project. I expressed public doubts, however, that the monetary union called for in this treaty could be long sustained without movement toward fiscal and, thus, political union. Recalling how Helmut Kohl's offer of monetary union to the East Germans had led so quickly to unification, I opined that Kohl and Delors may have had a similar objective in view in pushing European monetary union.

Once the Soviet Union disappeared, I became less concerned about the European Community taking on greater defense and security functions. I remained worried, however, about the introduction of non-NATO members like Sweden, Austria, and Finland into the EC. Would this mean that our NATO allies would become responsible for defending those countries, a commitment that might inextricably draw the United States into conflict not of its making while these new EU member countries would have no reciprocal responsibilities toward NATO or the United States? I was even more skeptical about the extension of NATO membership to former Warsaw Pact countries. The neutral states of Western Europe, Sweden, Finland, and Austria, the same ones now lining up to join the European Union, had fared quite well throughout the Cold War, achieving very high levels of political freedom and economic prosperity while remaining outside the European Community and NATO. Why couldn't the states of Eastern Europe advance along this path, becoming prosperous and democratic while remaining neutral? Why antagonize a friendly and increasingly democratic Russia by moving NATO up to its doorstep, something we had implicitly promised not to do only a few years earlier, in the negotiations over German unification?

As 1992 progressed the Bush administration turned its attention to domestic politics and the president's reelection campaign. Jim Baker reluctantly left State to run both the campaign and the White House. Zoellick, Tutwiler, and Ross went with him. A couple of days before the election I called on Bob in the White House and was somewhat surprised that he had time to spare for me. I found him in a reflective and rather downbeat mood as he acknowledged that the election was probably lost.

To this day I find it amazing that a president who had successfully negotiated the reunification of Germany, promoted the liberation of Eastern Europe, handled the peaceful dissolution of the Soviet Union, and secured the liberation of Kuwait should be summarily turned out of office. This happened to Winston Churchill at the end of World War II, but Great Britain had been subjected to a generation of economic privation. The same could hardly be said of the United States in 1992. Twelve years later I would become equally bemused that George W. Bush could be reelected after invading Iraq by mistake and then so badly mishandling its reconstruction.

Returning to Brussels I awaited the new administration with equanimity, assuming that, as a career officer, I would be allowed to finish out my three-year tour in Brussels. Anticipating the new team's likely review of European policies, I pulled together my thoughts on the topic. Integrating Russia into a democratic European order struck me as the top priority, much as integrating a defeated Germany into such an order had been the signal achievement of American post–World War II policy. Accordingly I wrote and began to speak in favor of an assistance program modeled on the Marshall Plan that would include Russia along with the other newly independent states of Central and Eastern Europe. I gave a paper to this effect to Strobe Talbott, who had just been named by the new administration to oversee relations with Russia and the other states of the former Soviet Union, but I never received a reaction.

Was I influenced by the Sonnenfeldt Doctrine, which held that Europe would be more stable and reliably peaceful if Moscow and its neighboring states lived in mutually beneficial dependency? Perhaps, although I did not make that connection at the time. In any case, American policy went in a very different direction, bringing the former Warsaw Pact nations into the European Union and NATO, while effectively treating Russia as a non-European state, unqualified by reason of its size and history for membership in either organization.

In February Warren Christopher, the new secretary of state, came to Brussels for his first set of NATO and European Community meetings. I greeted him at the airport, and was somewhat disconcerted to discover that I knew no one else who got off his plane. Then, of all people, Dennis Ross emerged. Asked how he came to be traveling with the new secretary, Dennis explained that he had been invited to stay on. He kindly invited me back to his hotel and spent an hour describing the new set-up and the various personalities involved.

The following day I went to NATO, where Christopher was speaking. Whenever Baker had come to Brussels I joined his entourage whether he was at NATO or a European Community event. Although never part of his innermost circle, I was by then a familiar and well-regarded member of the next tier and was greeted affectionately by the rest of his entourage. With this new group I was and felt a complete stranger.

On his second day in Brussels Christopher came to my side of town to meet with the twelve EC foreign ministers, all but one of whom, the Irish, he had already met on the previous day at NATO. Given that he had only been in office for several weeks, Christopher spoke in generalities about the major European preoccupation, the still-widening conflict in the Balkans.

Shortly thereafter my NATO colleague Reginald Bartholomew was pulled back to Washington to become Christopher's senior adviser on Balkan affairs. A couple of months later Christopher returned to Brussels, this time with Bartholomew in tow, to promote an American solution to the Bosnia conflict. We met in a large conference room, each minister bolstered by half a dozen aides. Christopher urged that the United States and Europe should lift their arms embargo so as to be able to supply weapons to the beleaguered Muslim forces. NATO planes should also begin hitting Serb targets. Lift and Strike, as this proposal was christened, proved wholly unacceptable to the Europeans. They had troops on the ground as part of the United Nations peacekeeping force that had been deployed to separate the combatants and protect the civilian population. Lift and Strike would deprive this force of its neutrality. European troops would be left to deal with the Serb reprisal while America would be engaged only in the air.

Bartholomew, after only a matter of weeks in his new position, had somehow managed to get himself nominated to become the ambassador to Italy. Although this meeting with the European foreign ministers was conducted almost entirely in English, Reg donned earphones and listened to the exchanges as interpreted into Italian. On his return to Washington, he called to ask if I would be willing to replace him as the administration's Balkan envoy. I declined, finding the Clinton administration's approach to that still spreading conflicts no more effectual than that of its predecessor. The person who did replace Bartholomew made little progress, as I expected. He was, nevertheless, rewarded after a year of dutiful service by being made ambassador to Germany.

I soon found myself leaving Brussels earlier than anticipated. The news came in the most tactless fashion, via an instruction to the head of our administrative section to put together a briefing book for my successor. Stuart Eizenstat had been Jimmy Carter's senior domestic policy adviser a decade earlier. He was one of several former Democratic officials who had not contributed lavishly enough to be sent to Paris or London, but who had, nevertheless, earned a respectable European posting, which turned out to be mine. I had to acknowledge that Stu was impressively credentialed for the post, and, in fact, he did an outstanding job. This did not make me feel any happier. I was, as it developed, the last career officer to hold this position, it having been treated as a patronage posting ever since.

Learning I was again at loose ends Bob Blackwill called. He was teaching at the Kennedy School at Harvard. The dean of that school, Graham Allison, had just been nominated to be an assistant secretary of defense, and Bob said Graham wanted me to join him at DOD as his principal deputy. A stint within the Defense Department struck me as a new and challenging experience. I knew and respected new Secretary of Defense Les Aspin, who had visited Bonn several times in his capacity as the top Democrat on the House Armed Services Committee. He had impressed me with his serious interest and broad knowledge of the field, as well as his gregarious and unpretentious demeanor. Frank Wisner, a Foreign Service colleague who had just taken over as under secretary of defense for policy, sent me a message urging that I cut short my remaining weeks in Brussels, insisting that the new Pentagon team needed me immediately.

I showed up in Washington a couple of weeks later only to find Aspin's personal staff, brought with him from Capitol Hill, were vetting all senior appointments and had yet to approve mine. For months on end nothing happened.

While awaiting some resolution of my status at the Pentagon I prevailed upon the State Department to lend me to the RAND Corporation, a large national security think tank with offices in Santa Monica and Washington. At RAND I headed a study commissioned by the Pentagon on policy options for Bosnia. Allison slowly moved through the Senate confirmation process, and I was invited to the ceremony at which Aspin was to administer the oath of office. The secretary was running late, and after an hour, I moved to leave for another engagement. As I collected my coat Aspin stepped off the elevator. He recognized me and we chatted briefly. He then entered the room full of Allison's friends and future colleagues only to announce to the startled celebrants that he had just been fired. His late arrival was due to an unanticipated White House meeting in which he had been so informed. With Aspin went any prospect of my own move to the Pentagon.

FOURTEEN

Black Hawk Down

FOUR DAYS AFTER TWO U.S. Army Black Hawk helicopters were shot down over downtown Mogadishu I received a call from Peter Tarnoff, the under secretary of state for political affairs. The choppers had been ferrying Army Rangers and Special Forces on a mission to capture associates of the local warlord, former general Mohamed Farrah Aidid. As a result of the downing nearly 100 American soldiers found themselves trapped overnight in an intense battle with Somali militia. Eighteen Americans were killed, seventy-three wounded, and one captured. Uncounted thousands of Somalis also died. In reaction, President Clinton decided both to send more troops to Somalia and to withdraw them six months hence. Ambassador Robert Oakley, who had been my immediate boss in the Embassy Paris political section twenty-five years earlier, was in Mogadishu negotiating the release of the one American soldier taken prisoner. I was asked to take over from Oakley and manage the diplomatic and the bureaucratic aspects of the planned withdrawal.

Over the next few days I familiarized myself with the policies and personalities that had brought us to this point. President Bush, in the waning days of his administration, had dispatched some 20,000 soldiers and Marines to Somalia with orders to protect the delivery of food and medicine to a population threatened by famine. Perhaps 100,000 lives were saved as a result of the assistance provided under cover of this American-led intervention. Although the country had already descended into civil war and had no national government, this large and capable American-led force met no significant resistance.

In May of 1993, four months after Bill Clinton took office, the United Nations resumed lead responsibility for international efforts in Somalia, deploying a force of 16,000 soldiers. The United States withdrew the bulk of its troops but provided logistic support to the UN and retained a small combat force of around 1,600 in-country. These Americans were not placed under UN command. Subsequently, the Clinton administration also dispatched a smaller number of Army Ranger and Special Forces. These were to operate independent of both the UN and the U.S. command in-country. Their mission was to capture or kill General Aidid. Three separate military forces were, thus, operating simultaneously from the same base (Mogadishu airport) into the same city.

The overall United Nations effort was headed by retired American admiral Jonathan Howe. Jon had succeeded Rick Burt as head of State's PM Bureau a decade earlier, and gone on to become President Bush's deputy national security adviser after Bob Gates moved to head the CIA. Howe's selection for this post was designed to ensure that United Nation's and American operations in Somalia remained closely linked. In fact, his assignment probably represented a source of confusion as to who was really in charge, the UN or the United States. Washington thought Somalia was now primarily a UN problem, whereas New York was continuing to look to Washington for guidance and support. Each tended to regard Howe as a representative of the other.

The shift from American to UN leadership and the consequent reduction in overall international military capabilities was accompanied by a vast expansion in the international mission. The original American force had had a limited, purely humanitarian mandate, with no nation-building component. The successor American force had the mission of supporting a UN-led program of grassroots democratization that was bound to antagonize every warlord in the country.

In Mogadishu UN troops found themselves challenged by fighters loyal to the local strongman, former Somali general Mohamed Farrah Aidid.

Howe asked the United States to capture or kill Aidid, and in response President Clinton dispatched the Rangers and Special Forces for this purpose. It was this element that became stranded in downtown Mogadishu after two of its helicopters were shot down.

I took up residence in the front office of the Africa Bureau headed by George Moose. Our bureaucratic relationship was somewhat anomalous, as George was a member of the interagency committee I was to head, but I was also a guest in his organization, supervising elements of his staff. Moose was heavily focused on the upcoming transition in South Africa from a white apartheid regime to a government headed by Nelson Mandela, and he was happy enough to have someone else take on Somalia, so we got on well.

Richard Clarke was the NSC senior director who had been running the interagency process in Somalia. Dick was less inclined to yield his authority. In addition, we had a history of friction, stemming from when Clarke had been a colleague back in Rick Burt's PM Bureau. On his arrival Burt reorganized the bureau, and one aspect of this was to move me into the office Clarke had occupied under the previous administration and Clarke into a less desirable space, one without a window. This annoyed Dick to the point that he refused to speak to me for several months. Despite this unpromising beginning, we formed a close partnership. Dick was smart and capable, and I saw the value in having the NSC closely engaged in my efforts, recognizing that only the White House could move the Defense Department when disagreements with State arose. Clarke and I agreed to alternate chairmanship of the Somalia Executive Committee and to share responsibility for interagency management. This worked remarkably well, perhaps because both of us recognized that our careers and reputations were on the line. A second Black Hawk Down-type fiasco could finish us both.

Our mission was to extract remaining American forces from Somalia by the following March and to do so without further setbacks or embarrassment. We also wanted to avoid having the American retreat turn into a rout with the rest of the United Nations force following us out the door. We therefore wanted the UN troops to stay behind after ours left.

President Clinton dispatched substantial reinforcements to Somalia in the immediate aftermath of the Black Hawk Down incident. Clarke and I secured an interagency agreement that these forces would be used to begin establishing a more secure environment in the capital, Mogadishu, to improve the position the United Nations would occupy when American troops departed. On learning of this intended move, Tom Donilon, chief of staff to Warren Christopher, became agitated. Donilon insisted that the only mission for American forces in Somalia was to deter attacks on themselves. Self-protection, in other words, was the only American mission. He engaged Christopher and succeeded in getting the impending operation scotched. For their remaining months in Somalia, American troops would do nothing except avoid casualties. Force protection would dominate American military operations for the rest of the decade, although never to quite such a paralyzing degree.

As noted, Washington was eager that the UN force not leave when we did. Abandoning the country so comprehensively would compound the impression of defeat and retreat. I was assigned a presidential mission aircraft and sent on a voyage to recruit as many troop contingents as could be persuaded to cover our withdrawal. I first consulted with Kofi Annan, then the UN under secretary general for peacekeeping, who agreed that an American effort in this regard would be helpful.

We began in Rome. Somalia had been an Italian colony before the Second World War, and Italy had a contingent of troops there with the United Nations. Reg Bartholomew, now our ambassador, met with me on arrival but chose not to accompany me to the foreign ministry. He regarded my mission in Rome as doomed to failure, and he was right. The Italian foreign and defense ministry representatives insisted that their forces would be leaving with ours. They had no intention of risking Italian troops in an environment judged too dangerous for Americans.

Fortunately other potential troop contributors proved less faint-hearted. The next stop was Islamabad. After breakfast there we went on to lunch in New Delhi, had tea outside Cairo, and dinner in Sicily. The next day it was on to Rabat. In the end Pakistan, India, Egypt, and Morocco pledged to keep their troops in Somalia. On my return to Washington I reported success to the NSC deputies committee. "I have helped put together several international coalitions in the past," I noted, "but this is the first I helped form that we did not not intend to join."

As the American engagement in Somalia reached its conclusion, I flew to Mogadishu with General John Shalikashvili, chair of the joint chiefs of staff. Shali, as he was universally known, was the most impressive and warm-hearted military commander I had encountered, with the possible exception of his immediate predecessor, Colin Powell. That the U.S. Army could produce two such formidable leaders, one right after the other, struck me as an impressive tribute to its system of selection and promotion.

Shali's purpose in visiting Mogadishu was to thank the national contingents that had soldiered with the United States throughout the intervention, and most particularly those that would be staying on after our departure. I spent my time with the United Nations' civilian leadership, discussing efforts to broker some kind of peace settlement among Somalia's numerous warring clans. When Shali left for Washington, I flew on to Nairobi, Kenya, where most of the Somali warlords had taken up residence in the city's luxury hotels. I met with General Aidid, and several of his adversaries. All the warring clan leaders listened politely, but the United States was on its way out, and our views counted for little. Aidid did promise there would be no interference with the U.S. troop withdrawal, but otherwise my discussions yielded little.

My Somalia mission was, within its limited mandate, successful. After six months American forces left without suffering further casualties. Thousands of UN troops remained, providing Washington just the sort of "decent interval" Henry Kissinger was said to have sought for the American withdrawal from Vietnam. A year later the U.S. Navy returned to lift the remaining UN forces out. Somalia, the classic failed state, was left to its own devices. The civil war resumed, eventually sucking in two neighboring states, Ethiopia and Kenya. The country became a haven for pirates who preyed on shipping that transited one of the world's major trade routes, that from the Suez Canal to the Far East. Eventually the conflict attracted the attention of Al Qaeda, which established one of its largest franchises, the Al-Shabaab insurgency.

Less than two weeks after the last American troops left Somalia, the Rwandan genocide began. The mass slaughter was sparked by the death of that country's president, whose plane was shot down on its approach to the capital. As the slaughter mounted it became increasingly evident that a campaign of extermination of Tutsi civilians by Hutu-led government forces was underway.

At the end of the Somalia mission my responsibilities were extended to cover all peacekeeping-related issues, and I attended an NSC deputies meeting that wrestled with the crisis in Rwanda. The United Nations peacekeeping force in the capital of Kigali was too weak to do more than shield a comparatively small number of the potential victims. The Pentagon was opposed to a UN request that this small force be expanded, citing the difficulty of deploying and supplying such a command in the middle of a hostile city against the wishes of the local government. Memories of Mogadishu remained keen. No one was willing to risk another such fiasco.

Madeleine Albright, then the American ambassador to the United Nations, encouraged me to explore what could be done. I was able to secure tentative Pentagon support for an alternative plan that would have established logistic hubs in a couple of neighboring countries and then pushed peacekeeping forces from outside into Rwanda along the border areas, gradually increasing secure zones within the country into which fleeing Tutsis could take refuge. The Defense Department was not prepared to commit American combat troops inside Rwanda, but it was willing to consider providing logistic support from the neighboring countries. I thought this proposal better than nothing. Once American troops were committed to the operation, even in such a peripheral role, I thought we would inevitably be drawn into more meaningful participation.

Iqbal Reza, Kofi Annan's deputy in the UN's Peacekeeping Department, came to Washington seeking help. I briefed him on this concept, stressing that this was the most he could expect from the United States at present. Reza rejected my proposal categorically, insisting that additional forces needed to be inserted directly into Kigali, the capital. In consequence the United States argued in New York for the full withdrawal of remaining UN troops. This was not done, but neither was the small UN contingent in Kigali reinforced until two further months had passed, by which time the killing had largely come to halt, leaving up to 900,000 dead.

Eventually the French did just what I had proposed, establishing bases in neighboring Zaire and extending safe zones into Rwanda, eventually occupying nearly a fifth of the country and, thereby, saving thousands of lives. I continue to believe that an American-supported effort of this sort mounted two months earlier, while not as effective as the course the United Nations was advocating, would have rescued a far larger number of people. I also believe that even limited American military involvement of this sort would have attracted others, and eventually led the United States itself to expand its commitment. But Rwandans paid the price for the Somalia debacle. Additionally the Clinton administration was moving toward a different military intervention.

The young expatriate, just
arrived in Manila in 1953.
American prestige was
at its height, the dollar
was super strong, and life
was very comfortable.

Graduation Day at Officers Candidate
School in Newport, Rhode Island,
November 22, 1963. My mother,
pictured, and father, behind the camera,
and I drove into town in a celebratory
mood, only to learn that President
Kennedy had just been shot to death.

Flight Operations on the deck of the USS *Bon Homme Richard*, CVA 31, in the South China Sea, early 1964. Some months later the two Gulf of Tonkin incidents—one a genuine firefight with destroyers under our ship's tactical command, the other perhaps imagined—would greatly escalate American involvement in the Vietnam War and the pace of our operations.

On New Year's Eve 1969, Toril and I were married in a staved wooden chapel on the Holmenkollen ski slope outside Oslo, Norway.

Toril shows First Lady Barbara Bush around the Bonn American School, during George H. W. Bush's first and last presidential visit to West Germany in May 1989. On Bush's next presidential visit, in November 1990, West Germany had become simply Germany.

With Undersecretary of State Bob Zoellick in Germany,
late 1990. Bob and I spent a day touring the East German
countryside, meeting with locals and getting a first
impression of the newly unified country.

Briefing President Clinton aboard Air Force One on our way to Venezuela, Brazil, and Argentina, October 1997. National Security Adviser Sandy Berger and his deputy, Jim Steinberg—both to Clinton's left—are also in attendance. U.S. relations with its hemispheric neighbors were at a high point, and Clinton had particularly close contacts with the Brazilian and Argentine presidents, Henrique Cardozo and Carlos Menem.

With my security detail on the airstrip at Bagram, November 20,
2001. My meetings there with the Northern Alliance leadership
confirmed their attendance at the Bonn Conference where the
first post-Taliban government was formed. (Craig Karp)

With Hamid Karzai at the Presidential Palace in Kabul,
December 14, 2001. Karzai had arrived in Kabul the previous day
and would be inaugurated as the head of Afghanistan's Interim
Administration a week later. (Craig Karp)

With Toril and Secretary of State Colin Powell,
who marked my departure from the Foreign Service
with kind words and a large medal, April 2002.

Lifting glasses in 2006 after receiving the Federal Republic of
Germany's Order of Merit from Wolfgang Ischinger, the German
ambassador to Washington. During Toril's and my years at the
American Embassy in Bonn, Wolfgang, then an aide to Foreign
Minister Han-Dietrich Genscher, had been a good friend.

FIFTEEN

Entering Haiti

THE SOMALIA DEBACLE WAS NOT the only reason President Clinton failed to do anything about Rwanda. Administration attention was fixed on the Caribbean, where thousands of Haitian refugees were taking to small boats in an effort to reach the United States. Just as the killing in Rwanda was gearing up, Deputy Secretary of State Strobe Talbott asked me whether I would serve as deputy to former congressman Bill Gray, who was being appointed as President Clinton's special envoy for Haiti. Talbott told me President Clinton was determined to use force if necessary to topple the military regime in Port-au-Prince and restore the freely elected president, Jean-Bertrand Aristide. Gray, a former house majority whip and chair of the Congressional Black Caucus, was being brought into the administration to prepare the way for such an operation. Talbott wanted me to play largely the same role I had in Somalia, chairing the interagency group that would prepare this operation.

I asked whether I could do this while continuing to work on Rwanda, noting the still-undetermined nature of our response to that unfolding tragedy. No, I was told; Haiti had precedence and I would have to devote full time to it.

Gray insisted on being offered several candidates for the deputy position. After interviewing three of us, he chose me. He exhibited visible reluctance in doing so, commenting sourly that I seemed to be the administration's preference. This was the beginning of a painfully fractious relationship.

In addition to acquiring a difficult boss, I also stepped into a partisan minefield, a new and unwelcome experience. Congressional opinion on European and East-West issues had always been divided between hawks and doves, but not between Republicans and Democrats. Scoop Jackson, a Democrat, had been harshly critical of Nixon, Ford, and Carter's efforts at détente, which many in his party supported. Bob Dole, Clinton's opponent in the 1986 presidential campaign, was also a strong champion of Clinton's Balkan interventions. With respect to Haiti, however, Clinton would get no Republican help whatsoever. Congressional support for this intervention was concentrated in the Congressional Black Caucus and there were no black Republican members of Congress. The Black Caucus, and with less passion other congressional Democrats, favored American action to restore Aristide. No Republicans did so; most were bitterly opposed to it.

This partisan divide extended to the hemisphere as a whole, and it had not begun with the Republicans. Democrats had been harshly critical of President Reagan's Cold War campaigns against leftist regimes and Soviet-backed insurgencies in Central America. They charged his administration with backing dictators, death squads, and abusive military establishments. Career diplomats working on Central America under Reagan had their subsequent careers blighted by vengeful Democratic congressmen. The fervor with which congressional Republicans sought to frustrate and denigrate Clinton's Haiti policies became a form of payback for this earlier rancor, and Gray's appointment only widened the partisan divide.

Haitian society was also badly divided. Jean-Bertrand Aristide was a former priest and a student of liberation theology. He had been elected president in early 1991 only to be forced to flee the country eight months later in a coup led by the Haitian Army chief, General Raoul Cedras. Aristide accused the United States of having helped engineer his ouster. Nevertheless, after temporarily taking refuge in Argentina, he moved to

Washington, from where he and his numerous American supporters pressed for his return.

Shortly after the coupe President Bush joined in an embargo on trade with Haiti imposed by the Organization of American States (OAS), and President Clinton further tightened the American economic sanctions. In July 1993 American and UN mediators brought Cedras and Aristide together on Governor's Island in New York harbor and successfully brokered an accord between the two providing for Aristide's return.

On October 20 of that year the U.S. Navy troop transport *Harlan County* arrived in Port-au-Prince. Aboard were a couple hundred American soldiers and a smaller number of Canadian Royal Mounted Police. This contingent was to begin reforming the Haitian military, one of the steps agreed to at Governor's Island leading to Aristide's return. On the pier awaiting their arrival was Vicki Huddleston, the American charge d'affaires (the ambassador being out of the country), surrounded by a crowd of armed and noisy Haitians. Huddleston informed Washington that these Haitians, members of a pro-government militia, seemed in a festive mood and would probably disperse once the troops began to debark. Ignoring this advice, the White House directed the USS *Harlan County* to turn around and sail back to the United States. Huddleston was left to make her own way back to the embassy.

This retreat occurred a week after the Black Hawks went down in Mogadishu and four days after President Clinton announced his intention to withdraw all American troops from that country. Over subsequent months Clinton came under mounting pressure from Aristide, members of the Congressional Black Caucus, political activists (one of whom was staging a well-publicized hunger strike), and assorted movie stars urging him to take a tougher line against the Haitian government and a softer line on Haitian migrants.

Thousands of Haitians took to boats and makeshift rafts in attempts to get to the United States. Cubans who behaved similarly were automatically granted refuge in the United States, but Haitians were summarily returned to Haiti by the U.S. Coast Guard. All Cuban migrants were deemed to be fleeing oppression, all Haitians to be fleeing poverty. But the Haitian regime was arguably just as repressive as the Cuban. The more the United States and the rest of the world castigated the Haitian regime for its human rights violations, the harder it was to discriminate between Cuban and Haitian migrants.

In the days immediately preceding Gray's appointment, Clinton decided to turn up the pressure on the regime in Port-au-Prince by further ratcheting up sanctions and implicitly threatening a military invasion. He also decided to stop the forced return of those fleeing Haiti. I would spend the next five months trying to implement both these new policies.

Gray did not mesh well with the rest of the Clinton team. He had been asked personally by the president to take his new position and did not regard himself as subordinate to, or even on the same level as, those who were actually running the policy. These included Deputy Secretary of State Talbott, Deputy Defense Secretary John Deutch, and Deputy National Security Advisor Sandy Berger. Decisions were needed on a daily basis and Gray was sometimes unavailable and often uncomfortable with the decisions being reached, but uninterested in proposing alternatives of his own. He became increasingly resentful of my role in keeping the interagency machinery rolling forward. Coming from a congressional background, he was used to having a staff that revolved around him and to picking and choosing the issues and the times at which to engage, whereas he now occupied a pivotal spot in a hierarchical structure charged with a fast-moving crisis that required issues to be staffed up the line and decisions to be passed down reliably and expeditiously. Occasionally he took a clear position, but more often he failed to provide guidance and then complained when I proceeded without his input. Finding Gray difficult, unresponsive, and often unavailable, Talbott and Berger routinely dealt directly with me, which only increased Gray's unhappiness.

I met early each morning with Talbott to go over the upcoming day's activity, following which I went on to cochair an interagency meeting. Dick Clarke continued to act as my partner in this new enterprise, replicating the pattern we had established on Somalia. Throughout the day I directed the operations of the State Department's Haiti Working Group, with a staff of about a dozen. Most evenings Talbott, Gray if he was available, and I would attend a deputies meeting chaired by Berger. I tried on multiple occasions to brief Gray in enough detail to get the kind of guidance that would see me through the typical day of crisis management in which dozens of small decisions and incremental actions would need to be taken but he would not engage at this level.

And a genuine crisis is what we had, albeit largely self-imposed. By easing its treatment of fleeing Haitians while tightening the sanction regime, the Clinton administration had put itself on a path that led almost inexorably toward invasion. The ever harsher sanctions further impoverished the population, the ever more strident rhetoric made it hard not to treat fleeing Haitians as genuine refugees, and the knowledge that those picked up by the U.S. Coast Guard would no longer be automatically returned to the island incentivized tens of thousands of additional Haitians to join the exodus.

The administration dispatched a U.S. Navy hospital ship to the waters off Haiti to provide a place where the Coast Guard could bring fleeing Haitians to have their claims to refugee status adjudicated. We were also trying to charter an ocean liner on which the growing number of fleeing Haitians could be accommodated. These efforts were soon overwhelmed, as thousands of Haitians took to the sea in vessels designed not to get to the United States more than 600 miles away, but just to get them to the U.S. Coast Guard cutters stationed immediately offshore. Soon the administration felt compelled to announce another policy change. Henceforth even Haitians found qualified for asylum, which is to say those who could establish a credible fear of persecution if returned, would not be admitted to the United States, but would instead be collected in refugee camps somewhere in the Caribbean.

Even this disincentive did not stem the flow. Soon we were looking for places to put tens of thousands of Haitian refugees. The Defense Department, with considerable reluctance, was persuaded to reopen a camp at the U.S. Naval Base at Guantanamo Bay, Cuba, where the Bush administration had, during an earlier such crisis, deposited some 30,000 Haitians. This facility was soon overflowing, and we began desperately searching for additional locations. To save time, it was decided that Gray and I would separately visit two prospective countries where we would seek agreement to open further refugee camps. We were each assigned a presidential mission aircraft, he to fly to Barbados and I to Panama.

On arrival in Panama City I first went to the U.S. Southern Command headquarters from where General Barry McCaffrey oversaw American military operations throughout Latin America. I explained that my mission was to secure Panamanian government permission for his command to construct a camp large enough to house 10,000 to 20,000 Haitian refugees. McCaffrey replied that the Panamanians would never agree and offered several practical objections as well. This was not a project he wished to take on.

I then went to see Panamanian President Guillermo Endara. It being Saturday evening, the president received me in his private home, where I explained that President Clinton was determined to restore democracy to Haiti, much as President Bush had restored democracy to Panama some five years earlier. The many Haitians still fleeing their island would soon be able to go home. In the interim, however, we needed additional facilities in which to hold them, as the one in Guantanamo was filling up quickly. Rather to my surprise, Endara, after consulting briefly with several of his advisers, agreed to my request. He said he would announce his decision first thing in the next morning.

I returned to the embassy and called Gray in Barbados. He had failed to persuade the government there to accept Haitian refugees and was put out that I had succeeded. I explained that Endara intended to announce his agreement the following morning. "No," Grey insisted. "We need to announce these two together." I protested, but he was adamant. I, therefore, passed a message to Endara asking that he hold off on his announcement.

Two days later the Panamanians informed us they had changed their minds. Whether McCaffrey's obvious lack of enthusiasm for the project had anything to do with the reversal, I don't know. I am sure it would have been more difficult for the Panamanians to withdraw their permission had Gray's childish petulance not caused us to delay their announcement.

We also wanted Caribbean governments to contribute personnel to the invasion force we were assembling to secure Aristide's return. Gray and I visited several of these island nations for that purpose, the largest being Jamaica. As a result of these visits we were able to cobble together something called the CARICOM Battalion. In actuality this unit was not larger than an infantry company, made up as it was of contingents of one or two dozen soldiers from half a dozen micro-states. The "battalion" was worthless militarily, but of considerable political importance, demonstrating as it did that the intervention had regional backing.

I accompanied Talbott and Aristide to a meeting of the Organization of American States held in Belem, Brazil. The city stands near the mouth of the Amazon, in the midst of a rainforest, on Brazil's impoverished north coast. It was hot, muggy, and rundown. On the way in from the airport someone told me that our hotel had rubber sheets on all the beds. "Must be one of the Hotel Incontinental chain," I commented.

We emerged from Belem with hemispheric endorsement of a military effort to restore Aristide to power, and action moved to the United Nations. Following the Governor's Island agreement, the Security Council authorized a peacekeeping force for Haiti and this authorization remained valid. Our intention was to assume command of this UN force, staff it with a strong American contingent, and employ it to oust the existing regime in Port-au-Prince. To do this we needed the agreement of UN Secretary General Boutros-Ghali. Lieutenant General Wesley Clark, who headed the plans division of the joint staff, accompanied me to New York to brief Boutros-Ghali. As we walked across First Avenue from the U.S. mission to UN headquarters, Clark informed me that his instructions were to tell the secretary general that this plan was infeasible.

"You will do no such thing," I insisted. Wes heard me out and found a telephone. He called back to the Pentagon and rejoined me, agreeing not to voice these reservations about our intended employment of the UN peacekeeping force. We then joined Madeleine Albright for our meeting with the secretary general.

Boutros-Ghali had his own reservations, which were not dissimilar to Clark's. The United Nations did peacekeeping, the secretary general insisted, not invasions. Ousting the coup regime and reinstalling Aristide should be done by a nationally-led force, following which the United Nations could take over responsibility for maintaining security. I pushed back, noting that we had a Security Council mandate for a UN force, not for a nationally-led one.

Back in Washington we debated this matter over the next several days. I remained opposed to Boutros-Ghali's proposal because I did not think we could get Security Council approval for an American-led invasion and did not think President Clinton would act without the Security Council's backing. Talbott heard me out but said Madeleine Albright felt she could get a resolution authorizing the use of "all necessary means" to restore Aristide. "If Madeleine thinks she can do it," I relented, "let's give it a try."

We still hoped the mere threat of force combined with ever more severe economic sanctions would suffice. Gray and I flew to Santo Domingo to persuade the Dominican Republic's long-time President Joaquín Balaguer to strengthen sanctions enforcement along his country's long land border with Haiti. Balaguer agreed to accept the presence of an Organization of American States (OAU) monitoring team to help with border enforcement.

The desperation of our efforts at this point can be illustrated by the fact that the sanctions evasion we were seeking to stem consisted of single individuals hand-carrying jerry cans of gasoline across the shallow river that divided the two countries.

Another example of our mounting desperation was the employment of Commando Solo, a fleet of antiquated Air Force cargo planes that had been configured in the midst of the Cold War to broadcast radio programming to otherwise unreachable populations. These planes now cruised around the Caribbean broadcasting messages from Aristide to the small number of Haitians who had radios that could pick up such transmissions. I located a Creole-speaking Foreign Service officer to vet the scripts and make sure nothing outrageous was said via this expensive and largely ineffective medium.

To my delight and astonishment Madeleine Albright delivered the first Security Council resolution ever to authorize one country to invade another; even Russia voted in favor. American planning for the intervention gathered speed. Wes Clark and his colleague, Lieutenant General Jack Sheehan, met with the rest of our interagency group to discuss the operation. They wanted to know whether the Haitians would resist. They asked me if this would be a forced or a permissive entry.

"You won't know until you step off the helicopter whether the Haitians reception committee will shoot you or invite you to lunch," I answered.

Sheehan did not like this answer. "If we don't know, we will have to assume the worst and kill anyone carrying a weapon," he responded. This conjured up pictures of arriving American troops driving through Port-au-Prince shooting bank guards and traffic cops.

"You will have to plan for both contingencies," I insisted.

Throughout this period the CIA was critical of the proposed intervention. Agency representatives painted gloomy pictures of sustained Haitian resistance to the foreign troop presence, and some of this was picked up by the media and congressional opponents of the operation. Images of American forces being subjected to voodoo spells were conjured. Aristide was accused of being an extreme leftist, based in part on what the press claimed to be leaked intercepts of his phone conversations. He was also portrayed as drug addicted and mentally deranged based on the supposed contents of his medicine chest.

As D-Day approached Admiral Paul Miller, the Atlantic command chief in overall charge of this operation, invited the relevant Washington agency representatives to a "rehearsal of concept," or ROC drill. I envisaged us clustering around a sand table moving model soldiers around simulated terrain. Instead this ROC drill employed no sand, no table, and did not even include a briefing on the intended operation. Miller wanted to know what other agencies would contribute as the operation unfolded, but he would provide no information whatsoever on what his forces would be doing. The meeting was a minor fiasco: far too many people in the room, no clear agenda, and complete opacity regarding our military's intentions.

In fact the planners had done exactly what I had recommended. Two separate forces had been assembled. The 82nd Airborne Division was readied for an air assault on the island and units of the 10th Mountain Division were loaded onto an aircraft carrier, which moved off the coast of Haiti ready to put them ashore via helicopter if the Haitian military offered no resistance. The forces could be employed sequentially, first an invasion, then an occupation, or the 82nd could be stood down and the job left to the 10th Mountain if no resistance were offered.

The military was treating these sensible precautions with a degree of secrecy comparable to that for the Normandy invasion, making any synchronization of civil and military actions difficult. There was one aspect of our military's intentions about which we were informed. The Pentagon insisted that American troops would assume no responsibility for public order. I protested to Shalikashvili that Haiti had no civilian police force, that public order was in the hands of the Haitian Army whose leadership we were proposing to overthrow and whose style of policing was abusive. The Haitian Army could not be trusted to exercise its police functions with the restraint that the United States, as the occupying authority, would insist upon. Shali responded that policing was a civilian function and it was, therefore, up to the State Department to fill this gap.

As a result, we at State spent much of the summer recruiting international police for Haiti. Ray Kelly, the former (and future) New Your City police chief, agreed to head the force. Eventually we were able to secure contingents from several Latin American and Caribbean countries, numbering about 700 individual policemen. But these would take weeks to arrive once the initial military intervention took place.

By this time Bill Gray was fading from the scene, reluctant to take responsibility for the administration's increasingly controversial decisions. He was also doing his best to make life difficult for me, at one point forbidding me to continue meeting with President Aristide, whom I was trying to prepare for his return.

On September 15 President Clinton issued an ultimatum. In a televised address to the American people, he declared, "The message of the United States to the Haitian dictators is clear. Your time is up. Leave now or we will force you from power." The *New York Times* and the *Wall Street Journal* reported that two thirds of the American people opposed the intervention. On Saturday morning, two days after Clinton's ultimatum, I arrived at the office to find that President Clinton, in one last effort to arrange a peaceful entry, had dispatched former president Jimmy Carter, accompanied by former senator Sam Nunn and former chair of the joint chiefs Colin Powell, to Port-au-Prince.

Talbott was not particularly happy about this move. Nunn and Powell could be expected to adhere to President Clinton's guidance. Carter, however, was notoriously independent. True to form, on his arrival in Port-au-Prince, Carter insisted on excluding the American ambassador, Bill Swing, from his meetings. In Washington we spent that weekend in some suspense. Talks in Haiti remained deadlocked into a second day, at which point President Clinton ordered the planes carrying the 82nd Airborne paratroopers to take off and head toward the island. American TV cameras broadcast their take off.

This news produced the desired effect. Cedras signed an agreement in which he promised to step aside and to accept the dispatch of an American-led "military mission." President Clinton recalled the planes and went on television to announce both the accord and the dispatch of a 15,000 member multinational force, the lead elements of which would arrive in Haiti the following morning.

Cedras and his top lieutenants were not expecting things to move so fast. They were startled the next morning when told that Lieutenant General Hugh Shelton and advance elements of this force would be arriving at the Port-au-Prince airport momentarily. After alerting Cedras to the arrival, Ambassador Swing rushed to the airport to avert a possible clash.

Shortly thereafter American troops debarking from transports in Port-au-Prince harbor were greeted by a friendly crowd of onlookers. The American soldier then watched passively as Haitian military police brutally chased off the crowd, swinging clubs and breaking heads in full view of American network television cameras. The next day the Pentagon dispatched several hundred MPs to the island and accepted interim responsibility for maintaining public order.

Three days later a more deadly incident occurred. U.S. Marines patrolling the northern town of Cap Haitian encountered a group of armed Haitian soldiers outside a local police station. Perceiving hostile intent on the part of the Haitians, the Marines opened fire, killing nine. This was the last and only violent resistance to the American intervention, if resistance it was.

Mark Gearan, the chief of White House communications, convened a meeting in the Situation Room of administration spin doctors, including David Gergen and George Stephanopoulos, to discuss how best to maximize the impact of Aristide's impending return. One participant proposed that the U.S. should suggest to Aristide several initiatives he could announce on his arrival. As the group began to mull over possible policies for inclusion, Stephanopoulos leaned toward Gearan and whispered, "Gays in the military?" referring to President Clinton's first out-of-the-gate blunder on the day after his inauguration. Discussion faltered and the idea was dropped.

On October 10 General Raoul Cedras made his farewell speech, largely drowned out by raucous abuse from the crowd milling outside army headquarters. He then departed for Panama. Four days later we flew Aristide back to Port-au-Prince, accompanied by Secretary Christopher, numerous members of the Congressional Black Caucus, and so many other of his American supporters that the Air Force had to lay on two large passenger planes to take us all. At the airport Aristide was met by a rapturous crowd, most of whom then walked back to the Presidential Palace three miles distant to hear him speak.

SIXTEEN

Exiting Haiti

WITH ARISTIDE BACK IN HAITI and the American-led multilateral force firmly on top of the security situation, my mission was over. I was eager to move on to something else, ideally somewhere with a peaceful population and a temperate climate, but this was not to be. Having helped get the U.S military into Haiti, my next assignment was to get it out.

At least Bill Gray was gone, and with him the need to serve two masters, and my workload also slowed. For the past five months I had left the house each morning before dawn and returned well after dark. Crisis management involves occasional big decisions, like President Clinton's to launch the 82nd Airborne, but mostly it consists of thousands of smaller steps, carefully calibrated incremental actions designed to advance the policy, respond to unanticipated events, and keep multiple bureaucracies working in harness. The crisis was now past, but the situation remained fluid and unfamiliar, requiring continued tending, albeit at a less frenetic pace.

Extricating the American military from Haiti was to proceed in stages. Clinton had promised the American-led operation would be turned over to the United Nations within six months, but American troops would remain as part of that UN force. This UN-led phase was to last a further eighteen months, following which all international forces were to leave.

The mission for both the U.S. and UN forces was well defined. The peacekeepers would provide a security envelope within which presidential, parliamentary, and local elections would take place, then the new president, new legislators, and new mayors would take office. While the political processes went forward, the United States, with help from France and Canada, would build a new civilian police force that could assume responsibility for domestic security when the international forces departed.

All this was achieved. Every objective was reached, every deadline was met, and no resistance was encountered. The United Nations took over the operation in early 1995; national elections were held later that year; a new president, parliament, and local officials were inaugurated; and the last American troops were gone by early 1996. Yet although the intervention was almost a perfect success within the parameters set for it, the whole effort accomplished little of enduring value.

Much of the responsibility for that failure rests with President Aristide. In the months leading to his return Aristide had been on his best behavior. Bill Gray and I met with him regularly, as did other American officials, and he assembled a group of moderate advisers, picked a levelheaded businessman for his prime minister, briefed me on his market-oriented economic reform plans, and approved our proposals to build a new police force and reform the Haitian Army. Once back in office, however, he gradually moved away from this line of conduct, dumping his reformist prime minister, abandoning his market-oriented economic program, abolishing rather than reforming the Haitian Army, and creating an abusive personal security force.

In person Aristide could be quite engaging. His personal story, a poor reformist priest disciplined and ultimately expelled from the church, threatened and eventually overthrown by the Haitian establishment for championing the interests of Haiti's impoverished masses, was compelling. His commitment to this cause seemed sincere, and he remained accessible and generally easy to talk to throughout this period. Shortly after his return, Tony Lake and I had dinner at his private home just outside the city. Thereafter Aristide and I met every few weeks. His responses to most requests and suggestions were positive, although follow-through was erratic.

American objectives during these two years were: first, to maintain security throughout the country, which proved easier than anticipated; second, to build and reform Haitian capacity to assume this responsibility, which proved difficult; third, to hold elections, which was also difficult; and last, to promote economic growth, which proved impossible.

The great majority of Haitians were docile, unarmed peasantry, long dominated by small bands of officially sanctioned thugs. The thugs were quickly neutralized by arriving American and international forces. The United States opened a police academy at a former Haitian military post outside the capital and began a national recruitment campaign. French Gendarmes and Royal Canadian Mounted Police joined the academy faculty, and the U.S. military began a parallel effort to reform the Haitian Army.

The first sign of trouble came a few weeks following Aristide's return, when he told Ambassador Swing that he intended to disband the army. This occurred in the immediate aftermath of a violent altercation over pay and related benefits that took place at army headquarters, within earshot of the presidential palace. This disturbance was quickly put down by U.S. troops. Three Haitian soldiers were killed and several wounded, and the incident underscored for Aristide his own vulnerability once international forces departed.

Aristides's decision to disband the army threatened to throw off our timetable for departure. We needed to leave behind some institution for public order, and a brand new police force was now all we had. For Haiti, too, disbanding the army was a striking departure. The Haitian state was the creation of the Haitian Army. During the American Revolution, the Continental Army was created by the Continental Congress. Haiti's experience was the reverse. The painting dominating the chamber of the Haitian Parliament symbolizes this relationship. It is of the Haitian Army and its leaders celebrating victory in the 1791–1804 war of liberation from France.

Jack Sheehan and I flew to Port-au-Prince the day after Aristide's conversation with Swing. Sheehan had by this time pinned on a fourth star and moved from his position on the joint staff to replace Admiral Miller as the head of the U.S. Atlantic command. Sheehan was a tall, rangy Marine who moved with a swagger and spoke with the confidence of command. We were met on arrival by Swing, who said he agreed with Aristide that the army should go. It was corrupt, abusive, and incompetent. Haiti had no external enemies and no need for an army. Swing's position complicated Sheehan's and my effort to persuade Aristide to reverse his decision.

Aristide listened politely but remained adamant; the army must go, and immediately. On return to Washington, I began working with USAID on a program to disarm, demobilize, and reintegrate the soon-to-be former soldiers into civilian society. The army had already been largely disarmed; ex-soldiers were provided a stipend for the first six months to cover living costs and offered vocational training. Given the high level of unemployment in the country, there was little hope that most would find gainful employment thereafter, but by the time the reintegration program cut them loose, their former units would have been disbanded and they would have difficulty offering any organized resistance.

The next major bump in the road came in late March, just three days before President Clinton was scheduled to visit Port-au-Prince. A prominent conservative critic of Aristide, Mireille Durocher Bertin, was gunned down in broad daylight. Swing persuaded Aristide to request assistance from the FBI to investigate what had all the appearances of a politically motivated hit. Two days later the first FBI agents arrived and this gesture was enough to take the pressure off the Clinton visit, but many subsequent complications would arise.

Clinton intended his visit to mark the formal transfer of responsibility for peacekeeping in Haiti from the United States to the United Nations. The remaining American troops in Haiti would serve under UN command but many in Congress and the U.S. military were opposed to such a move. The Somalia experience had reinforced this chauvinistic stance even though it was the very independence of the American Black Hawk Down force that complicated its rescue and increased its casualties. Eventually we resolved this dilemma by determining that the American general commanding the new UN force would take strategic direction from his UN civilian superior but remain under the operational control of Jack Sheehan at Atlantic Command in Norfolk. Under more demanding circumstances, this rather artificial construct would have fallen apart, but Haiti remained an extremely tranquil environment.

Lakhdar Brahimi, a former Algerian foreign minister and experienced UN troubleshooter, headed the UN mission in Haiti (UNMIH). Brahimi had mediated an end to the Lebanese civil war and would go on to serve as the first UN mission head in post-9/11 Afghanistan and, later still, help the United States form the first post-invasion Iraqi government, in 2004. Brahimi was low-key, soft spoken, and pragmatic. He and I quickly formed a strong partnership. In preparation for the change of command, we cochaired two large, all-day meetings bringing together his senior staff and all the relevant American civilian and military officials, including American general Joe Kinzer, who would serve under him. The first of these sessions took place in Blair House, across the street from the White House, the second in Haiti the day before President Clinton's visit. Thereafter, Brahimi and I met every few weeks with President Aristide to align U.S., UN, and Haitian government activities.

Leslie Delatour, the head of the Haitian Central Bank, alerted me to the next sign that Aristide was deviating from the promised path. Still in his mid-forties, Delatour had already twice been the country's finance minister. Educated in the United States and a World Bank consultant, he was a strong proponent of what was then labeled "the Washington consensus" in favor of trade liberalization and the privatization of corrupt, money-losing, state-owned businesses. He pulled me aside on one of my early visits to warn that Aristide was reneging in the promises he had made both to me and to Delatour to support such a program.

The American strategy for Haiti's development relied heavily on promoting foreign, particularly American, investment. Privatization of the port, telephone, and electric power monopolies was key to this strategy. These monopolies were terrifically inefficient, costing the state money while providing ludicrously poor service. For instance, Haiti had the highest per ton port costs in the entire western hemisphere, despite also having the lowest labor cost. Electricity was erratic. The country had no cell phone service and it could take years to be hooked into a landline. There were, nevertheless, strong constituencies associated with all these enterprises. The port was a source of corruption, and the telephone monopoly put money in the government's coffers. While electricity was intermittent, it was also effectively free for most of those hooked up to the grid. Even the former employees of completely defunct public enterprises strongly objected to their sale while pressing the government to reopen them.

Haiti's low-wage labor and proximity to U.S. markets offered an attractive opportunity to investors in light manufacturing, particularly in the garment assembly sector. Sanctions had driven most such investors out of the country in the early nineties, and our hope was to lure many of these back. But undependable power, extraordinarily high port costs, and unavailable telephone connections were serious barriers.

Our efforts at economic development failed. Resistance to privatization proved too strong, particularly once Aristide turned against it. In less than a year Aristide replaced his pro-reform prime minister. None of the state enterprises were privatized or even reformed. The garment assembly industry that had moved to Central America never came back, and it took the rest of the decade just to bring the Haitian economy back to the state it was in before the United States and others imposed sanctions in the early 1990s. Those sanctions had failed to displace the coup regime, while further impoverishing the poorest country in the Western Hemisphere. The damage they caused was repaired largely at the expense of the U.S. taxpayer. The same would occur a few years later with Afghanistan and Iraq.

In the fall of 1995 Haiti held parliamentary elections. These went off peacefully, and with no more mismanagement or fraud than was normal for countries at Haiti's abysmal level of development. Aristide's supporters won. Most international observers, the International Republican Institute (IRI) aside, found the process free and fair, if messy. IRI actually jumped the gun by issuing a statement declaring the elections fraudulent a day before the balloting. Senator John McCain, the chair of IRI's board, publicly disparaged this premature rush to judgment, although not the judgment itself.

Aristide was precluded by the Haitian constitution from running for a second consecutive term. His supporters argued that his three years in exile should not count toward his five years in office, but the U.S. administration remained adamant and Aristide himself did not protest. His handpicked successor, Rene Preval, who had been prime minister during Aristide's brief 1991 tenure, was elected president.

Among my last responsibilities as the administration's special Haiti coordinator was to persuade Canada to take over leadership of the UN peacekeeping mission and to convince the Haitian government to request an extension of this force's mandate. Aristide's decision to disband the Haitian Army had left the country with no security institution whatsoever. We accelerated our program to build a new police force, even going so far as to open a second police training facility at the U.S. Army base at Fort Leonard Wood, Missouri, to supplement the academy we had created in Port-au-Prince, and a couple thousand brand new police were on the beat by the end of 1995, but in addition to being far too small, this was a raw, untried force.

In April 1996 the last American troops left Haiti. Within the terms set by President Clinton, the mission was a complete success. The United States had restored a democratically elected president and helped organize new elections that resulted in the installation of a new president, parliament, and local officials. There had been no resistance. All this was accomplished within two years. As was the case in Somalia, the Canadians provided a decent interval, after which they and the rest of the UN force also departed.

In the longer light of history, this intervention achieved little. Aristide was reelected president in 2001 and was again overthrown in 2004, this time with the help of a few dozen ex-members of the army he had disbanded a decade earlier. American troops again invaded Haiti. This time they remained only a few weeks before turning the operation over to the United Nations.

The Clinton administration's Republican critics turned out to be more right than wrong about Aristide. He was not the drug-crazed psychotic as sometimes alleged, but he was unreliable and unwilling to work with his domestic opposition. He even abandoned his own political party when it showed signs of independence. He also kept bad company, either condoning the abuses of associates or exhibiting excessive loyalty in protecting them from accountability. His government was less corrupt and abusive than its immediate predecessor, the coup regime of Raoul Cedras, but it was not so much better as to justify the efforts to which the United States went on his behalf. A better alternative would have been to have accepted his original removal back in 1991 and to have pressed the resultant regime to hold new elections for a new president, the more normal response to Latin American coupes. But the administration of George H. W. Bush chose to join in a hemisphere-wide demand for Aristide's return, thus making it hard for the Clinton administration to do less.

The Clinton administration's ephemeral success in Haiti paid one dividend. The fact that the operation appeared to be achieving all its stated goals without encountering resistance gave the administration confidence and credibility when it chose to mount the much larger, more challenging, and more enduringly successful intervention in Bosnia at the end of 1995.

SEVENTEEN

A Lesson in Divided Government

THE MOST TROUBLING ASPECT OF Aristide's behavior was his reliance on individuals associated with serious human rights violations. Aristide had accorded the United States a free hand in recruiting the new police force, and we had successfully rebuffed his efforts to place several of his corrupt associates in command positions. Aristide proceeded in parallel, however, to build his own presidential security force in which the main criterion for recruitment was personal loyalty. As time went on we became concerned that members of this force might be involved in lethal attacks on the political opposition.

A first sign of trouble on this score was the lack of cooperation the FBI received in its investigation of the Bertin murder. Deputy Associate Attorney General Seth Waxman and I flew to Haiti, along with Deputy Assistant FBI Director William Perry, to see what we could do to move the investigation forward, but when we arrived at the offices of the local FBI team, Waxman said I could not join the briefing. He maintained that it would be inappropriate for anyone outside the Department of Justice to be privy to the contents of this ongoing investigation. I found this a dubious rational since the investigation was being conducted at the request of the State Department and was not intended to lead to American legal proceedings but, rather, to assist a foreign government. Nevertheless, I didn't argue.

Some weeks later Dick Clarke asked Waxman to report to the Haiti Executive Committee on this investigation. Waxman declined, again insisting that this information could not be shared outside the Department of Justice. Later still the issue arose at a deputies committee meeting. Berger asked Jamie Gorelick, the deputy attorney general, whether the contents of the investigation would eventually be shared with Congress. Gorelick said that, too, would be inappropriate.

Although not privy to anything the FBI might have uncovered, we at State did press the Haitian government for greater cooperation. We eventually succeeded in creating a special investigative unit within the new Haitian police force to assist in this and similarly sensitive inquiries. In testimony before a subcommittee of the House Foreign Affairs Committee I informed its chair, Congressman Dan Burton, of this step. Burton then turned to the FBI's investigation of the Bertin case, and asked, "Have they found anything yet?" I responded, "The FBI has not briefed me, or as far as I know, anyone else in the administration, on their findings. They are still conducting their investigation, and as far as I know have not come to a conclusion."

Several days later, unbeknownst to anyone at State, Bill Perry, the FBI official who had accompanied Waxman and me to Port-au-Prince, took the initiative to brief congressional staffers on the status of the Bertin investigation. The FBI efforts were stalled, he said, as a result of official Haitian obstruction. "Have you told anyone at State?" the staffers asked. Perry responded that the FBI had kept State fully informed. On this basis Congressman Burton sent a letter to the secretary of state alleging that I had lied to his subcommittee.

In less partisan circumstances this allegation might have been disposed of fairly easily. I had briefed the subcommittee on the creation of the special investigative unit, which its staff knew was intended to help overcome obstacles to the investigation of which they were already aware. When asked what the FBI had found, I assumed Burton was inquiring regarding the bureau's findings, of which I was ignorant.

Immediately following my testimony the FBI finally acceded to Clarke's request that they brief the interagency group on the investigation. There was little to report. The FBI's efforts had been stymied by a lack of coop-eration on the Haitian side, which of course raised suspicions. But the bureau officials told us they had no active leads. One arrest had been made a few months earlier, which I had mentioned to Burton, but the bureau was advising the Haitian authorities to release that individual. The FBI with-drew its agents from Haiti, although the case remained open for a while longer.

The full House Foreign Affairs Committee held a hearing on the topic, which turned out to be an organized lynch mob. Perry, Waxman, and I were all ostentatiously sworn in, something seldom done with administra-tion witnesses, the obvious purpose being both to highlight a level of dis-trust and to establish the legal basis for charges not just of lying but of perjury. Waxman and Perry neither corroborated nor contradicted my testimony. It has never been clear to me why both these officials failed to acknowledge that they had not shared the FBI's findings, such as they were, prior to my earlier testimony. In Perry's case, he told the committee staff that the FBI had kept State fully informed on the course of the inves-tigation, by which he meant informed on the obstacles it was encounter-ing rather than the content of any findings. He may not have wished to correct the misimpression he had left. Waxman, who went on to become solicitor general, may simply have wanted to steer clear of any controversy. He also proved unable to remember denying Dick Clarke's request to brief the Haiti Working Group on the FBI investigation, although a number of others present recalled his refusal distinctly.

Burton opened the hearing with an attack so lengthy and vituperative that it completely filled his allotted time, making it impossible for me to respond. The other Republicans had all been supplied with similar talk-ing points. No one from the administration troubled to brief the Demo-crats, so they were of little help. One outraged member of the audience rose up to call the proceedings a travesty and was ejected from the room.

Republican motivations for staging this bit of theater were obvious. Throughout the 1980s the Democrats had scourged the Reagan adminis-tration for allegedly covering up evidence of death squads acting on behalf of its Central American protégés. Now the table was turned and the Re-publicans were delighted to be able to make the case that the Clinton ad-ministration was now guilty of the same thing in Haiti.

As they departed Haiti the FBI told us they had matched the ballistics on the weapon that killed Bertin with those used in another execution-style killing on the island. This suggested that the Bertin murder was part of a larger conspiracy. George Tenet, then the NSC senior director for intelligence issues, convened a meeting to discuss Haiti at which I pressed the CIA to step up the investigation. Berger convened a small meeting with Talbott, Clarke, myself, and John Deutch, who had just become the CIA director. Again I urged that we press forward to determine who was behind these killings. I acknowledge that we might not like what we found and that whatever we found would certainly become public, but I argued that we should, nevertheless, persist. Clarke concurred and it was so agreed.

Someone complained to the Hill that I was seeking to politicize intelligence in an effort to cover up these killings. This led the House Permanent Select Committee on Intelligence to hold a classified hearing on the matter. Congressman Burton preempted the occasion by issuing a press release announcing the hearing and repeating his charges. This annoyed the chair, Republican Congressman Jerry Lewis, who opened the hearing by regretting this breach of protocol by a non-member of his committee. Several witnesses were then called, including myself. No one from the CIA, or anywhere else, corroborated the charge that I had sought to suppress or distort the inquiry. On the contrary, it became clear that I had consistently pressed the agency to step up its collection. At the session's conclusion Lewis made a gracious closing statement that stopped just short of an apology.

Eventually we were able to assemble enough intelligence information to conclude that one or more members of Aristide's palace guard force were likely implicated in at least some of these murders. I traveled to Haiti to see Aristide and apprised him of this fact. Normally Aristide responded in a quiet and composed fashion even to unwelcome advice, but in this instance he reacted angrily, demanding evidence, which of course I could not provide, and rejecting the allegation.

Rene Preval, Aristide's successor, was honest and direct, but not a strong or decisive personality. He governed under the shadow of his patron, his predecessor, and his eventual successor. Six months after his election, two further political killings took place, and this time the links to members of the presidential guard force were more clearly established. Tony Lake, Talbott, Sheehan, and I flew to Port-au-Prince.

We asked Preval to come alone to Ambassador Swing's residence in the hills above the city, a highly unusual request of a head of state. Preval complied and appeared genuinely shocked by our revelations. Unlike Aristide, he made no effort to refute them. He immediately agreed to our proposal that American law enforcement officers should take over responsibility for his security while we also vetted and thoroughly reorganized the presidential guard force. Fearing for Preval's safety should this plan become known to those currently responsible for his security, we asked him to say nothing about it until we were ready to move.

Organizing the follow-through on this agreement fell largely to me. Protecting foreign leaders in their own country was a new mission for the U.S. government and no agency was eager to assume the responsibility. After a good deal of cajoling, we were able to put together a team of twenty-two State Department diplomatic security agents, plus an equal number of law enforcement personnel from the Department of Defense. These arrived unannounced two weeks later, at which point Preval fired the head and deputy head of presidential security and placed the rest of the 200-man force under American control. Canadian soldiers, part of the UN peacekeeping force, took over perimeter security at the palace. Over the next several months the presidential guard force was purged and reorganized under new leadership.

These events naturally provided an occasion for our congressional critics to say "We told you so," which was true, and to charge that we had ignored their warnings in an effort to cover up this death squad activity, which was not.

For several years the official inquiry into my 1995 testimony continued. The State Department's inspector general took more than a year to complete the investigation requested by Congressman Burton. The resultant report concluded that my testimony had been seriously misleading and possibly perjurious. This shocked Robert Ponzo, the very investigator who had handled the inquiry. Ponzo had conducted all the interviews upon which these conclusions were based and then drafted his report. Shortly thereafter he retired to join an investment bank. I contacted him on being apprised of the report's conclusion, and he told me the report he had drafted had found my testimony to be truthful. He surmised his draft had been altered by his superiors to reach a conclusion more likely to satisfy Congress. I informed the head of State's office of personnel and also the department's deputy legal adviser that the report had been so doctored, but they declined to take any action. The altered report was accordingly transmitted to the Department of Justice for possible prosecution.

The inspector general's finding also surprised Senator Helms' staffer handling Latin America. This individual approached me with a proposal to move forward my nomination for chief of mission in Argentina, which had been on hold for two years in light of Helms' opposition, in exchange for favorable administration action on another personnel matter of interest to the senator. I informed Helms' staffer of the inspector general's finding, which he admitted was not what he expected. We agreed that this made the deal he was proposing unfeasible.

Another year passed, at the conclusion of which the Justice Department returned the inspector general's report to the State Department, indicating that it was declining prosecution. This left any disciplinary action up to State. At this point I was given access to the full report, including the interviews upon which it was based. I was pleased to find that Seth Waxman and William Perry had confirmed in private what they avoided saying in public, that I had testified truthfully when I said the FBI had not informed me of their findings. Instead of taking this information at face value, the inspector general relied on the testimony of another FBI agent, located in Florida, who had never met me and who speculated that I must have known about the FBI's findings in the Bertin case. The report contained dozens of other discrepancies, distortions, and inaccuracies.

The State Department concluded that the report did not support the charge it had leveled. I was, nevertheless, sent a "letter of admonishment" stating that, while I had testified in good faith, I should have been more forthcoming. This letter concluded with a paragraph explaining that the admonishment was not a formal disciplinary action, would not be put in my official file, and would be destroyed after one year. I remained dissatisfied with this grudging exoneration and decided to appeal the case further.

In March 2001, nearly five years after the testimony in question, my appeal was heard. I submitted a statement by the investigator, Ponzo, who testified that the inspector general's report fundamentally misrepresented his findings, that he had in fact found no evidence I had misinformed the Congress. I also submitted a statement by the previous (and as it turned out, subsequent) head of the inspector general's office. Commenting on the report, this official found "the presentation of the underlying evidence to be unbalanced and its main conclusions to be unsupported."

The three-member grievance panel found in my favor. The State Department accepted the result and agreed to take a number of corrective steps involving, among other things, a sizeable financial settlement.

This exoneration cut no ice with Congressman Burton or Senator Helms. The latter used his position as chair of the Senate Foreign Relations Committee to block confirmation of three further appointments throughout the remainder of my career.

EIGHTEEN

Hemispheric Interlude

INSTEAD OF GOING TO ARGENTINA in 1996 I moved to the National Security Council where I became special assistant to President Clinton responsible for the Western Hemisphere. This proved a good time to be working on Latin America and a fascinating time to be on the White House staff. Relations with our hemispheric neighbors were approaching an all-time high. Relations with the Republican-dominated Congress were approaching an all-time low.

Within the White House, my closest collaborator was Thomas "Mack" McClarty. Mack was a close friend of the president, a relationship dating back to their time together in kindergarten in Hope, Arkansas. Mack had been President Clinton's first chief of staff. Clinton's initial few months in office had been rocky and Mack accepted some of the blame. Replaced as chief of staff by Leon Panetta, Mack was named counselor to the president and "special envoy for the Americas." Having such a well-connected figure in the White House with responsibilities overlapping my own could have resulted in certain tensions, except that Mack was determined otherwise. His highest priority was promoting hemispheric trade and investment. These were areas where I was happy to follow his lead and grateful for the additional weight he could bring to bear. On security-related issues, he looked to Lake, Berger, and me, although always willing to use his own contacts and influence to advance policy. Mack was also just about the most courteous and considerate person I ever met. This might explain why his tenure as White House chief of staff was so brief, but it certainly made my relationship with him a pleasure.

When he entered office Clinton pushed the North American Free Trade agreement through Congress and spent the rest of his tenure seeking to promote a somewhat similar arrangement for the hemisphere as a whole. This objective had been embraced by other regional leaders in the first summit of the Americas, held in Miami in 1994. Negotiations continued for over a decade, eventually foundering on the desire of South American governments to establish their own common market, one that would exclude the United States. While the interest lasted, however, Clinton's initiative gave regional leaders a good deal to talk about and became the centerpiece of an unusually intense hemispheric dialogue.

The issues of trade, immigration, drugs, and democracy drove hemispheric relations. Mexico was especially important because of its size and proximity. Haiti and Cuba were two special problem cases. By the late 1990s every country in the western hemisphere except Cuba had a democratically elected government although, naturally, the quality of these democracies varied. Military coups, dictatorships, and civil wars were still fresh memories, so this happy condition was by no means taken for granted. The civilian leaders of these countries were proud of what they had achieved, eager to avoid any roll-back, and ready to act in concert to maintain their gains. It was this democratic solidarity that led the Organization of American States to impose sanctions on the coup regime in Haiti, then to send a human rights monitoring team into that country, and, finally, to endorse a military force to restore President Aristide.

I had only been at my post for a few days when a new challenge to hemispheric democracy emerged. Around midnight I was awakened by a call from the president of Paraguay, Juan Wasmosy. The president had just taken refuge in the residence of our ambassador, Robert Service, fleeing a threatened coup by his army commander, Lino Oviedo, whom he had tried to fire earlier in the day. Jeff Davidow, my State Department colleague, was also on the line. Between the two of us we calmed the president, urged him not to resign, as he seemed inclined to do, and assured him that help was on the way.

Help initially took the form of Caesar Gaviria, the secretary general of OAS, whom Davidow succeeded in rousing in the middle of the night. Gaviria started immediately for Paraguay and arrived the next day. I chaired an early morning meeting in the White House Situation Room to coordinate the U.S. reaction, and through the following twenty-four hours we worked in Ascuncion, in Washington, and through our embassies elsewhere to mobilize all the regional powers, particularly Paraguay's two big neighbors, Argentina and Brazil. Talbott went before the OAS council to announce that the United States was cutting off assistance to Paraguay and was ready to apply economic sanctions. The Argentine foreign minister and senior officials from Brazil and Uruguay flew into Asuncion. President Clinton called Wasmosy to express support, as did other hemispheric and European leaders.

Parallel with this rapid and unanimous international reaction, large crowds in Asuncion turned out to protest the threatened coup. Buoyed by these expressions of support, Wasmosy persuaded Oviedo to step down as army chief with the promise of promotion to defense minister. Public reaction to this proved so negative that Wasmosy subsequently withdrew that offer, leaving Oviedo with no official position. Oviedo was eventually tried, convicted, and jailed for staging a coup, only to be released several years later on the basis of testimony from army officers denying there had been a coup attempt. Oviedo subsequently ran twice for president, losing on the first try and dying in a helicopter crash during the second campaign.

Mexico was my most important account. NAFTA had come into effect in 1994 but remained highly controversial. At that time, Mexico was the largest source of illegal immigration into the United States, always a hot button issue, and the most important transit point for illegal drugs. On a more positive note, Mexico was emerging from a major financial crisis, assisted by a $50 billion bailout package put together by President Clinton over congressional objections. The country was also in the midst of a peaceful transition from one-party rule to genuine democracy.

As with Haiti and Cuba, there was a strong overlay of American domestic politics involved in our relations with Mexico. Hispanics, particularly those from Mexico, were becoming an ever larger portion of the American electorate and these new voters tended to support Democrats. In California, Republican Governor Pete Wilson successfully promoted a ballot initiative to establish a state-run citizenship screening system, only to see this initiative ruled unconstitutional in federal court. The drug certification process became another bone of partisan contention. Passed in 1986, this law required that, each year, the administration certify whether major drug producing or transit countries, most of which were in Latin America, were "cooperating fully" with American law enforcement. A negative certification could force a cut-off of American aid. Hemispheric governments found this requirement unbearably humiliating, whether they received a passing grade or not.

President Clinton's drug czar was retired general Barry McCaffrey, whom I had first met in Panama and who now headed the Office of National Drug Control Policy (ONDCP). McCaffrey was in a perennial turf battle with the Department of Justice and the law enforcement agencies under its authority, most notably the Drug Enforcement Agency (DEA). The Justice Department was unwilling to be directed or even coordinated by ONDCP, though it was more willing to listen to the NSC staff, which was thought to speak more directly for the president and was regarded as a benignly neutral arbiter rather than a bureaucratic rival. This irritated McCaffrey, who could never quite accept that he could not both be a protagonist in these bureaucratic struggles and expect to mediate their resolution.

On one thing, we agreed. McCaffrey was committed to building cooperation with Mexico, and this brought us both into conflict with the administration's chief anti-drug warrior, Tom Constantino, the head of the DEA. In 1985 a DEA agent working in Mexico was kidnapped and tortured to death, and the Mexican police were implicated in the disappearance. They had, subsequently, obstructed the investigation into his murder. This led the DEA to have two of the suspects kidnapped and brought to the United States where they were tried in federal court. A decade later the affair still rankled on both sides. Constantino regularly pushed to decertify Mexico and was publicly very critical of the Mexican government. McCaffrey insisted on deleting such criticism from one of Constantino's congressional testimonies, a removal that was immediately leaked to the press. A year later, again testifying before Congress, Constantino said Mexican drug traffickers posed the worst threat to the United States he had seen in his forty years of law enforcement. Two days later, Secretary of State Albright announced that Clinton had once again certified Mexico. Shortly thereafter Constantino resigned, subsequently stating:

"The policy makers from the National Security Council and the State Department started with the premise that they were going to certify Mexico."

I spent a lot of time refereeing these bureaucratic turf wars. Within the White House, Dick Clarke and I shared responsibility for putting together recommendations regarding certification to the president. The most controversial cases were always Mexico and Colombia. In Mexico, President Zedillo and his top officials cooperated fully, but Mexico's law enforcement establishment was riddled with drug-related corruption. For instance, just two weeks before one year's certification announcement, the Mexican government arrested and charged McCaffrey's opposite number with drug corruption. By contrast in Colombia we had the opposite problem: cooperation at the bottom, corruption at the very top. The president of Colombia, Ernesto Samper, had taken a substantial campaign contribution from the Cali Cartel. But the Colombian national police were mostly honest, competent, and willing to work closely with American law enforcement. Year after year, as long as Zedillo and Samper were in office, we chose to certify Mexico and decertify Colombia. One year the House of Representatives voted to override the president's certification. This failed in the Senate, but only after the administration promised to subject Mexico to even greater scrutiny.

I found the inconsistencies in our policy toward Colombia particularly frustrating. The country was both a narco-state and one of Latin America's longest running and most firmly established democracies. Not only were we sanctioning its president while working closely with its police, we were also backing the government's war on drugs while refusing to support its conflict with drug-financed leftist insurgents. Chairing a series of interagency meetings I began to move the administration toward a more consolidated set of policies. The election of a new, untainted president in Columbia, Andres Pastrana, allowed me to make the case for a State visit in late 1998. I also sought to remove barriers between aid to Colombian counternarcotics programs and its counterinsurgency campaign. These efforts came to fruition more than a year after I returned to State in Plan Colombia, a long-term comprehensive program of American support for peace and democracy in that country.

Clinton formed a particularly close relationship with his Mexican counterpart, Ernesto Zedillo Young, Yale educated but with almost no political experience. Zedillo was picked unexpectedly by his party to run for president when its original candidate was assassinated in the midst of the 1994 campaign. The Institutional Revolutionary Party (PRI) had not lost an election for seventy years. While in office Zedillo successfully weathered a major financial crisis with help from Bill Clinton, peacefully resolved the festering Zapatista rural insurgency, and began putting in place electoral reforms that would end his party's uncontested hold, first, on the Congress and then, in 2000, on the presidency.

Clinton and Zedillo were in frequent contact, regularly visiting one another and speaking by telephone. Increasingly the U.S.-Mexican relationship was conducted in this channel, either directly between the two presidents or via their staff, which in the U.S. case meant me. My Mexican counterpart and I scheduled visits, arranged agendas, drafted joint announcements, and identified areas of convergence that could become the basis for joint initiatives. State would have preferred these communications move through its channels but accepted, and perhaps even recognized, the value of this more direct relationship.

Clinton and Zedillo met with a single note-taker on each side. Both men were super smart, articulate, and visibly enjoyed the other's company, and the results were among the warmest, most stimulating diplomatic exchanges in my experience. Zedillo was patently sincere in his efforts to move Mexico forward, to modernize the economy, fight corruption, break the one-party monopoly, and align the country more closely with its North American partners. Working in Washington to help him and his key advisers progress toward these goals made Mexico my favorite portfolio.

Cuba was the hemisphere's odd man out. Here even more than with Haiti domestic American politics dictated American policy, leaving the administration little room for innovation. Damage limitation was the most we could achieve, and even that was difficult. With the end of the Cold War and the conclusion of the proxy conflicts in Central America and Southern Africa in which Cubans had been involved, the foreign policy case for isolating Cuba evaporated. Castro was no longer spreading communism, aiding the Soviet Union, promoting terrorism, or fomenting insurgencies. The regime's human rights record was lamentable, but no worse than that of several American allies elsewhere in the world. The American embargo on all trade with Cuba had not forced improvements in human rights or weakened the regime. On the contrary, the embargo almost certainly contributed to the longevity of Fidel Castro's rule. Cuban Americans were increasingly divided. Many of the newer arrivals, who still had family and friends on the island, were interested in easing travel and trade restrictions. It was the older generation, those who left the island in the 1960s, who supported the strictest possible application of the embargo. This latter group of Cuban Americans was not more numerous but did care more intensely, and in contrast to more recent immigrants, it had more money and the incentive to use it to make the weight of their opinions felt in Washington.

In 1994, just as the flood of Haitian boat people was reaching its peak, Castro exacerbated our problems by permitting a large outflow of Cubans. These people took to improvised rafts to reach the United States, but most ended up in Guantanamo like the Haitians had. Faced with this flood of would-be immigrants, the administration abandoned the longstanding American policy of granting asylum to any Cuban who made it out of that country and began returning to Cuba those intercepted at sea by the U.S. Coast Guard.

Nevertheless, fear remained that Castro might unleash another flood of boat people and refuse to accept their return. Shortly after my arrival on the NSC staff, Lake and Berger sought my views on how such a challenge might be handled. They asked what I thought about the idea that the United States should seize one of Cuba's smaller islands to which any Cubans picked up at sea could be returned. "You mean we would invade Cuba but not overthrow Castro?" I asked skeptically. Fortunately, Castro mounted no such provocation. In fact immigration issues became one of the few areas where we were able to establish a reasonably constructive dialogue with the Cuban government.

The more militant elements of the Cuban American community regularly sought to provoke Cuban American confrontation. The Cuban American group Brothers to the Rescue flew light aircraft to spot and direct rescuers to Cuban rafters, but once the United States began to return those rescued to Cuba, the outflow largely ceased. Brothers to the Rescue redirected their efforts to dropping anti-regime leaflets, ignoring warnings from both Cuban and American authorities about violating Cuban airspace. On February 24, 1996, the Cuban Air Force shot down two of these planes, killing the pilots. This led to vigorous American protests, a condemnation by the UN Security Council, and legislation introduced by Senator Jesse Helms and Congressman Dan Burton that formalized and extended the embargo on trade and other contacts with Cuba. This

Helms-Burton Act was passed by Congress within ten days of the shoot-down, and was signed by President Clinton shortly after.

Among the most troubling features of this law was a provision that allowed American citizens to sue in U.S. courts any foreign companies that had invested in formerly American-owned properties that Cuba had confiscated after the revolution. This set up a serious confrontation with America's principal trading partners—including the European Union, Canada, and Mexico—all of which passed their own laws allowing their citizens and companies to sue in their courts to recover damages inflicted by American court decisions. The EU also brought a case against the United States in the World Trade Organization, which our trade lawyers said we would likely lose.

Not satisfied with the analysis I was seeing on this dispute, I read through the actual legislation. I found that the president could waive this extraterritorial provision if he found "that suspension is necessary to the national interests of the United States and will expedite a transition to democracy in Cuba." I urged the president to exercise this authority by securing in exchange an agreement from EU member states to step up their efforts to promote democratic reforms in Cuba.

The president assembled a group of us to debate this alternative. Berger, McClarty, and I advocated the waiver. George Stephanopoulos, the president's chief domestic adviser, made the counter case, but without great conviction, recognizing, he said, that Clinton was going to decide in favor of the waiver. This he did, thereby averting a transatlantic trade war. President George W. Bush continued to reissue this waiver annually throughout his term.

While the shoot-down of the two Brothers to the Rescue planes ended violations of Cuban airspace, a related Cuban American group sought to create a confrontation by violating Cuban territorial seas. This group began sending Freedom Flotillas of small boats to enter Cuban territorial waters. The administration recognized it had been a mistake not to have prevented the Brothers to the Rescue overflights and determined to forestall any repeat at sea. This put me at the center of a negotiation involving New Jersey Congressman Robert Menendez, acting on behalf of the Flotilla organizers, and the U.S. Coast Guard, which was directed to prevent any incursion into Cuban territorial waters. The easiest way to do that was to prevent the craft from leaving port, which the Coast Guard was prepared to do. I spent a couple of weekends on the telephone between Menendez and the Coast Guard securing commitments about the Flotilla's behavior as a condition for its leaving port. These were eventually forthcoming, and as a result the Coast Guard escorted the boats to the edge of Cuban waters and then back to the United States. After a couple such pointless voyages this activity also petered out.

Helms and Burton were open adversaries of the administration, and their happiness was of small concern to the White House and even less to me. Menendez was another matter. A Democrat who eventually became vice chair of the party's caucus in the House before moving up to the Senate, he was, on most issues, an important administration ally. It fell to me to fend off, firmly but politely, his repeated efforts to tighten up various aspects of the embargo. He was particularly upset when I informed him of the president's intention to waive the extraterritorial aspects of the Helms-Burton Act. He insisted irately, and probably correctly, that Congress had not intended to construct the loophole I had discovered in the act.

In January 1998 Pope John Paul traveled to Cuba, and hundreds of America journalists flew to Havana to cover the big story only to abandon the pope mid-visit for something bigger when the story of President Clinton's affair with Monica Lewinsky broke. When I arrived for work on Monday morning, I looked down from my office onto the front lawn of the White House to see the area swarming with camera crews and broadcast reporters. It was also teeming rain, and journalists huddled under umbrellas. Cameras were planted in ever-enlarging mud puddles. I took a bit of satisfaction in their discomfort, but the White House grounds staff were less amused. The journalists and camera crews did so much damage they were, henceforth, forbidden to set up on the front lawn.

In my experience the Clinton White House was a very happy work environment. The president could be impatient and testy with his most immediate staff, but he treated the rest of us as if we were potential donors and he was running for a third term. He remembered names, paid small compliments, and, to the great distress of his schedulers could easily be diverted into extended conversations not immediately relevant to the business at hand. He was also smart, quick, curious, and indiscreet. All that made talking with him, or watching him engage with foreign leaders or work an audience, a real pleasure. Here was a chief who listened to advice, acted on it effectively, and achieved meaningful results.

I had a rather opposite reaction to Vice President Gore, whom I first met in Bonn when he was a visiting senator. In personality Gore was the antithesis of Clinton. He had proved a disappointingly dull dinner companion, and during his White House years he treated subordinates curtly and even discourteously. At one state dinner my wife and I were waiting along with the other attendees to be introduced to the president, Mrs. Clinton, and their guest of honor, the president of Colombia. The vice president moved down the line, speaking briefly to each prominent couple in turn, skipping over mere White House staff without even a smile of recognition, something Clinton would never have done. He was also the worst public speaker I ever encountered, whereas Clinton was the best.

The president was particularly accessible on foreign travel. Earlier in the decade *Air Force One* had been upgraded to a new, specially configured Boeing 747. Under the somewhat more formal George H. W. Bush, the plane was organized like a small version of the West Wing. The president kept to his quarters, and the large conference room in the middle of the plane was limited to its designated purpose and usually empty. In contrast, both President and Mrs. Clinton tended to circulate through the plane, greeting staff, asking questions, and distributing sweets. On most trips, someone would be having a birthday, and this became an excuse for an impromptu party with all the staff assembled in the conference room for cake and a chorus of "Happy Birthday." At other times one would find the president there playing cards or watching a movie with anyone who chose to join.

By the second term, lines of authority in the White House were well established. Berger, who replaced Lake as national security adviser, was unchallenged in his domain, and our relations with the domestic and political sides of the White House were collegial. We on the NSC staff were not unaware of the domestic ramifications of the issues we managed, but we were not expected to allow this to slant our advice. Like everyone else we were surprised and disappointed at successive revelations regarding the president's personal behavior, but the larger effect of the impeachment process was to create a sense of comradery in adversity as we worked together to see the country through a grave constitutional crisis, carrying on with the nation's business as best we could.

Far from distracting the president from his international responsibilities, the mounting Lewinsky scandal redoubled his attention to them. At moments of greatest stress, Clinton took refuge in his in-box. Normally I would get back from the president at most one or two documents a month with some marginal notation indicating he had read and agreed or disagreed on some point. On only two occasions did I get back multiple marked-up memos on the same day. The first instance was that rainy Monday following the weekend the Lewinsky revelations broke. The second came some months later, on the Monday following the weekend when the president was preparing for his grand jury testimony. In both cases Clinton seems to have sought distraction by churning through and annotating weeks of accumulated staff memos, which, if my allocation was any indicator, must have numbered in the dozens.

I reaped another unanticipated advantage from the domestic crisis. Normally an NSC senior director would campaign for months to secure an Oval Office call for one of his charges. A presidential visit to his region was an even more sought-after prize, and an invitation for a state visit to Washington would take years to obtain. But for the rest of 1998 the president was effectively precluded from domestic travel or any unscripted public appearances during which he would face both protests and unwelcome questions, and this freed up more time for international trips and foreign visitors. The White House chief of staff office was soon calling me for suggested destinations and foreign leaders to invite.

One of my less fortunate initiatives was persuading Clinton to meet with Hugo Chavez, who had just been elected president of Venezuela. Talbott and I had visited Caracas a year earlier and been unimpressed with the quality of its superannuated leadership. Maybe, I thought, Chavez would be an improvement despite his having led a failed military coup in 1992 and spending the following few years in prison as a result. The meeting was billed as a "drop by." This meant that it would take place at Berger's office but with the promise that President Clinton would briefly stop in. Chavez arrived in a state of high excitement, and he could barely contain himself once Clinton joined. Chavez literally never stopped talking. It's hard to shut down Bill Clinton, but our president could hardly get a word in before Chavez would be off again, breathlessly outlining his many plans for Venezuela. The session went way overtime and left an unsettling impression of a personality devoid of self-control.

Latin Americans watched with wonder as revelations about the president's private life led to his impeachment and trial. That a national leader might have extramarital affairs seemed to them normal, that he would lie about these if asked certain. What else could a gentleman do? After each new revelation the president would receive telephone calls from his main hemispheric buddies, Ernesto Zedillo in Mexico, Fernando Cardoso in Brazil, and Carlos Menem of Argentina. Each leader would manufacture some excuse for the call, but the real message was one of solidarity and encouragement. At the height of the scandal, in another sign of hemispheric support, President Clinton was named Man of the Year by the city of Rio de Janeiro.

There were somber moments as the House voted on impeachment and later, when the Senate trial loomed. In the White House it was clear that the most senior staff were under strain, but morale remained strong. While there was regular collaboration between the domestic and national security side of the White House on presidential travel and foreign visitors, there was also a careful effort to conduct the nation's business abroad in as normal a fashion as possible. The effect, I think, was to make my colleagues and me even more aware of the gravity of our responsibilities and the privilege of service in this difficult time.

The year of Monica ended on February 12, 1999, when the Senate voted against conviction on all of the four charges brought by the House. Two days later on a trip to Mexico for a state visit President Clinton, clearly euphoric, wandered around *Air Force One* chatting with senior and junior staff alike. I had proposed he give a speech from the balcony of the Merida town hall where the visit was to take place, but this was nixed by his domestic staff who felt it would present too triumphalist an image. There were, nevertheless, large, enthusiastic crowds in the streets as we drove in from the airport. On arrival at a reception hosted by President Zedillo, the president moved from group to group, by this point seeming a foot or two off the ground. Coming up to a circle of Mexican officials with whom I was chatting, he threw his arm around me and told everyone, apropos of nothing in particular, what a terrific guy I was.

The next morning I briefed the president for an upcoming press conference. Throughout the Lewinsky year, these briefing sessions had been carefully orchestrated to separate the foreign from the domestic policy components. Previously, we NSC staffers would lead with our issues and then leave the room before advice was offered on how to handle the scandal- and impeachment-related questions. This time, this practice was abandoned in favor of the more normal mix of domestic and foreign briefers in a single session. Following my review of the Mexico-related questions he might receive, discussion turned to U.S. domestic politics and, specifically, to rumors circulating that Hillary Clinton was considering a run for the Senate. The president listened as Chief of Staff John Podesta and other advisers suggested how he could deflect this question. Clinton then went out to the waiting journalists and did the exact opposite.

"I think she would be terrific in the Senate," he responded to the anticipated query. "But it's her decision to make. I will support whatever decision she makes enthusiastically." Needless to say, Hillary's candidacy, rather than anything to do with Mexico, became that day's story.

NINETEEN

War in Kosovo

UPON OUR RETURN FROM MEXICO, I moved to a new position. A few weeks earlier Strobe Talbott had called to say the president was ready to authorize a military intervention in Kosovo and to ask whether I would take over the Balkan portfolio. The title was suitably grandiose: special adviser to the president and secretary of state. As a practical matter I would work for Secretary Madeleine Albright, and my responsibilities would encompass the ongoing NATO peacekeeping operation in Bosnia as well as the new front that was about to open in Kosovo. Talbott said both Berger and Secretary Albright supported the move and explained there was just one more hurdle to be surmounted. I would need to interview with Dick Holbrooke.

Dick was, at this point, a New York banker. He was awaiting confirmation to become our ambassador to the United Nations. Dick had negotiated the 1995 Dayton peace accord that ended the war in Bosnia and continued to maintain a proprietary interest in the region. We breakfasted in the Hay Adams hotel across Lafayette Park from the White House and the discussion went smoothly. It had been nearly a decade since I had dealt with the Balkans and I was genuinely eager to learn from him. On parting, I complimented him on *To End a War*, his book on the Dayton negotiations. Dick offered to sign my copy and was annoyed to learn I had borrowed the volume from the State Department library.

In contrast to my Somalia and Haiti assignments, I was in this case stepping into an existing position, one with established lines of authority and a substantial supporting staff. Holbrooke had left the government in 1996 shortly after brokering peace in Bosnia, and for a time his successor, as assistant secretary of state for Europe, assumed responsibility for implementing that agreement. Eventually a separate office was set up for the purpose, initially headed by Bob Gelbard, whom I was to succeed. Dick continued to pop in and out of Balkan diplomacy throughout the intervening years, much to Gelbard's annoyance. Both were assertive, occasionally choleric, personalities, and this resulted in a fractious rivalry. On one occasion they arrived together in Sarajevo, and the embassy officer there to meet them signaled back to Washington that "the egos have landed."

I met with Jim Pardew, Gelbard's principal deputy and soon to be mine. Pardew, a retired army officer, had been on Holbrooke's Dayton team, and I asked him whether he continued to seek Dick's counsel. Pardew laughed. "Calling Dick for advice is like calling in artillery on your own position."

Yugoslavia had been made up of six republics, of which by 1995 only two remained: Serbia, the largest of the original six, and Montenegro, the smallest. Slovenia, Croatia, Macedonia, and Bosnia had all become independent states. Kosovo was an "autonomous province" of Serbia, one overwhelmingly populated by Albanian-speaking Muslims. The Kosovars had also wanted independence, but Slobodan Milosevic, the Serbian strongman, moved in the opposite direction, revoking the province's autonomy, suppressing its separate institutions and governing Kosovo directly from Belgrade. Some had criticized the Dayton settlement because it failed to address the plight of Kosovo's Albanian-speaking majority, and in the years since there had been mounting Kosovar resistance and Serb counter-repression, growing refugee flows, and international condemnation of both Kosovar violence and Serb human rights violations.

There was no possibility of resolving this incipient conflict through negotiation in 1995, and Holbrooke was right to make peace when and where he could. There remained little prospect of resolving the Kosovo conflict peacefully in 1999, although people were still trying, but President

Clinton was now preparing to force the issue, much as he had in Haiti in 1994 and Bosnia in 1995.

No sooner had I taken up my new position than I was on my way to France with Madeleine Albright. We were headed to the French presidential chateau at Rambouillet, outside Paris, where negotiations were taking place to end the escalating conflict in Kosovo in a conference convened by the United States, France, Italy, the United Kingdom, and Russia. Serbia and the Muslim population of Kosovo, generally referred to as Kosovars, were represented. The six convening governments all agreed Serbia should grant Kosovo "substantial autonomy." The Western powers were also insistent that the Serb army and police should withdraw from Kosovo and be replaced by NATO troops.

The dominant view in Washington was that the parties were too far apart for these talks to succeed but that they needed to fail in a manner that was clearly Serbia's fault so as to provide a rationale for NATO military intervention. Chris Hill, who had worked with Holbrooke at Dayton, was one of three lead mediators, along with a Russian and a European Union representative. Chris had not entirely abandoned hope that an agreement could be reached, but he was realistic enough to regard it as a long shot. Several of our Western partners were lukewarm about NATO military action, Italy being particularly unenthusiastic. Russia was entirely opposed to such a step.

Upon our arrival we met first in the Quint, or Western caucus, which included the foreign ministers of France, Germany, the UK, and Italy. We then reconvened in the Contact Group format, which added a Russian representative. Albright and I then met with each of the two sides. Albright warned Milan Milutinovic, the president of Serbia (Milosevic had become the president of what was left of Yugoslavia and was, thus, Milutinovic's superior) that the threat of NATO military action was real. She spent more time with the diverse Kosovar Albanian delegation. Its most prominent member was Ibrahim Rugova, the head of the province's largest political party, but its most influential figure was a twenty-nine-year-old newcomer, Hashim Thaci, who represented the Kosovo Liberation Army.

This conference took place in unusually comfortable circumstances. The rooms of the chateau were well appointed and the surrounding park offered tree-shaded walks around an island-dotted lake. Liveried waiters served multi-course meals of classic French cuisine with a selection of red and white wines well suited to the fare. One could see why the participants might not be anxious to return to Belgrade, still less to the raw Kosovar capital of Pristina.

Two days of effort on Albright's part brought the parties no closer together. Nor was she able to persuade the Kosovar delegation to accept the Contact Group proposals and, thus, isolate the Serbs. The convening powers were offering "substantial autonomy" but the Kosovars wanted full independence, a step even our European allies opposed. On her return to Washington Albright was subjected to a barrage of press criticism. This seriously upset her, not least because some of it seemed to come from unnamed American officials. Albright felt particularly vulnerable as she was known to have favored the Rambouillet process while others, notably Holbrooke, had been unenthusiastic. She called Under Secretary for Political Affairs Tom Pickering, me, and several others to her office for an extended, rather emotional tongue-lashing. Albright must have known her criticism was misdirected, but we were the targets within range and would have to serve as surrogates for the real culprit.

We returned to Rambouillet two days later determined to bring the Kosovars to yes on the Contact Group proposal. In the interim Chris Hill had flown to Belgrade to meet with Milosevic in an unsuccessful attempt to move the Serb position. Senior French and British officials had also gone to see Milosevic with similarly negative results. Albright now sought to sweeten the promise of "substantial autonomy" in the draft agreement by offering the Kosovars a unilateral American assurance that they would be able to conduct a referendum on independence. She also promised to open an American consulate in Pristina. Jamie Rubin, Albright's press spokesman, struck up a friendship with Thaci that was to prove helpful throughout the coming months. We also wheeled Wes Clark, now NATO's supreme commander, into action. The French prohibited Clark from coming to the chateau out of deference to likely Russian objections, but arranged, instead, for him to meet the Kosovar representatives at a nearby French military airfield. I accompanied Thaci and several other Kosovars to the meeting, where Clark promised NATO air strikes against Serb targets if the Kosovars accepted the Contact Group proposal and the Serbs did not.

To Albright's considerable frustration, the Kosovo delegation still balked. They asked for and were accorded a recess to return home and consult their constituents, the most important of whom were the Kosovo Liberation Army (KLA) commanders.

During this lull Hill flew back to Belgrade, but this time Milosevic re-fused to see him. Holbrooke was, therefore, tapped to go. I asked Dick if he would like me to join him and he said I was welcome but that most of the discussion would probably be limited to him and Milosevic. I appreci-ated this warning and remained in Washington.

At the conclusion of his meeting with Milosevic, Dick telephoned Washington to report the result. His call was to Pickering, who asked me to join. When Dick learned I was also on the line, he insisted I drop off, saying the matter was too sensitive to share with anyone but Tom. When excited, Dick was prone to these dramatizations. In fact, Milosevic had given no ground; the trip had only served to demonstrate that we were still trying to reach a peaceful solution and that the Serb side was still obdu-rate. There was no reason to keep this secret; quite the contrary.

On his return Dick joined a principals meeting in the White House Situation Room. When he entered, he noticed that no place had been set for him at the table. He was, after all, still a private citizen. Without a word he sat down behind my nameplate. Had he asked, or even smiled apolo-getically, I would have ceded the place to him willingly enough, as he was only a few weeks from assuming a cabinet-level position and the failure to set a place for him was likely an oversight.

In the course of recounting his conversation with Milosevic, Dick com-plained bitterly about alleged press leaks from Washington, comments that, in combination with his behavior a day earlier on the telephone, I took to be directed at me. He also took a swipe at Madeleine Albright, and she emerged from the meeting quivering with rage. Asking me to join her on a couch in the adjoining anteroom, she said she was determined that she, not Dick, should direct our Balkan diplomacy. I said that could be ar-ranged provided she would back me, and she readily agreed.

On March 15 the Kosovo negotiations resumed, this time in Paris. I headed the U.S. delegation while Hill continued in his role as conference mediator. We met in the same conference center on Avenue Kleber as the Vietnam peace talks had occurred twenty years earlier. Thaci asked to see Chris and me, and he reported that the KLA had designated him to take over the political leadership of Kosovo through and beyond the approaching conflict. He assured us we would find in him a loyal and will-ing partner.

On March 18 the Kosovar delegation signed on to the autonomy plan, and the Serbs refused. Milosevic immediately began to move additional military and police units into Kosovo, and the hundreds of international observers who had been deployed to Kosovo four months earlier were withdrawn. With NATO poised to open its bombing campaign, Holbrooke was dispatched to Belgrade one last time. Albright, Talbott, Pickering, and I met with Dick in the secretary's office to prepare him for the trip, and Albright made as clear as she could that the purpose of this mission was not to extort some minor concession from Milosevic that could provide an excuse to restart the negotiations. Rather it was to offer Milosevic one last chance to accept the agreement the Kosovars had already signed, to remove Serb forces from Kosovo, and to allow their replacement by NATO troops. Dick was to deliver an ultimatum, not reopen negotiations. Dick did not demur, but he clearly hoped for some more positive outcome.

On March 22 Holbrooke and Hill were back in Belgrade. Milosevic gave no ground, but said he would submit the accord already signed by the Kosovars to his parliament the next morning, along with the proposal for the NATO deployment. Dick and Chris stayed overnight, hoping for but not really expecting some positive development, and they departed as soon as the parliament had roundly rejected the agreement. By late evening Washington time Dick was in Budapest, connected to the White House via a secure video link, again in a state of great excitement. His attention had turned to Bosnia, which he feared would explode once NATO started bombing Serbia. He insisted we take a number of preemptive steps I thought unnecessary, or at least premature. Discussion went on interminably, and Dick could not be talked down from his adrenaline high. Eventually I grew weary of the discussion and departed, leaving others to carry on an increasingly repetitive conversation. Bosnia remained calm throughout the subsequent air war.

On March 24 President Clinton addressed the nation, explaining the need for military action but pledging there would be no employment of American ground troops. NATO began bombing Serb military targets in Kosovo, and some days later started hitting sites within Serbia as well. The planes flew well above the range of Serb air defenses, which prevented NATO casualties but also limited their effectiveness. Based on the experience with Bosnia four years earlier, the United States and other allied governments hoped that a few days of bombing would suffice to secure Serb agreement to the Contact Group and NATO conditions. Instead Milosevic responded by launching a massive campaign of ethnic cleansing, eventually driving more than half the Kosovar population out of their homes and most out of Kosovo altogether.

Over the previous few weeks we had been following a policy course set before my arrival. With the advent of the air war, the administration moved into unexplored territory, and I established a certain routine to deal with the changes. Early each morning, by which time it was early afternoon in Europe, I would arrive in the office, familiarize myself with the latest developments, draw up a to-do list for the day, and meet with Albright. The first couple of these meetings were large and unwieldy. Thereafter Albright disinvited everyone except myself, Tom Pickering, and Mort Halperin, the head of her policy planning staff. I would come armed not just with an update on the situation but with half a dozen or more proposed steps to take. Tom and Mort were invariably supportive, the secretary usually agreed, and I left armed with the necessary mandate to get a number of things done in the course of the day.

State's input into the military campaign occurred through daily meetings at the deputies and principals level and, more rarely, from principals meeting with the president. State had the lead responsibility for maintaining alliance unity, persuading other governments around the world to support or at least not criticize the air campaign, and working with the Russians on a way to end it satisfactorily. State also managed a media campaign to build public support across the alliance and beyond.

Albright and I spoke to our Quint colleagues every day or two. Before and after her calls, I would work with the other four political directors, my equivalents in the Quint group, to prepare and follow up on all decisions taken. Late in the afternoon, by which time my European colleagues would have gone to bed, I would send a fax (this was the pre-email era) with further thoughts and proposals for them to consider on their arrival in the office while I slept. Their reactions would be on my desk first thing the next morning to help form a basis for my meeting with Albright.

While I worked with Albright on the alliance front, Strobe Talbott took the lead with the Russians. Jamie Rubin, the department press spokesman, also held daily calls with his Quint counterparts to coordinate a common press line.

There were continuous debates on the range of permissible NATO targets. I urged an initial focus on military targets in Kosovo lest a more rapid escalation on our part divide the alliance. It soon became evident that from 20,000 feet, where our planes flew to avoid Serb air defenses, they could spot few purely military targets and hit fewer still. Wes Clark understood the alliance dynamic, but some of his Air Force subordinates became impatient with what they labeled "war by committee." They urged a rapid expansion of the bombing campaign to extend throughout Serbia and to include a wide range of war-related civilian facilities such as bridges, power stations, government ministries, and even Milosevic's political party headquarters. Vice President Gore echoed these calls for escalation, even advocating the destruction of the Serbian electrical grid. French President Chirac weighed in on the side of restraint.

Throughout the eleven-week air campaign we constantly had to put out media fires. NATO bombing was not always accurate, and a number of civilians were inadvertently hit. The worst incident came the day our planes destroyed the Chinese Embassy in Belgrade. This was not a result of inaccuracy, but rather of mis-targeting; U.S. planes hit the spot they were aiming at, but their maps had incorrectly identified the building in question. Profuse apologies followed, never entirely accepted by the Chinese government, which had a hard time believing the strike was accidental.

The speed, scope, and brutality of the Serb offensive against the Muslim population of Kosovo took everyone by surprise. In 1995 a short, sharp NATO bombing campaign against Serb forces in Bosnia quickly brought Milosevic to the bargaining table. Most American and allied officials hoped, naïvely perhaps, that this effect would be repeated with Kosovo.

The State Department subsequently estimated that about 10,000 Kosovars were killed by Serb military police and paramilitary units over the ensuing weeks. Over a million—more than half the Muslim population of Kosovo—were driven from their homes, with some 800,000 fleeing into Albania and Macedonia. In Pristina Serb authorities rounded up Kosovars, loaded them into sealed railroad cars, and transported them to the Macedonian border.

This Serb offensive produced three effects. First, it put NATO governments on the defensive before their own publics. Second, it produced a massive refugee crisis. Third, it firmed up wavering allied government support for the air campaign.

In the short term NATO bombing clearly made life worse for the Kosovars. Any let-up in the bombing, therefore, would be seen as a victory for Milosevic. This left NATO leaders with little option but to persist and gradually escalate the attacks until the alliance objectives were achieved and the refugees could go home. In the interim there was no disguising the fact that NATO governments had miscalculated the likely Serb reaction.

In a phone call with Albright, German Foreign Minister Joschka Fischer, his voice quavering with outrage, compared the sealed trains carrying Kosovars out of their country with the manner in which the Nazis had transported Jews to the concentration camps. Although heading a pacifist party on the left of Germany's political spectrum, Fischer became the single most powerful champion of the war in his country and throughout Europe. On April 7 he held a press conference in which he produced a copy of a Serb operational plan for the ethnic cleansing of Kosovo dated a full month before the bombing campaign began.

Dealing with the sudden flow of refugees became our most pressing problem. The Albanian government was eager to help its Albanian-speaking neighbors but lacked the capacity to do so. The Macedonians lacked both willingness and capacity. Albanian-speaking Muslims were a significant minority in Macedonia, and the addition of hundreds of thousands of Kosovars could radically shift that country's ethnic balance. The government in Skopje was, hence, denying the Kosovars entry, leaving tens of thousands huddled without shelter in the cold and rain on the other side of the border.

Eventually, after prodding from Washington and other European capitals, the Macedonian government agreed the refugees could be interned on its side of the border provided someone could immediately organize the necessary camp. Julia Taft, the State Department's head of refugee affairs, insisted this task be left to the United Nations' high commissioner for refugees. I argued that UNHCR could not possibly respond in time, no matter how much money we provided, and urged that U.S. and NATO militaries be mobilized to build the necessary camps in both Macedonia and Albania. The argument became heated enough that Albright urged me to stop being so hard on Julia, but she also agreed to call in the military, which was done.

Even as the war expanded, we pursued an effort to secure a settlement. Holbrooke favored opening a direct line to Milosevic for this purpose, but almost everyone else in Washington and among the allies preferred to work with and through the Russians. I pointed out that even if the Russians failed to persuade the Serbian government to accept the Contact Group and NATO conditions, Moscow could deliver a UN Security

Council resolution endorsing these objectives, which would greatly relieve alliance tensions and blunt wider criticism of the air campaign.

One obstacle to engaging Moscow was Russia's refusal to continue Contact Group meetings, which they had quit as a protest against the bombing. The Russians did prove willing, however, to discuss Kosovo within the G-8 group, which was holding meetings preparatory to a June summit in Cologne, Germany. This forum included Japan, Canada, and the European Union in addition to the Contact Group countries. As all of these were sympathetic to the NATO objectives in Kosovo, we readily agreed to this shift in venue.

On April 12 Albright and I visited NATO headquarters. In addition to meeting with all the member state representatives, she had a private breakfast with Wes Clark. We also had dinner with foreign ministers from all the non-NATO member states that bordered what was left of Yugoslavia, including Albania, Macedonia, Bulgaria, and Romania. These states were as hostile to Milosevic as any of the allies, and their solidarity in support of the NATO operation effectively cut Serbia off from any concrete external assistance.

The following day Albright, Steve Sestanovich, her chief adviser on Russia, and I met with the Russian foreign minister outside Oslo, Norway. On our arrival the minister looked up, saw a new face, and offered his hand, saying with a smile, "Hello. I am Igor Ivanov, the Russian foreign minister." In three hours of discussion Ivanov pushed for at least a temporary halt to the bombing, urged that we reengage with Milosevic, and suggested the UN should control any peacekeeping force for Kosovo. Albright rejected all these suggestions, but the two ministers were able to agree on several other elements of a settlement, and both announced a narrowing of their differences during the ensuing joint press conference.

In person, Ivanov was soft-spoken, courteous, and very pleasant. He and Albright got on well. Occasionally when Ivanov was at a loss for some word, they shifted into Russian, which left me in the dark. Dealing with Ivanov's correspondence was less agreeable. He would regularly send tirades full of tendentious arguments, inaccurate assertions, and unjustified accusations. I would draft equally heated responses, full of sound arguments, accurate assertions, and justified accusations, and Sestanovich would then strip these from the draft and Madeleine would send the blandest of replies. Steve was right. Ivanov was establishing a record and letting his subordinates, who undoubtedly drafted these missives, blow off stream. There was no point in seeking to score points in reply.

On April 14 Russian President Yeltsin named as his personal envoy for Kosovo his former prime minister, Victor Chernomyrdin. In that earlier capacity Chernomyrdin had worked closely with Vice President Gore on a wide range of U.S.-Russia issues. He proposed now to do the same with Kosovo.

In late April a long-planned NATO summit took place in Washington. The air campaign was entering its second month, and its only visible effect was a million displaced Kosovars. British prime minister Tony Blair signaled his intent to use the occasion to urge NATO leaders to open a ground campaign to liberate Kosovo. Albright and I had been arguing for such an escalation of the war for some weeks. "Until we take the plunge on ground troops," I had written to Albright and Berger, "any efforts at a negotiated settlement can be no more than delaying or diversionary tactics intended to occupy the allies and placate the Russians. Only once the threat of ground forces is real can we expect our diplomatic efforts to produce real movement in Belgrade, Moscow and New York." I argued that preparing for and, if necessary, employing ground forces was the only course of action that offered a good chance of attaining NATO's objectives and urged that we seek to have the NATO summit endorse such a step.

Wes Clark was of a similar view, but his superiors in the Pentagon, Defense Secretary Bill Cohen and Joint Chiefs Chair Hugh Shelton, were strongly opposed to a ground campaign. President Clinton was on record having ruled out the possibility. Accordingly, Berger met with a small group of us to search for a formula that could satisfy Blair without pitching this issue into a gathering of nineteen heads of state and government. We agreed that Wes Clark should quietly be authorized by NATO Secretary General Solana to "reassess" plans for a possible ground war. Blair accepted this formula, Solana issued the instruction on his own authority, and the issue was not raised among the assembled NATO leaders.

Preparing for this summit meeting, I was reminded of the famous "don't talk about the war" skit in *Faulty Towers*, the one where John Cleese cannot stifle repeated mentions of World War II before a group of German guests. In this case, however, the injunction stuck. Western leaders, Blair excepted, were all eager to avoid any substantive discussion of the unpopular and at that stage apparently unsuccessful war they were waging. I joined other officials in drafting an anodyne restatement of NATO policy on Kosovo, which the leaders duly issued. But the bulk of the discussion and the resultant communiqués were all about the alliance's past triumphs and future prospects rather than its troubling present.

Early May saw a couple of important developments. Chernomyrdin visited Washington for talks with Gore and Talbott. Chernomyrdin suggested that a European figure should be nominated to work with him in mediating a peace settlement between NATO and the Yugoslav government, and Talbott suggested the president of Finland, Martti Ahtisaari. Chernomyrdin agreed and, subsequently, Ahtisaari did as well.

Three days later Albright met with her G-8 colleagues outside Bonn, where they issued a declaration that aligned Russia with most of the NATO demands, including the withdrawal of both the Serb army and police from Kosovo and the introduction of an international force, without specifying that this force would be NATO-led. The ministers also directed us political directors to begin drafting a United Nations Security Council resolution that would give effect to this agreement.

Dick Holbrooke continued to deprecate the utility of working with the Russians on these issues; he favored a direct approach to Milosevic. In one principals meeting he characterized the extraordinary efforts Albright and Talbott were making as "worse than useless." Dick charged that "Madeleine and Strobe's efforts are actually lengthening the war," by running after the Russians and conveying to Milosevic a sense of American desperation. I found this statement remarkably insensitive as well as substantively incoherent. If engaging with the Russians encouraged Milosevic to believe he held the stronger hand, would not engaging him directly do so even more?

Dick, still awaiting Senate confirmation, chaffed at being left on the sidelines throughout this critical period, but his remarks did reflect a mounting sense of desperation that was seeping into administration and NATO discussions. The bombing campaign was expanding largely because it was proving impossible to find and hit true military targets. Repeated incidents of collateral damage and civilian casualties were the most obvious result, generating controversy and opposition to the war. It was impossible to gauge what effect the air strikes might be having on Serb morale and Milosevic's calculations. Albright had been blamed in the media for the alleged failure of Rambouillet; now press commenters were labeling the air campaign "Madeleine's war."

As May wore on the debate within the administration over a possible ground offensive intensified. A million Kosovars were homeless, and a couple hundred thousand of these were still in Kosovo hiding in the hills from Serb army and police. This internally displaced population would have difficulty surviving a winter without shelter. Preparations for a ground operation would need to begin shortly if it was to be conducted before snows covered the mountain passes through which the troops would need to move.

Clinton bemoaned his earlier promise not to use ground forces and, in one meeting he angrily reproached Berger for inserting this line in his address to the nation that had opened the air bombardment. "If I go ahead and employ ground forces I will be branded a liar but if I do not we will lose the war."

The American defense establishment remained divided. Clark wanted to move from planning to preparation for a ground assault, but both Bill Cohen, the secretary of state, and General Hugh Shelton, the chair of the joint chiefs, were still opposed. Albright also supported preparation for a ground offensive, but felt at a disadvantage arguing the military aspects of the case with the secretary of defense.

The situation was complicated by the poisonous relationship between the defense secretary and chairman on the one side and Clark on the other, and the fact that Albright and Clark were of the same mind only seemed to increase the antagonism. At one point Shelton called Clark to convey an instruction from Cohen, telling Wes to "get your fucking face off television."

As a result of these tensions, Clark was excluded from all Washington policy discussion. In the course of a telephone conversation on some other matter I mention to Wes something that had come up in the previous day's principals meeting, assuming he would already have heard of it. He had not and asked whether I could call him occasionally with updates on the Washington debates. "Why don't you call me?" I asked. "Because I can't," he replied. "I have been told that I can receive calls from Washington, but that I cannot make any except to the Pentagon."

The White House Situation Room was equipped with secure video connections both to Clark's headquarters in Mons, Belgium, and our mission to NATO in Brussels. Sandy Vershbow, our ambassador to NATO, routinely participated via this video line in principals and deputies meetings, but Clark never did. Clark's views and recommendations were presented by his Pentagon critics, who were usually arguing against them.

Berger put the issue of ground troops on the principals agenda. John Podesta, the White House chief of staff, attended, his only appearance in one of these meetings throughout the war. Ideally the debate should have pitted Clark against Cohen and Shelton, but Berger felt that would undercut the latter's authority. State would have to stand in for the commander in the field. Albright was uncomfortable with challenging Cohen on his own ground, so the burden for making the case for a land invasion fell to me. Cohen argued that a force of at least 200,000 would be needed to invade Kosovo, mostly through Albania, and that it would be impossible to deploy such numbers in that mountainous, undeveloped terrain before winter set in. He cited, among other reasons, the lack of necessary ships to transport troops from the United States. I pointed out that from a standing start, the United States had taken ten months to mount an amphibious invasion of North Africa in 1942. Surely we could do better in 1999, when the United States already had over a 100,000 military personnel in Europe and NATO had even larger numbers of allied forces already on that side of the ocean. I recalled that Britain alone was offering to provide 50,000 troops for the offensive.

Additional U.S. and NATO forces were sent to Albania and Macedonia. In response to media questions about the use of ground forces, Clinton said, "We will not take any option off the table." Cohen himself attended a secret meeting of Quint defense ministers in Germany to discuss the possibility of a ground campaign. Slowly the administration was edging toward a decision to move from planning to preparation for a ground offense, including positioning the necessary forces.

Louise Arbour, lead prosecutor of the Hague Tribunal, told us confidentially that she was nearing a decision to indict Milosevic for war crimes in Kosovo. Albright expressed concerns about the timing of such an announcement, and Arbour said she would consult further before acting, but she did not. On May 27 she announced the indictment, and our immediate concern, and that of the other Quint officials, was that this step would strengthen Milosevic's determination to resist.

Talbott worked intensively to equip Chernomyrdin and Ahtisaari with a common proposal, really an ultimatum, to present to Milosevic. On June 2 the two envoys traveled to Belgrade and delivered the desired message, and to nearly everyone's surprise Milosevic said he would put the

NATO demands to his parliament and recommend they be accepted. He did so the next morning and the parliament did as he advised.

The next two weeks became even more hectic as we tried to consolidate this breakthrough. Two things were still needed to end the war. Serb and NATO military authorities had to conclude an agreement covering the actual removal of all Serb forces and the entry of NATO troops, and the G-8 governments had to draft a UN Security Council resolution determining how Kosovo was to be governed, and by whom, once the Serbs were gone. This latter task fell to me.

We political directors had already met once to begin drafting the necessary Security Council resolution. With Milosevic's concession, our work intensified. We met in a German government guesthouse located on a hill, the Petersburg, across the river from Bonn, which was then still the country's capital. In the early 1950s the allied high commission had occupied this same building, from which the American, British, and French authorities exercised ultimate authority over the newly emergent West German state. I was familiar with the site, having hiked its wooded slopes on many occasions. I now looked down from this hilltop at the home across the river where my family had spent four happy years.

Over the next several days and nights we developed a text that would set up a United Nations-led governing authority for Kosovo and authorize an international security force under NATO. Our Russian colleague raised endless objections, but gradually we were able to put most of the essential pieces into place, producing a text thirty-three paragraphs long. Even so we still faced twenty Russian objections.

On June 8 we were joined by our foreign ministers, who went to work dealing with these remaining obstacles. Everyone was aware that bombing would continue until full agreement was reached. I admired how Albright handled her colleagues on this as on other occasions. She was very conscious of being a woman in a man's world and used this to advantage. Some successful women seek to operate as if gender made no difference, but Albright, in subtle ways, did the opposite, emphasizing in dress and mannerism her femininity even while bargaining tenaciously. Her ability to negotiate in fluent French and Russian helped. She and the other ministers had spent a lot of time together over the past several months, and a degree of collegiality had developed, even including the Russian. Over time a dynamic evolved in which her negotiating partners also became her suitors. There is a picture from this Petersburg meeting that captures this dynamic, with Madeleine, as she was universally called, seated with all the other ministers clustered around her appearing to vie for attention.

One by one, through a process of grit and charm and the threat of continued bombing, the remaining Russian objections were cleared away and a full text sent to New York for Security Council promulgation.

I flew to New York to consult with UN Secretary General Kofi Annan on the United Nations' new task. Kofi was not pleased at being handed such an unusually broad and unprecedented set of responsibilities with no prior consultation or even notice. He and his staff, nevertheless, moved quickly to deploy the necessary assets.

Two days later Albright and I were back in Europe, visiting a refugee camp on the Macedonian border. It was hot and humid, and there was not a tree or substantial structure in sight, just a hillside covered with small, makeshift tents in which whole families sought shelter from the burning sun. Albright assured them that their brief exile was almost over.

On arriving back at the Skopje airport we were met by Lieutenant General Sir Michael Jackson, the NATO commander whose troops were preparing to enter Kosovo. Striding across the tarmac from his helicopter, Jackson informed us that several hundred Russian troops that had been stationed with the NATO command in Bosnia had suddenly departed their post, driven into Serbia, and were, even as we spoke, on the road to Pristina.

"I assume they are going for the airport," Jackson said. He explained that he had already informed the Serbs that NATO would enter Kosovo in several stages to give Serb forces time to leave before NATO troops arrived. Under this arrangement NATO did not intend to enter Pristina until day three of the intervention. We discussed whether NATO troops should preempt the Russians by jumping straight into Pristina and Jackson warned that this could lead to fighting with Serb forces. I said the Russian challenge should be dealt with diplomatically, not militarily.

We quickly extended the conversation, tying in Berger in the White House and Talbott on a plane flying out of Moscow. Strobe reported that he had met earlier that morning with Vladimir Putin, Yeltsin's new national security adviser, and Putin had told Talbott to ignore the threats of a deployment into Kosovo emanating from the Russian military. Putin promised to issue a positive public statement within the hour. Albright called Ivanov, who similarly denied that Russia was trying to steal a march on NATO, promising that "there will be no surprises."

Despite this assurance Strobe turned his plane around and returned to Moscow. Jackson strode off to lead NATO's advance into Kosovo. Albright and I flew back to Washington. I tried to sleep during the flight but was continually woken with the latest updates. The Russians were coming! The Russians were not coming! The Russians were already there! Ivanov has just announced that the Russians were leaving!

By the time our plane landed in Washington it was clear the Russians had beaten NATO forces to Pristina, where they seized Kosovo's only airport. Nor were the Russians showing any sign of leaving. The Russian troops soon found themselves surrounded by a vastly larger NATO force and Moscow sought to fly in reinforcements. In Washington we coordinated an intense diplomatic campaign, successfully persuading every one of Serbia's neighbors to deny Russia requests for overflights. Clark ordered Jackson to block the Pristina airport runways, but Jackson refused, responding angrily, "I am not going to start World War III for you." This confrontation escalated to capitals, leading JCS Chairman Hugh Shelton to back Jackson.

Signals from Moscow were mixed, and the apparent confusion there became ominous. In a phone call with Clinton, Yeltsin was more than normally incoherent. Ivanov, who was clearly out of the loop, first publicly denied there were Russian troops in Kosovo, and then claimed it was all a mistake and that they were leaving, which they were not. Washington was left wondering if this was a rogue operation, if the Russian military was no longer under civilian control, and if some sort of rolling coup was underway.

Eventually things calmed down. The few Russian troops at the Pristina airport were isolated and without hope of reinforcement. On June 16 I accompanied Albright and Cohen to Helsinki to meet with their Russian counterparts, where the Russians said they wanted their own sector and did not want to fall under NATO command. In the end it was agreed that the Russian contingent would be distributed among the three sectors, each commanded by a NATO member country officer who would have authority over the Russian troops in his sector.

Albright and I stayed on for dinner with President Ahtisaari, who was to play a pivotal role in arranging for Kosovo's eventual independence a decade later. The next morning we flew to Paris to brief the Quint on the just-concluded agreement with the Russians.

It was a lovely late spring afternoon. The five ministers and their political directors gathered in the garden courtyard of the Quai d'Orsay, the French Foreign Ministry. For the past several months career-ending failure had been in prospect for all five ministers until, almost miraculously, victory had been grasped from the jaws of defeat. The dominant mood was less one of triumph than of lingering wonder and immense relief. Liveried waiters appeared with buckets of iced Champagne, and Joschka Fischer raised his glass and proposed a toast "to Madeleine's war."

TWENTY

Peace in Kosovo

FOR SEVERAL MONTHS CLINTON'S NATIONAL security team had been doing all Kosovo all the time. Now they were able to devote themselves to a wider range of issues, so meetings with Albright were as needed rather than every morning. Deputies still met on Kosovo at the White House one or two times a week, principals less often. The Quint and Contact Group remained active but mostly at the political directors level.

Kosovo was the fourth of the Clinton administration's nation-building efforts. It was the NATO's second. Somalia had been an unqualified disaster. In Haiti we had avoided outright failure but produced little of enduring value. Peace in Bosnia was proving a more enduring achievement. Through a process of trial and sometimes costly error the United States and its allies had learned a good deal about how to organize and manage post-conflict operations. These lessons we were able to apply in Kosovo. The by now familiar division of labor between State, Defense, USAID, Treasury, and other agencies could be applied with little need for adjustment. Similarly at the international level, the roles for NATO, the United Nations, the European Union, the OSCE, and other institutions could be adapted to the new circumstances rather than negotiated anew. The air war had been messy, but implementation of the subsequent peace enforcement mission went more smoothly than any of the Clinton administration's earlier such efforts.

UN Security Council (UNSC) Resolution 1244 provided the basic framework. NATO was authorized to secure Kosovo and the United Nations to govern it. The resolution recognized, nominally at least, continued Yugoslav sovereignty, but it granted NATO and the UN all the actual attributes. Unlike most such mandates, this one had no termination date and, therefore, no need for periodic renewal. Thus the Russians could not employ their veto to block or alter these arrangements.

I followed NATO troops into Pristina several days later. A U.S. Army Black Hawk helicopter took me low through the steep hills that separated Kosovo from Macedonia, difficult terrain that invading forces might have had to fight through had a land invasion proved necessary. Evidence of bomb damage was everywhere, but the Kosovars were already back out in their fields. One family, seeing us directly overhead, dropped their farm implements and waved excitedly. I had seen no signs of gratitude for what the United States had tried to do in Somalia or Haiti, but here in Kosovo Bill Clinton, Madeleine Albright, and Wes Clark would become national heroes. During the air war there had been a lot of criticism of its effect on Kosovo's civilian population, but the Kosovars bore the war stoically, were delighted with the result, and never reproached us for the sacrifices it had entailed.

On arrival I met with Mike Jackson, a colorful, swaggering figure, who chided my young escort, a U.S. Army captain, for wearing his flak vest and helmet, noting that his British troops were patrolling downtown Pristina in soft hats and summer uniforms. Jackson provided an upbeat account of the situation. Serb army and police were entirely gone. The situation was largely peaceful. Many Serb civilians had fled, however; some all the way into Serbia proper, and others into and around the northern city of Metrovica.

Kofi Annan had dispatched his top troubleshooter to Pristina to establish the UN presence. Sergio Vieira de Mello, a career UN administrator from Brazil, was impressive. Smart, charming, movie star handsome, Sergio created an immediate impression of competence and vigor. The United Nations had already brought in a hundred international police from Bosnia and was just beginning to staff its many responsibilities, the most pressing being humanitarian relief. The return of Kosovars was going exceptionally well, but the flight of Serbs was troubling.

I traveled from Pristina to join Albright in Brussels. There I received a phone call informing me that NATO Secretary General Solana had just announced that Wes Clark was to be replaced by Joe Ralston, the current vice chair of the joint chiefs. I telephoned Vershbow and asked what the hell was going on, and Sandy said he had received overnight an instruction from Secretary Cohen to inform Solana that President Clinton had named Ralston to replace Clark, asking that Solana announce the change forthwith. I demanded angrily why Vershbow had not checked with Albright before carrying out this instruction, recalling that American ambassadors were explicitly precluded from accepting direction from anyone other than the secretary and her designees. Vershbow reminded me that at NATO he represented both the secretaries of state and defense. Nevertheless, had Albright been alerted in time, I believe she might have been able to avert this abrupt and unceremonious curtailment of Clark's career.

Madeleine was upset. So was President Clinton, who told his staff that he thought the change of command he had signed off on was routine, to be executed at the conclusion of Clark's normal term rather than requiring Wes to leave his post early. A few days later we all found ourselves in Sarajevo, where Clinton had a private conversation with Clark, subsequently awarding him the Presidential Medal of Freedom. Thus ended the military career of the only American general to win a war without losing a single soldier, sailor, or airman.

In 2004, when Clark was seeking the Democratic nomination for president, Hugh Shelton told a reporter Clark's early dismissal "had to do with integrity and character issues." This low blow, offered without a shred of evidence, illustrates how Clark's relations with his immediate superiors had deteriorated.

Creating a functional international administration for Kosovo took time, but it proceeded more quickly and smoothly than had comparable efforts in Bosnia five years earlier. In the mid-nineties American and European officials were operating under the bizarre notion that they were competing for influence in the Balkans, as if Bosnia were a prize to be won rather than a burden to be borne. Since Washington wanted an American to command the NATO mission, the Europeans insisted on a European heading the civil administration with the title of high representative.

Washington successfully sought to weaken this position by having substantial civil responsibilities assigned to other fully independent institutions, notably the United Nations for police training and the OSCE for
democratization and elections, both of which were eventually headed by
Americans. The result was excessive institutional competition and frequent
paralysis.

In designing arrangements for Kosovo, I persuaded my G-8 colleagues
to mandate a more streamlined structure in which all nonmilitary entities
would serve under a single UN head. The United Nations mission in
Kosovo (UNMIK) would have four pillars. The European Union took
charge of economic development, the OSCE handled democratization and
elections, the UN's High Commission for Refugees conducted humanitarian relief efforts, and the UN secretary general's personal representative
and his immediate staff were in overall charge. This hierarchical structure
did not eliminate institutional rivalry, but did channel the competition
more constructively.

The most immediate policy issue was what to do about the Kosovo Liberation Army. Resolution 1244 had charged NATO with "demilitarizing"
the KLA, whatever that might mean. On this first visit to Pristina, I called
on General Agim Ceku, the KLA chief of staff. Ceku, a native of Kosovo,
had once been a captain in the Yugoslav Army, but defected to fight for
Croatia in its war of independence. Ceku returned to Kosovo at the outset
of the bombing campaign to assume command of the KLA. He impressed
me as moderate, mature, and professional.

These were not characteristics generally associated with the KLA. This
organization was regarded with great suspicion in Washington and outright hostility throughout most of Europe. Smuggling and other forms of
criminality had long been a source of livelihood for Kosovars, and this was
the milieu from which the KLA emerged. As an insurgent group, the
KLA had regularly been accused of attacks on Serb civilians; that is to say,
terrorism. U.S. and NATO military authorities had been reluctant to coordinate their air strikes with the KLA during the conflict, and Washington
had repeatedly considered and rejected proposals to provide arms. Every
few days throughout the air war Hashim Thaci called Jamie Rubin, with
whom he had struck up a friendship, to relay targeting information, which
Jamie passed on to U.S. military authorities. That was pretty much the
extent of our wartime collaboration.

A French officer attached to NATO's Kosovo Force, KFOR, head-quarters proposed that the KLA not be disbanded, but rather repurposed as a civil defense organization charged with responding to floods, fires, and other natural disasters. It could retain a military-like structure, but would not be armed or conduct military training. Whenever Kosovo's final status was determined this organization could, then, become the basis for a real defense force.

I found this an elegant solution, meeting the Security Council's require-ment that the KLA be demilitarized without dispersing several thousand unemployed young men practiced in the use of arms into the civilian pop-ulation at a time of high unemployment and continued tension between the Albanian-speaking and the remaining Serb populations. I secured NSC and Pentagon backing, briefed Albright on the proposal, and trav-eled to Europe where I gained the reluctant agreement of the other Quint political directors. Walking back to my hotel I received a call from Al-bright. She had Dick Holbrooke on the line and said Dick was opposed to retaining the KLA in any form. I responded impatiently that I had just convinced the French, British, Italian, and German governments to back the scheme she and I had discussed, that this move had been fully cleared in Washington, that I had no intention of reversing our position on the matter, and that the administration would need to find a new Balkan envoy if it wanted that done.

Pursuant to the Quint decision, the KLA was disarmed, rechristened the Kosovo Protection Corps, and retrained in civil defense and conserva-tion tasks. This kept its remaining members largely out of trouble for over a decade, until Kosovo achieved its independence and could begin slowly to constitute its own defense capability.

Another pressing problem was what to do about the remaining Serb population. It is an irony of peacekeeping in a divided population that, hav-ing intervened to defend one group from persecution, the intervening power then must spend most of its effort protecting the former persecu-tors from retribution. Roughly 10 percent of Kosovo's prewar population had been Serb. Something less than half of these had fled to Serbia. Many others had moved to the northern fringe of Kosovo, adjacent to the border with Serbia. There remained, nevertheless, a number of Serb villages dotted throughout the rest of the territory, and NATO's principal secu-rity mission over the next decade was not protecting Kosovo from Serbia, which never presented a threat but, rather, protecting the remaining Serbs from the Kosovars.

Much of the Albanian-speaking population in the north had fled or been pushed out during the Serb offensive that accompanied the opening of the air campaign. When Serbs from the south fled north, they moved into homes vacated by the departed Kosovars. I urged the UN to build temporary housing for the displaced Serbs so the displaced Kosovars could reclaim their homes. No one took up this suggestion, and I was not convinced of its feasibility. Intermixing highly antagonistic populations in this manner tends to sustain violence rather than produce tolerance. In both Bosnia and Kosovo the international community sought to reverse the process of ethnic cleansing that had taken place during the just-concluded conflicts. The failure of these efforts has probably contributed to the uneasy peace that has prevailed in both countries since.

The Metrovica Serbs organized their own security force and employed it to prevent Kosovars from entering their half of the city. Thousands of Kosovars marched in protest, threatening a large-scale sectarian riot. The local French commander moved to separate the two sides, asking for reinforcements from other KFOR sectors, most notably the American. The Pentagon instructed the American commander to refuse, fearing the negative publicity that might flow from having U.S. soldiers clubbing or, worse yet, shooting people they had only just liberated.

This led to an acrimonious discussion in the White House Situation Room. I pointed out what a poor example we had just set, particularly given that American officials had for years been criticizing other allies for opting out of certain NATO missions. The Pentagon contended that American troops "don't do crowd control." Now, I responded irritably, the Pentagon's risk aversion was extending beyond minimizing casualties to avoiding bad publicity.

My complaints produced no apology, but we also had no further challenges from the Pentagon to the necessity of U.S. and other NATO troops ensuring public order until enough UN police could be deployed. In Bosnia, the international civil authorities had possessed no capacity to ensure public order and the NATO military had no mandate to do so. This left a power vacuum that was filled by extreme nationalist and criminal elements. To avoid a repetition of this situation, I had successfully inserted a provision in UNSC Resolution 1244 to make internal security a joint responsibility of NATO and the UN. NATO was mandated to take the lead in assuring public order until the United Nations had time to recruit and deploy enough international police to assume responsibility for routine policing. This hand-off proceeded gradually over the following year. As soon as there were enough UN police in a given district, there was a formal hand-off of lead responsibility from NATO to UNMIK. Eventually over 4,000 international police were deployed. Both NATO and the United Nations also recognized the need for international units trained in riot control and public order duties. Both organizations stepped up the deployment of gendarmerie contingents with these specialized capabilities, and these arrangements provided space and time for the much slower process of raising a completely new and genuinely multiethnic Kosovo Police Service.

Moving Kosovo toward economic recovery and substantial self-government proved more difficult. In negotiating UNSC Resolution 1244 I had given way to my European colleagues' desire that the European Union should be the lead agency for reconstruction. The EU had never before undertaken such a task and proved very slow to assign the necessary personnel and mobilize the needed resources. Several months into the endeavor the Brussels bureaucracy had sent only one official to Kosovo. Recognizing the need to fill this gap, I had half a dozen American development experts assigned to the EU office, leading to the anomalous situation in which, for the first year, the United States provided most of the staffing for the EU pillar of the international civil presence.

A more serious obstacle to development was posed by the Russians, who insisted that the government in Belgrade would need to approve any substantial changes in Kosovo's economic or political life. Resolution 1244 had recognized continued Yugoslav sovereignty over Kosovo, but clearly assigned the exercise of those sovereign powers to the UN and NATO. Moscow used its influence at UN headquarters in New York to slow UNMIKs execution of its mandate, causing months of delay as every new step toward market economics and democratic self-government was scrutinized and debated by UN lawyers in New York.

In Pristina, Sergio de Mello had been superseded by Bernard Kouchner, a dapper, flamboyant, and media-savvy Frenchman. Kouchner was the founder of Doctors Without Borders, one of the world's largest and most courageous humanitarian agencies. He and Albright became instant friends, and we were pleased to find Kouchner's views on Kosovo's future status closer to those of the American government than his own.

Not that the American government was of one mind on this matter. One of the tasks assigned to the United Nations under Resolution 1244 was to promote the establishment of substantial autonomy and self-government in Kosovo pending a final resolution of the territory's status. The resolution was silent on what that final status should look like, other than referring to the Rambouillet accord, which had explicitly left this to be decided by some undefined future international process. France was opposed to independence for Kosovo and not eager to see early progress toward even limited self-government. Washington was divided on the ultimate objective, but unified in supporting early movement toward the development of democratic institutions.

Personally, I was sure the Kosovars, having experienced years of Serb persecution followed by a massive campaign of ethnic cleansing, would never again accept even the most limited form of Serb oversight. Independence was, therefore, the only viable final status for the society. Strobe Talbott resisted this conclusion, concerned about how the precedent of a disputed separation of Kosovo, not just from Yugoslavia but from the Republic of Serbia of which it was part, might affect the territorial integrity of several fragile post-Soviet states. Events proved us both right. Despite strong and consistent Serbian and Russian objections, Kosovo became independent almost a decade later. Shortly thereafter Russia recognized two small breakaway Russian-speaking enclaves within Georgia as independent states, citing the Kosovo precedent. Years later Russia cited the Kosovo precedent yet again in defending its annexation of Crimea.

There was general agreement in Washington that the sooner effective local institutions for governance could be established the quicker NATO troop strength in Kosovo could be drawn down. This meant overriding Serb and Russian objections. Albright backed this position, and so, too, did Kouchner, who joined Washington in pressing the UN lawyers in New York for maximum leeway to reform the economy, organize elections, and empower local officials.

I suggested to my Quint colleagues that we make a joint visit to Pristina. We gathered in Rome, where the American ambassador hosted a dinner for us at his lovely residence, and the next morning the Italian Air Force flew us to Pristina. The plane was fitted out like a luxury yacht, all burled walnut and velvet plush. During the short flight we drank freshly brewed cappuccino served by white-liveried stewards, then the five of us met with Thaci and other local leaders in an attempt to encourage multiethnic participation in Kosovo's emerging political institutions.

KFOR's northern sector, where most of the Serbs were congregated, was commanded and staffed largely by the French. U.S. officials felt the French forces were excessively tolerant of the Serb attempts to bar entry to Albanian speakers, set up independent institutions, work directly with Belgrade authorities, and effectively partition the city of Metrovica. Seeking to counterbalance French influence, I persuaded Kouchner to appoint a retired American general as the UN administrator for that region. I visited the city myself, meeting both with the Kosovar mayor, Bayram Rexhepi, a medical doctor and moderate politician, and Oliver Ivanovic, the most prominent Serb leader. Ivanovic, speaking American-accented English, was easy to talk to but unyielding on the basics. The Serbs would not recognize Kosovo institutions, would continue to work with the government in Belgrade, and would continue to police their side of the city. For this latter purpose Ivanovic had helped organize the Bridgewatchers, a group of toughs who prevented Kosovars from crossing into the Serb half of the divided city.

Like so many aspects of nation-building in divided societies, the Serb-Kosovar antagonism was a problem to be managed rather than solved. Rexhepi went on to become Kosovo's first elected prime minister. Ivanovic developed into one of the more moderate Serb politicians. He was, nevertheless, arrested in 2014 and tried by a European Union court for war crimes, eventually receiving nine years in prison for ordering the murder of Kosovars during the NATO air campaign.

With the end of fighting in and over Kosovo, I was able to spend more time on Bosnia. The country was then, and remains today, governed under the constitutional arrangements put in place at Dayton. This document recognized three peoples—Muslim, Serb, and Croat—and two entities—the Muslim-Croat Federation and the Serb Republic. The country has three presidents and all three must agree on any new legislation, which they almost never do. The system only holds together because the internationally-appointed high representative has the power to impose laws unilaterally when necessary and to remove uncooperative officials from office. This clumsy and undemocratic arrangement was the best that could be achieved in 1995 and has since proved impossible to alter.

After nearly a year's wait, Holbrooke was confirmed as our UN ambassador, and he immediately moved to reinvolve himself in our Balkan diplomacy. He met with me to say he intended to continue to work on Balkan issues and expressed the hope we would be able to collaborate. I agreed, while cautioning that Albright remained sensitive about her leadership on these issues. Dick waved this concern aside, insisting there were no differences between him and Madeleine.

A few days later I learned that Holbrooke was planning to make his first trip as UN ambassador to Bosnia, Kosovo, Albania, and Macedonia. I called and urged him to make his maiden voyage to some other troubled region of the world, again warning that Albright would not be happy with such an early resumption of his Balkan diplomacy. Dick angrily denied that Albright would have any difficulty with his travel and refused to discuss the question further.

In the course of his tour of the region Dick invited Bosnia's Muslim, Serb, and Croat leaders to UN headquarters in New York for a celebration of the fourth anniversary of the Dayton accords. He staged this event without reference to Albright, me, or anyone else in Washington, then became upset when I sent Jim Pardew rather than attend personally. The three leaders addressed the Security Council and issued a joint declaration. This event was characteristic of Holbrooke's approach to diplomacy, which tended to move from one media event to the next. He used these as pressure points for impelling movement. This technique was sometimes quite effective, but in this case, the movement was slight.

Dick did an impressive job at the UN. His most notable achievement was persuading Jesse Helms and other skeptical American legislators to pay off the large and longstanding arrears in U.S. dues to that organization. He also persuaded the rest of the UN membership to agree to a small reduction in future U.S. contributions and, thus, a corresponding increase in everyone else's. But he could not leave Balkan policy to those of us who were now responsible for it.

Tony Blair came forward with a proposal for building on the Kosovo precedent to secure a United Nations endorsement for humanitarian interventions more generally. This idea stimulated some interest in Washington. If successful it would represent an ex post facto legitimization of the air war and make Security Council agreement easier to achieve in future such cases. I scotched the idea, arguing that the Kosovo intervention was already regarded by most observers as legitimate, that we had established a useful precedent we could call upon in the future if need be, but that any Anglo American initiative to formalize this consensus would generate a heated reaction, not just from the Russians but from any number of other governments worried about the United States and its Western partners becoming the world's policemen. The resultant debate would make our actions in Kosovo more, not less, controversial.

Several years later the Canadian government advanced a similar idea in a more palatable form. In 2005 the United Nations General Assembly, meeting at the level of heads of state, promulgated what became known as the doctrine of "responsibility to protect" or R2P. The assembled world leaders declared that all governments had a responsibility to protect their populations from genocide, war crimes, ethnic cleansing, and crimes against humanity, and that when any government failed to do so, the UN Security Council should, on a case by case basis, authorize forceful measures to provide such protection. The Security Council has in the years since authorized a number of UN peacekeeping missions and raised the priority given in these missions to the protection of civilian populations. It also authorized the use of NATO airpower to halt the threat to civilians in Libya. So far, however, the Security Council has been unable to agree on a common approach to the slaughter of innocents in Syria, where the involvement of individual countries has only intensified and extended the conflict.

TWENTY-ONE

The Fall of Milosevic

THE KOSOVO CONFLICT STIRRED SEVERAL neighboring societies. Macedonia possessed a sizeable minority of Albanian-speaking Muslims, who had long been excluded from power by the Orthodox Christian majority. This Muslim population became more restive, some wanting to share power in Macedonia, others to secede and become part of Kosovo. There was also a small Albanian-speaking population in Serbia just across the border from Kosovo, in the Presevo Valley, which would have preferred to be within the newly autonomous, perhaps eventually independent, Kosovo. The leadership of Montenegro, the smaller of Yugoslavia's two remaining republics, had been hostile to Milosevic throughout the Kosovo conflict and now was moving toward a unilateral declaration of independence. These sentiments were all reminders that self-determination is a principal without inherent limits, particularly in ethnically, linguistically, and religiously divided lands like the Balkans.

The Kosovo conflict also reverberated within Serbia. The immediate effect of the bombing was one of national solidarity and, thus, a strengthening of Milosevic's political position. His loss of Kosovo began to reverse this dynamic, giving renewed hope to a weakened and divided opposition.

Following the conclusion of the air campaign, the issue of Western sanctions on Serbia arose. These had been put in place over a number of years and for a variety of reasons. With Serbia having met all NATO's demands regarding Kosovo, there seemed some logic in lifting at least those sanctions related to that conflict. In a meeting of Quint political directors, the five of us agreed to recommend such action to our governments. I briefed Albright, who seemed agreeable. A few days later I made the same case to a meeting of principals, only to find that Albright had changed her mind. She insisted the Balkans would never be stabilized as long as Milosevic remained in power; that he was now weakened and vulnerable, and rather than relaxing our pressures we should redouble them with a view to precipitating his early ouster. Berger agreed, no one demurred, and I found myself with a new assignment.

Although we tended to characterize the Milosevic regime as authoritarian, it would be more accurate to label it an illiberal democracy; that is, one where representative institutions were more than mere trappings but not yet sufficient to operate as an effective check on those in power. Corruption and criminality were rampant. Yet Serbia was not a closed society. The extreme nationalist parties that formed the government had a real following and their policies substantial public support. Yugoslavia held regular elections. Opposition parties were harassed but not banned. Media was largely, but not exclusively, regime-controlled. Citizens, including prominent opposition figures, could travel freely. Civil society and some foreign nongovernmental organizations could, with difficulty, operate inside the country.

Domestic opposition to the Serbian government was dispirited and divided. Its leaders felt the United States and Europe had let them down by courting good relations with Milosevic to secure and then implement the Dayton settlement. We had. This is the kind of invidious choice between competing objectives, short- and long-term goals, and principals and practicalities that one has to make all too often in diplomacy. The democratic opposition in Serbia had reason to believe they had been abandoned. But five years on, the situation had changed. Bosnia was calm. Kosovo was largely insulated from Serbian interference. Milosevic had been strengthened domestically by his role in the Dayton settlement, but had now been weakened by his loss of Kosovo. My first task, therefore, was to convince the opposition leaders that this time they had Western backing, that Milosevic was not going to be rehabilitated, and that they could, if they tried, defeat him at the ballot box.

The president of Montenegro, Milo Djukanovic, had already fallen out with Milosevic. He was ready to work with the United States and the Serbian opposition to unseat him. I paid Djukanovic my first visit in August 1999, and it felt strange entering a country with which we had only recently been at war. Arrangements for my visit were handled by the Montenegrin security service, who met us at an isolated border crossing on the Adriatic coast. We left our own vehicles on the Croatian side, switched to a couple of black Mercedes, drove for about an hour, crossed the Bay of Kotor on a car ferry, and met with Djukanovic in a Montenegrin government safe house in the seaside resort of Budva.

This pattern was repeated every few months over the next year. On the second of these visits Djukanovic arranged for a dozen prominent Serb opposition leaders to meet with me at one of the town's seaside hotels. It was winter and the hotel was otherwise empty. The most impressive of the assembled political figures was Zoran Djindjic, a young, charismatic leader accorded some deference by his elders among this group. On my next visit I met with retired general Momcilo Perisic, who had been the chief of staff of the Yugoslav army during the Bosnian war. He insisted on holding our discussion out of doors, apparently concerned about being overheard or recorded. Perisic made no promises in our conversation, but he ended up playing an important, positive role in the final days of the Milosevic regime. This did not prevent his subsequent arrest and trial before the Hague Tribunal for war crimes.

I met again with many of these same opposition leaders in Budapest. Here they were joined by Dragoslav Avramovic, the former head of the Yugoslav Central Bank, who was emerging as the likely opposition candidate to take on Slobodan Milosevic in the 2000 presidential election. Djindjic chose not to join this group, but instead asked to meet me the next day in a small Hungarian town just across the border from Serbia.

While in Budapest I also met with Doug Schoen, President Clinton's favorite political pollster. Doug was polling in Serbia on behalf of the opposition and had just briefed their leadership on his most recent results, which indicated that Milosevic was vulnerable and could be beaten. I asked that we stay in touch, as this was both valuable intelligence and a powerful argument with which to motivate a still wary and pessimistic opposition, most of whom had boycotted the last elections in 1996 and were tempted to do so again. Schoen's findings also proved essential in persuading skeptics in Washington that an opposition victory was feasible and worth backing.

In November Avramovic led a Serb opposition delegation, including Djindjic, to Washington where they met with Albright and others in the administration and in Congress. Albright promised that a change in government in Belgrade would lead not just to a lifting of American and European sanctions on Serbia but to substantial American and European economic assistance, as well.

One opposition leader who had not boycotted the previous parliamentary elections was Vuk Draskovic. After that election he had joined the government but was now once again in opposition. I met him for the first time at Djukanovic's safe house in Budva, where he was jumpy, histrionic, and only intermittently cogent. I met him again a few weeks later, shortly after a traffic "accident" that killed four of the people with whom he was traveling. He told me this had been an assassination attempt. I treated this charge with some skepticism at the time, but three years later several members of the Serb state security services were tried and convicted of murder for having arranged this attack.

I persuaded Draskovic to meet with Albright when both of them were in Berlin. On being introduced, Draskovic, with a characteristically theatrical show of old world courtesy, bowed and kissed Madeleine's hand. This gesture was photographed and publicized back home in Serbia where it went down badly, Madeleine's war still a living memory. In the end the courtship came to naught; Draskovic took refuge in Montenegro, where there was yet another attempt on his life. He and his party boycotted the September 2000 presidential ballot and played no role in the dramatic aftermath.

Draskovic was not the only opposition figure with reason to worry about his safety. Two others disappeared or were killed in the run-up to the 2000 election. Washington became increasingly concerned about Djukanovic's position. He controlled the Montenegrin police, but there were a number of Yugoslav military bases throughout his territory with army troops that Milosevic could employ to suppress the increasingly hostile Montenegrin regime. I consulted with Wes Clark, NATO's supreme commander at the time, about possible responses to any such move. Wes sketched out some possibilities, but I was skeptical that the administration would approve any military reaction. We did publicize NATO military exercises in the region in the hope this would raise some uncertainty in Belgrade about a possible NATO or U.S. response. We also provided Montenegro financial support. Nevertheless I thought we had to be candid about the dangers Djukanovic was running. Speaking to him privately during my next visit, I warned him that the United States would not be of any practical assistance should Milosevic move against him. He took the point but did not alter the course.

The most effective element of the Serbian opposition, and certainly the most appealing, was its youth movement, Otpor, or "Resistance." This student group, first organized in 1998, gained real momentum as the 2000 elections approached. It had a dispersed leadership, which made it more difficult to suppress, and practiced strict nonviolence. It organized increasingly massive rallies, often in the guise of rock concerts, and possessed a clear strategy to force regime change. This involved getting out the vote, defeating the government in the polls, and fostering a general strike in protest of the inevitable regime effort to fraudulently manipulate the outcome. We brought one of Otpor's young leaders to Washington, arranged meetings throughout the administration, and sent him back with enough funding to train and deploy 30,000 election monitors.

Doug Schoen's polling continued to favor an opposition victory provided its various factions united behind a single candidate. The State Department and USAID poured tens of millions of dollars into support for these parties. Most of this money went to civil society and independent media. The National Democratic and International Republican Institutes, both U.S. government-funded, provided political parties and activist organizations with advice, computers, and other material support. This aid was available to all parties. Milosevic's Socialist Party could have asked for a share but did not.

Other institutions independent of the American government lent support to the opposition. Prominent among these was the Open Society Foundation bankrolled by the American financier George Soros. We encouraged allied governments and nongovernmental organizations to become engaged. We also dispatched Bill Montgomery, a senior Foreign Service officer, to Budapest to coordinate the many strands of aid. Bill became, in effect, our resident representative to the opposition.

Serbia was surrounded by hostile neighbors. Hungary was a NATO member; Romania, Bulgaria, and Macedonia all wanted to be; Montenegro was moving toward secession; and Kosovo was garrisoned by 40,000 NATO troops. We coordinated efforts among all the neighboring governments, traded intelligence, and established a chain of radio and television broadcasts beaming anti-regime messages into what became known as "the ring around Serbia."

In the summer of 2000 I replaced Marc Grossman at the head of the European Bureau. Jesse Helms again blocked confirmation, but I, nevertheless, assumed the position on an acting basis and, subsequently, received a recess appointment from President Clinton. Jim O'Brien, a State Department lawyer and long-time aide to Madeleine Albright, succeeded me as the Balkan envoy, and Jim took over contacts with the Serb opposition. I continued to lead our participation in the Quint and Contact Group.

Jim and I had to deal with skeptics in Washington and Europe. Our intelligence agencies argued that Milosevic would win the election and remain in power, drawing both on history and an assessment of his capacity to mobilize voters and manipulate the process. They also cited polls that showed him leading. We were able to counter with the results of polling that Doug Schoen was doing for the opposition parties. If Schoen had not been Clinton's personal pollster with a record of success in calling races, I am not sure we would have won that argument.

Our key allies also had doubts. At a dinner with Quint ministers, several signaled their concern that we were overinvesting in a failing enterprise. Hubert Vedrine argued that Milosevic would manipulate the result whatever the actual vote count. I acknowledged that he would but said the discrepancies would be too large to disguise and the population would rise up to prevent him stealing the election. I urged we stay united behind a strategy that had a good prospect of success. Madeleine backed me, and the other ministers agreed to stay the course. By this time France had followed Germany in the presidency of the European Union. Gerard Errera, the French political director, and I worked closely together to ensure that the American and European advice to the Serbian opposition remained in synch.

Particularly aggravating was a report put out by the International Crisis Group just a few days before the Yugoslav election. The ICG is an independent analytical and advocacy organization with strong democratic credentials, and it urged the opposition parties to boycott the election. We hurried to counter this bad advice.

Events played out very much as hoped. Balloting for the presidency and other posts was held on September 24. Eighteen opposition parties had joined together to support the candidacy of Vojislav Kostunica after Dragoslav Avramovic fell ill. Otpor turned out enthusiastic crowds throughout the campaign. Its omnipresent slogan was: "He's finished." Voting put Kostunica well ahead of Milosevic, but the electoral commission claimed that neither candidate had surpassed the 50 percent threshold, thus requiring a second round of voting. The commission's figures were clearly fraudulent. As one example, it counted far more votes from Kosovo than there were Serb voters still living there.

Kostunica rejected the commission results, and workers, most notably the miners, went on strike. Thousands marched on Belgrade, some bringing along their heavy equipment. Massive crowds demanded Milosevic's ousting. Mayors and other local officials threw their support to the opposition. The demonstrations were largely peaceful, but some participants came armed. One striking miner used his earth moving wheel loader to force entry into the state television network, which was then taken over by the strikers. The uprising immediately became known as the Bulldozer Revolution. Momcilo Perisic urged the army to stay in its barracks, and the police refused to move against the demonstrators.

Igor Ivanov flew to Belgrade as concern about a violent denouement rose. Quint political directors debated whether Western governments should join Ivanov in trying to calm the situation. I insisted we do nothing of the sort. Events were playing out as hoped. We should allow them to take their course. Ivanov met with Milosevic, who agreed to step down, and Kostunica assumed the presidency. In December elections for the lower house of parliament were held, and Zoran Djindjic became prime minister.

A similar if less dramatic transformation was taking place in Croatia. Franjo Tudjman, the country's first president, had shared responsibility with Milosevic for the Bosnian civil war. Had he lived long enough, he, like Milosevic, would probably have been indicted as a war criminal. Tudjman was, however, already in failing health when I met with him in 1999. He remained unsatisfied with the Dayton settlement, and pressed me for the creation of a separate Croatian republic within Bosnia, which I dismissed as wholly unrealistic. His political party, the HDZ, maintained a strong criminal and political network among Bosnian Croats, thereby presenting a substantial obstacle to the healing of that country's ethnic divisions. In December Tudjman died, and in January 2000 the democratic, pro-European opposition won the parliamentary elections and formed a new government.

Following the fall of Milosevic, Dick Holbrooke paid another visit to Bosnia, where he publicly threatened to ban the largest Serb political party from competing in the upcoming national elections only weeks away. On his return Dick insisted the administration make good this threat, which he had discussed with no one in Washington. In a difficult Situation Room meeting I categorically refused to do so. Excluding the Serb Democratic Party from competing was not something we could do unilaterally. Our European partners were unlikely to agree, and banning a major political party didn't strike me as the best way for advancing democracy in the region, however offensive we found its leadership, record, and policies. Finally, I felt confident that the democratic changes that had just taken place in Croatia and Serbia made a breakdown of the Dayton peace much less likely.

TWENTY-TWO

Mending Transatlantic Relations

RELATIONS WITH EUROPE SOURED OVER Balkan policy during the first Clinton term. The Bush administration had been happy to leave that troubled region to Europe to sort out, and the Europeans had initially been pleased to try. The early Clinton administration, on the other hand, proved neither willing to follow the European lead nor to take on the burdens of leadership itself. Beginning in 1992 the Europeans committed troops under UN auspices to the war-torn regions of Bosnia and Croatia. Europe also backed a peace plan put forward jointly by a UN envoy, former American secretary of state Cyrus Vance, and an EU envoy, former U.K. foreign secretary David Owen. The United States neither committed troops nor supported the Vance-Owen peace plan. The preferred American alternative was to arm the Muslims and bomb the Serbs. With their troops on the ground vulnerable to Serb reprisal, the Europeans rejected this approach.

After several years of this transatlantic friction the Clinton administration bit the bullet and accepted the need to put American boots on the ground to enforce any settlement advanced by air power. This combination of air power and the promise of American ground forces to follow provided the leverage that allowed the United States to orchestrate the Dayton settlement. Dick Holbrooke's energetic and exigent style of statecraft produced results, but at the cost of some raw feelings. European governments were grateful for American leadership, but they were also humbled by their own collective failures. The most notable of these had been their failure to prevent the slaughter of more than 8,000 unarmed Muslim Bosniacs being protected by Dutch troops in Srebrenica.

This sense of inferiority and resentment lingered well beyond Dayton. The style of American diplomacy in the region did not change a great deal even after Dick returned to private life, not that he ever entirely withdrew from the field. American officials continued to see NATO and the European Union in some kind of competition for influence. Relations between the European high representative in Bosnia and the Americans heading the OSCE and UN missions were often strained. Washington continued to regard European efforts to bolster the European Union's capacity for security cooperation with suspicion.

In the Kosovo crisis allied unity proved the key to success. This was particularly the case once it became clear the bombing campaign was not going to yield quick results. Albright was very good at this task. Whereas her predecessor Warren Christopher came across as rather stiff and aloof, Albright was a warmer personality. In public, she adopted a tough, no-nonsense, straight-talking style, but in private she was a good listener and an amusing companion. She was direct and forceful when called for, but never patronized or talked down to her interlocutors. Her Quint and Contact Group colleagues remained the same throughout these years: Robin Cook for the UK, Hubert Vedrine for France, Joschka Fischer for Germany, Umberto Dini for Italy, and Igor Ivanov for Russia. The Kosovo air war created a bond among the Western ministers, each of whom recognized that their reputations, and perhaps their jobs, depended on the outcome. Ivanov was in much the same position. Years later, long after all these men had left office, Albright brought them together once a year to talk over world affairs and recall past collaboration.

I returned to European affairs after seven years working on Somalia, Haiti, and Latin America. The current Quint political directors were all unknown to me, though each was a rising star in his respective service. Indeed the Frenchman, Gerard Errera, had already achieved the highest professional slot in the French foreign ministry. On most issues the views of my British colleague, Emyr Jones Parry, were closest to my own, reflecting the general state of Anglo American relations. Errera and I, at least initially, were more frequently at variance. Gunter Pleuger, the German, generally tried to straddle these divides, while the Italian tended toward the French view and was always the most risk adverse.

Errera had previously served as the French ambassador to NATO, where he had been a thorn in the side of the American delegation and its Washington overseers. He was strongly committed to expanding the European Union's reach into foreign and security policy realms and saw NATO as an obstacle in this path, as, indeed, many American officials intended it to be. All my European colleagues, but particularly Errera, were constantly on guard for any sign that the United States was about to break ranks, engage in unilateral diplomacy, bully the Europeans into line, or seek to garner disproportionate media attention, all hangovers from the Dayton experience.

It quickly became apparent that if I could forge a good working relationship with Errera consensus within the larger group would follow. This turned out to be not all that difficult. I was more sympathetic to European aspirations for a better balanced transatlantic relationship than most American officials, and I had no patience with the common view that NATO and the European Union were locked in a zero sum contest for influence over issues of European security. Quint management of the Kosovo crisis had demonstrated just the opposite, that there was real synergy between the two organizations when their principal members were united and prepared to ignore the institutional jealousies that characterized both headquarters despite the fact they were located only a few miles from each other in Brussels.

Throughout the air war, these two organizations had marched in lockstep. NATO managed the war while, surprisingly, the European Union played the larger role in organizing the peace. European leaders and ministers met far more frequently in the EU framework than at NATO. At each such meeting statements were issued regarding the war and, in particular, the conditions for its cessation. Over time these conditions were refined and further defined, largely by the EU rather than NATO. The Western mediator who joined the Russian Chernomyrdin in bringing an end to the conflict was Finnish president Martti Ahtisaari. He represented the European Union, not NATO. Finland was not even a member of

NATO, yet its president was chosen in the first instance by Washington to represent the Western coalition in these negotiations.

The Finish president had been handpicked by Strobe Talbott precisely because his country was not belligerent. The United States was content to have the EU define and refine its war termination conditions because these issues were the topic of constant discussion within the Quint, where a strong consensus was developed and maintained, and the Quint's members had the preponderant weight within both NATO and the European Union.

Management of Western diplomacy throughout the Kosovo crisis was significantly aided by the happenstance that Germany was both president of the European Union and chair of the G-8 throughout the war. This dual leadership role ensured Quint influence over both the timing and content of discussion in both these forums, the latter of which included Russia. It also provided the Europeans two vehicles to profile their leadership through these critical months. Fischer and his team worked flat out to keep these forums aligned. Behind the scenes, Talbott was conducting some of the most critical diplomacy, but neither he nor anyone else on the U.S. side was seeking to hog the limelight.

Critics, including some who became influential in the next American administration, continued to refer dismissively to the Kosovo campaign as "war by committee," as if more unilateral assertion of American preferences would have yielded a better result. Given that NATO achieved all its original goals and suffered not a single casualty in the process, I regarded the Kosovo campaign as an unqualified success and an unexcelled model of coalition warfare, despite its rocky start.

On taking over the European Bureau in early 2000, I became responsible for the broader transatlantic relationship, including that between the United States and the European Union. Coincidentally, the French assumed the EU presidency, which meant that Vedrine would be Albright's counterpart for U.S.-EU relations and Errera mine. We had all played a role in the smooth NATO-EU collaboration throughout the Kosovo crisis, and I was convinced we could build on that experience to construct a more enduring link between those two organizations.

Errera was initially skeptical. He knew me, after all, as the author of the 1991 American démarche that bore my name opposing the development of a separate European defense capacity. This attempted American veto still rankled with committed Europeanists, but the subsequent disappearance of the Soviet Union and my own two years as representative to the European Community had altered my views considerably. I provided Errera with copies of the more forthcoming public remarks I had made on the topic during my Brussels assignment.

One of the silliest debates between Washington and its European allies was occasioned by American insistence that NATO should have "the right of first refusal" in meeting any particular crisis or demand for forces, with the EU able to act only if NATO chose not to do so. This position was logically flawed on several grounds. First, any such NATO decision would require unanimity and, thus, NATO could not exercise a "right of first refusal" if any of its EU members preferred the task to go to the EU. More fundamentally, however, this U.S. demand was premised on the view that the two organizations would vie for the privilege of taking on risky, demanding missions, whereas all experience demonstrated they would do just the opposite; that is, they would compete not to assume the burden. The whole history of Balkan diplomacy in the early 1990s demonstrated that buck passing rather than burden sharing was the default policy on both sides of the Atlantic. Finally, it was virtually certain that the Europeans would want the United States engaged in any costly, high-risk endeavor that might tax their capabilities, whereas the United States would be foolish to insist on joining any enterprise the Europeans were capable of mastering on their own.

Despite American opposition, the EU had made some progress toward defining a role for itself on defense and security affairs. An agreement between Paris and London reached in 1998 at St. Malo, France, had both advanced this EU agenda and led France to consider returning its forces to NATO's military command structure from which de Gaulle had removed them in 1967. Several intergovernmental bodies were created within the EU to give substance to these aspirations. The EU created the post of High Representative for Common Foreign and Security Policy, and Javier Solana left NATO to take up this new position. I felt there should be comparable movement on the NATO side to forge institutional links between the two organizations, but Errera feared that too close a NATO embrace would crush the delicate flower of Europe's Common Foreign and Security Policy (CFSP). Once he became persuaded that this was not my intent, however, we began crafting practical ways the two organizations could communicate and, ultimately, cooperate.

In September 2000 American and EU foreign ministers met on the fringes of the UN General Assembly session in New York for one of their regular exchanges. Vedrine, chairing the EU side, asked Errera and me to provide the ministers a brief overview on the state of the U.S.-EU relationship. Rather to the surprise of most present, both of us stated there were no outstanding differences between the two sides. This was certainly the first and maybe the last time such a report had been delivered to this audience.

By year's end Errera and I had put in place arrangements for NATO-EU collaboration that included regular meetings of the NATO Council with its EU counterpart and attendance by top NATO and EU representatives at the other organizations meetings. We had hoped to conclude an agreement for the use of NATO planning capacity and NATO common defense assets in support of EU military missions, but this ran into stiff opposition from Turkey. Ankara feared the European Union, influenced by its arch-rival Greece, might undertake military operations inimical to Turkey, for instance on behalf of Cyprus, which was itself on track to become an EU member. Ankara, therefore, opposed anything that might bolster European Union defense collaboration. The Turkish foreign minister was embarrassed and the Europeans pleasantly surprised when, at the December 1999 NATO foreign ministers meeting, Albright gave unqualified support to the proposed NATO-EU collaboration to which the Turks objected. The session went into several hours of overtime, but the Turks proved obdurate. The day ended, nevertheless, in the first-ever working dinner between NATO and EU foreign ministers.

A couple of months later I had another go at overcoming this impasse. My British colleague, Emyr Jones Parry, and I traveled to Istanbul for a meeting with our Turkish counterpart. The negotiation lasted into the early morning, and at its conclusion I was able to telephone Colin Powell, who had just taken over from Albright at State, to report success. The Turks had agreed to put in place the missing piece in the NATO-EU architecture. Unfortunately, by the time we all gathered in Brussels the following day, the Turkish military had vetoed what their foreign ministry had agreed to the night before.

Despite, even because of, this Turkish obstruction the United States conclusively demonstrated to its European allies that it was not opposed to the European Union assuming greater security responsibilities. Working together during the French EU presidency, Errera and I effectively concluded the long-running transatlantic debate I had helped open a decade earlier.

Since then the European Union has not sought to displace NATO as the guarantor of European security. Full institutional transparency between the EU and NATO continues to be blocked by Turkey and Cyprus. The EU has, nevertheless, conducted a number of military operations with varying degrees of NATO support, and EU troops took over from NATO peacekeepers in Bosnia in 2005, thereby freeing U.S. forces for other missions. The EU also took over a smaller NATO military mission on Macedonia, sent peacekeepers into Chad and the Democratic Republic of the Congo, and dispatched an anti-piracy task force into the Indian Ocean. The EU's military dimension remains modest but no one is blaming this lack of progress on the United States.

In January 2001 the Clinton administration was able to pass on to its successor a peaceful Europe and a healthy transatlantic relationship. The United States and the European Union had put in place a well-financed program for regional integration and economic growth, and Balkan governments were lining up for membership in the EU and NATO. Institutional rivalries between the two organizations had diminished, and modes of cooperation, formal and informal, had been established. Both of those institutions emerged stronger from the Kosovo experience, and each was cooperating with the other more closely than ever before. As a result of their joint efforts Bosnia had been pacified, Kosovo liberated, and Croatia and Serbia democratized. Serbia's democratic breakthrough created a new template for what later came to be labeled "color revolutions," in which Western support for civil society and democracy promotion helped bring about peaceful regime change.

TWENTY-THREE

A New Administration

I WAS, THEREFORE, SURPRISED AND disconcerted when the first issue the new administration placed on the interagency agenda was a proposal to withdraw American troops from Bosnia, and to do so entirely and immediately. Nothing could have done more to undermine what the United States had achieved in Europe from Dayton onward. Bosnia was hardly the most pressing issue facing the new administration. Indeed Bosnia was not even its most urgent problem in the Balkans. The NATO force in Bosnia originally had an authorized strength of 60,000, of which about a fourth were American, and these numbers had been drawn down over the subsequent five years by more than half. A further 50 percent cut was planned for announcement by NATO within a few weeks. But no one familiar with Bosnia thought the country would hold together and remain at peace without some continued peacekeeping presence.

Don Rumsfeld, the new secretary of defense, thought otherwise, however, or just didn't care. Rumsfeld was not alone in his disdain for the previous administration's efforts at nation-building. Many Republicans had sounded similar themes throughout the nineties. Condi Rice had written disparagingly of these operations during the recent presidential campaign and, as a candidate, George W. Bush had promised in a televised debate with Al Gore that there would be no nation-building during his administration. Rumsfeld's proposal was, thus, a logical extension of the campaign rhetoric and the Republican critique of nation-building.

Eight years earlier, when Bill Clinton succeeded George H. W. Bush, I had known almost no one among the incoming team, and I was treated by that team as a disposable hold-over. This time around, my position was even more precarious than it had been eight years earlier. I held a recess appointment as assistant secretary made by a Democratic president over objections from a Republican Congress, and I thought it likely I would be asked to leave on January 20 along with other Democratic political appointees, but this did not occur. Happily for me the Bush 43 national security team turned out to be heavily staffed by people I had worked closely with during Bush 41, including Condi Rice and Steve Hadley in the White House and Colin Powell and Rich Armitage at State. At Defense I knew the Deputy Secretary Paul Wolfowitz and Under Secretary for Policy Doug Feith. Paul had always been friendly, but Doug, during his stint as Richard Perle's deputy in the Reagan administration, had been a particularly tenacious opponent of pretty much anything the State Department wanted to do. He had mellowed somewhat in the intervening years without softening his ideological edge.

The Deputies Committee was convened for the first time by the new administration to discuss Bosnia. Steve Cambone, a senior aide to Rumsfeld, represented Defense, as I did State. Steve argued that the United States had intervened in Bosnia too early. If the fighting had been allowed to go on longer, greater exhaustion might have set in, a clearer outcome reached, and peacekeeping made easier. While the point had some analytical merit, it was politically, not to say morally, tone deaf. But I knew it would be futile to defend the Clinton record before a hostile audience, so I confined myself to noting that the administration could take credit for the 50 percent reduction in Bosnia troop levels tentatively planned for later in the year, while arguing that going beyond this could lead that country to unravel.

The issue next came before principals. This may have been Condi's first time in the chair, and she seemed slightly ill at ease. Powell and Rumsfeld had sat around this very table often enough before, whereas Condi had attended fewer Situation Room meetings and usually was in the back row.

Powell made the case for remaining committed in Bosnia on the grounds of alliance solidarity, arguing that the United States was committed to its NATO partners to see the mission through to completion. Whatever the new Pentagon leadership might think, these partners did not believe the mission had yet been accomplished. He left it to me to explain the operational need for a continued peacekeeping force.

Driving back to the State Department, I commented to Powell that Albright had sometimes looked to me to make the military case in these meetings, an area in which she was somewhat uncomfortable. I had not, however, expected him to do so. Powell replied that it wasn't that he knew too little about such matters but too much. Any attempt by him, a former chair of the joint chiefs, to challenge Rumsfeld on military grounds would only be resented and, therefore, doubly resisted.

On this occasion Powell's views prevailed. In a few weeks, when we traveled to his first meeting with NATO foreign ministers, he was able to assure his colleagues that "we went into Bosnia together and we will come out together."*

On the fringes of this NATO meeting Powell attended his first Quint dinner. Trouble was brewing in Macedonia, and this small country looked like the next bit of former Yugoslavia that could fall apart. Fighting had begun between ethnic Albanian militants and government security forces, and the Albanians, emboldened by the success of their kindred in Kosovo, were seeking some combination of autonomy and greater political rights, including making Albanian a second national language. At my suggestion we invited new EU High Representative Javier Solana to join our discussion. I knew the Bush administration would not be eager to take the lead in yet another nation-building venture, so I suggested to the ministers that Solana should be charged by both the United States and the European Union to mediate a solution to this crisis. Solana agreed to head for Skopje the very next day. I offered and he readily agreed

---

*In the event, this was not quite what happened. Four years later NATO turned responsibility for peacekeeping in Bosnia over to the European Union. Thus American troops left and Europeans stayed. But the troop levels required were even lower and the Europeans were eager to demonstrate their capacity for independent military operations under these less demanding circumstances. So the NATO mission ended happily for all concerned. And today, twenty years after the Dayton accords, a small peacekeeping force remains in Bosnia.

to take my deputy, Jim Swigert, with him. This partnership continued for the rest of the year, with EU and American envoys working in tandem, the European at the forefront, to halt the fighting and bring the conflict to a negotiated resolution.

Powell was less keen on foreign travel than Albright. I did, eventually, persuade him to make a visit to the Balkans, and to save time, we arranged for the foreign ministers of all the Balkan states to meet with Powell collectively in Skopje, the capital of Macedonia. This gathering had the virtue of sustaining international pressure on the Macedonian leadership to resolve their country's internal differences while, at the same time, providing Powell a quick exposure to the region as a whole. The Macedonian minister, who as host chaired the session, was clearly uneasy with this unfamiliar responsibility. He kept looking to me for guidance whenever anything unanticipated arose. Powell, who himself resisted working from prepared remarks, asked me with some amusement whether our Macedonian host was operating off a script I had provided him for the occasion. He was.

Several Balkan states were beginning to press for membership in the NATO alliance. Beginning as early as 1990 I had opposed taking former Warsaw Pact members into NATO. Such a step was inconsistent with the spirit, if not the letter, of assurances we had given Gorbachev in the context of German unification. Far from enhancing American security, the usual criteria for extending an alliance, expanding NATO would poison relations with Russia, the only European country that could conceivably threaten the United States. Sweden, Austria, and Finland had all lived in freedom and prosperity outside NATO throughout the Cold War, and I saw no reason the former Warsaw Pact countries could not do the same in its aftermath. On my return from Brussels in 1993 Holbrooke and I debated the issue before a wider audience; he for, I against. I also pressed my views with Talbott, who had just assumed responsibility for relations with Russia. But Russia was weak and the Central European states importunate. Their ethnic lobbies in the United States and Western Europe pressed for NATO membership. Perhaps most critically Germany decided it would like to have a buffer of allied states between it and Russia. And then, from 1993 to 1999, I was out of this loop, working instead on Africa, the Caribbean, and Latin America, and so without standing to engage further in the ongoing Washington debate. In 1997 Poland, Hungary, and the Czech Republic became the first Warsaw Pact member countries to join NATO.

Now the issue was posed again, this time regarding the Balkan and Baltic states. Almost a decade of conflict in southeastern Europe had convinced me of the need to integrate this fractious region into a larger whole via both NATO and EU membership. I was less convinced of the case for Latvia, Estonia, and Lithuania. These countries had not been Warsaw Pact members, but rather part of the Soviet Union, and earlier still, part of Imperial Russia, and had enjoyed only a brief period of independence between the two World Wars. Militarily, they were indefensible, too small to defend themselves and too isolated from the rest of NATO to be successfully defended by the United States and its allies. Like Berlin during the Cold War, only the threat of nuclear escalation could ward off a Russian attack, should it ever come to that. This did not seem to me to be a risk worth taking.

We discussed this issue among the Quint political directors. We were all agreed on the need to begin introducing Balkan members, and we were all doubtful about the wisdom of doing the same with the Baltics. I cautioned, however, that any expansion of NATO would require Senate confirmation, and said that the administration would be unlikely to get congressional support for bringing in Bulgaria and Romania without including Latvia, Lithuania, and Estonia, since the latter three countries had far greater sympathy and support among the American public. My colleagues took this aboard without enthusiasm. The following year all five of these countries plus Slovakia and Slovenia were invited to join the alliance.

The first foreign leader to visit President Bush was British prime minister Tony Blair, in a meeting held at Camp David. Bush, famously on time himself, was mildly impatient when Blair's helicopter arrived a few minutes late. After the initial introductions, a small group of us sat down for a working lunch. I had looked forward to an interesting tour of world issues, with Bush seeking Blair's views on any number of matters. This certainly would have been Bill Clinton's approach and, indeed, that of the older President Bush. Instead there was a carefully controlled exchange of pre-scripted talking points. The meal, like those in the White House itself, proceeded quickly, each course whisked away and replaced in quick succession. Bush read from a handful of 3x5 cards, and he asked no open-ended questions. Blair responded in kind, employing brief, carefully measured phrases, offering no unsolicited opinions. My sense was that the president, at this early point in office, was uneasy about venturing onto unfamiliar territory in front of a dozen people, half of whom he had never met, and that Blair, sensitive to this unease, was uncharacteristically reserved as well.

After the meal, Bush and Blair went for a long walk. At its conclusion, when asked by the press what he had learned, Bush replied that he had discovered they both used the same toothpaste. Clearly the two had bonded.

Powell was helicoptering back to Washington, and I was supposed to stay into the evening to participate in any further substantive conversations between the leaders. I thought these unlikely to occur and asked Powell to take me with him. On our way back, he told me of his pick for my successor, Beth Jones, a long-term Foreign Service colleague. She would be the first woman to head the European Bureau.

During these early months, Powell was holding his own against the more conservative and unilateralist elements in the administration. He prevailed on Bosnia, and the United States was supporting a modest nation-building effort in Macedonia, one that would eventually involve a small NATO military presence as well as American economic assistance. When an American military reconnaissance plane was forced to land in China, Powell took over the diplomacy needed to extract both plane and crew. Most remarkably, Powell secured administration agreement to scale back international sanctions against Iraq. Errera was frankly incredulous when I informed him of this intended policy shift for which I was seeking French support in the Security Council.

The hawks had won on two big issues. They persuaded President Bush to abrogation of the Anti-Ballistic Missile Treaty with Russia and they forced Powell to back off his plan to resume nuclear negotiations with North Korea. Yet within the administration the center was still holding, even on Iraq. This would change as a result of 9/11.

As I prepared to hand the European Bureau over to my successor, Colin Powell asked whether I would be willing to head our embassy in the Philippines. I readily assented, enchanted at this opportunity to return to my childhood home. I spent the next several weeks filling out the reams of paperwork needed to advance a presidential nomination and Senate confirmation. These forms were, of course, familiar, as I had completed the same for appointments to Argentina and the European Bureau, confirmation to both of which had been blocked by Jesse Helms. Three times lucky, I felt. This time I was to be nominated by a Republican president.

Further, the State inspector general's findings regarding my congressional testimony on Haiti five years earlier had finally been overturned on appeal.

Powell spoke personally to both Jesse Helms and Congressman Dan Burton. No luck. Helms made it clear that as long as he remained in office the Senate would never confirm me for this or any other post. Powell broke the bad news to me as gently as he could, assuring me he had every intention of continuing to find use for me in the department. I saw little prospect of meaningful work, however, and prepared to retire.

TWENTY-FOUR

Another War, Another Assignment

THANKS TO JESSE HELMS, I wasn't in Manila when the twin towers were hit. I was, in fact, on my way to my car's annual safety inspection. When news that the second plane had hit came on the air, the mechanic checking my brake lights shook his head. "I don't know why they do this," he said. "It will just drive us together." So true, at least for a while.

It was then reported that both the Pentagon and the State Department had been struck. I headed to the latter, worried about my son who worked directly across the street from the department. A confused policeman diverted my car onto a ramp that took me over the Potomac and directly in front of the burning Pentagon. Realizing that all the roads in this vicinity were likely to be soon blocked by police and emergency vehicles, I headed up the river, crossing over several miles upstream. By this time it was clear the State Department had not been hit, so I drove home and ascertained that Toril and both my sons were safe. I spent the rest of that lovely, sunny, late-summer day watching the horror unfold on national television.

232

The next morning I was back at the department, but with no work to do. I still had an office and a secretary, but no responsibilities. The next few weeks were painful, as everyone else in the building hurried about on work of national importance while I was entirely idle. Relief came in a call from Marc Grossman, who had replaced Pickering as under secretary for political affairs. Marc said Colin Powell wanted me to serve as the administration's envoy to the Afghan opposition. Powell was reflecting the wider administration concern that the diplomatic aspects of the Afghan campaign were not keeping pace with the military. Specifically he was worried the Taliban regime would fall before a successor government was ready to take its place. My assignment was to produce such a successor regime, thereby forestalling the necessity for an American military occupation.

I was eager to join the national response to 9/11 and happy to postpone retirement. I spent the next few days learning about the military and intelligence campaign already underway, and the thinking, such as it was, about our political objectives. Responsibility for developing policy on post-Taliban Afghanistan was somewhat dispersed. At State, Richard Haass, policy planning director, and Christina Rocca, head of the South Asia Bureau, both had a role. At the NSC, Zalmay Khalilzad worked the political side of the war while Frank Miller coordinated the military. All these people except Rocca were well known to me from prior administrations.

The administration did not want to govern Afghanistan even for a day if they could avoid it. Neither was there any desire to parlay with the Taliban. The intent was to drive the current regime from power, employing to the maximum extent possible local Afghan forces for that purpose, and to replace it with a new government drawn from the various strands of the opposition. This opposition was divided between expatriates and armed groups fighting within Afghanistan, between Pashtuns and non-Pashtuns, and between Royalists and non-Royalists. Our strategy required all of these divides to be bridged. This would be my job.

The United Nations would be critical to the success of this effort. John Negroponte had replaced Dick Holbrooke at the United Nations. John, like Dick, had been a colleague three decades earlier, during the Vietnam peace talks. We discussed the situation over lunch at John's club. Lakhdar Brahimi, my UN partner in Haiti, had already spent several years trying unsuccessfully to broker peace in Afghanistan, and in the aftermath of 9/11 Kofi Annan had brought Lakhdar back. He and Kofi had established a core group of interested countries comprising the six states bordering Afghanistan plus the United States and Russia. Foreign ministers from these eight countries were to meet in New York with Kofi and Lakhdar in a week's time.

Bob Blackwill also came to see me. He had recently returned to government as Bush's ambassador to India. Bob feared the Afghan crisis and the prominence it would give to Pakistan in Washington's eyes would distract the administration from its intended rapprochement with India. He stressed that India, too, was an important player in Afghanistan, having joined Iran and Russia in providing material assistance to the anti-Taliban resistance groups known collectively as the Northern Alliance.

Wes Clark, then in private life, called me to offer his services as my military adviser, the same role he had played for Holbrooke at Dayton. I was impressed with his desire to serve, even in a subordinate capacity, in this time of national crisis, but knew it would never fly. Wes was the poster boy for Clinton administration nation-building and war by committee. Rumsfeld and, particularly, Hugh Shelton, still the JCS chair, would be apoplectic. Tommy Franks, the regional commander overseeing the war in Afghanistan, would not be pleased either. I apprised Powell of the offer and he agreed it was a non-starter.

I spent a half day at CIA headquarters where John McLaughlin, the deputy director, and his staff briefed me on the activities of the agency's paramilitary teams operating in support of several insurgent commanders. These local forces were mostly drawn from non-Pashtun populations in the north of the country. There were also efforts, much less advanced, to mobilize armed resistance among the southern Pashtun tribes. The CIA teams had led the way with bags of money, and U.S. Special Operations Forces (SOF) were about to arrive on the battlefield. SOF would bring with them the capacity to more precisely mark Taliban units for aerial bombardment.

I next flew to Central Command headquarters in Tampa, Florida, to meet General Tommy Franks. While we were talking, one of his staff interrupted to say, "We have him. He is in a helo crossing the Pak border." Franks explained that his aide was referred to Hamid Karzai, a member of the Pashtun opposition in Pakistan. Karzai had recently entered Afghanistan in the hope of raising resistance to the Taliban, and the U.S. military had just rescued him from encirclement by Taliban fighters. This was the first I heard of Hamid Karzai.

Franks was under pressure from Washington to produce results and anxious about the slow pace of the campaign. I recalled the Kosovo air war, and advised that if he could make every day a bit worse for the enemy than the day before, at some point his adversary would crack. Franks seemed comforted by this observation.

From my reading of the intelligence it was evident that the pre-9/11 conflict in Afghanistan had largely been a proxy war between Pakistan, backing the Taliban, and Iran, India, and Russia, backing the Northern Alliance, a war that had largely been won by Pakistan and the Taliban. In a meeting with Bill Burns, then head of State's Middle East Bureau, I said I would have to work with Iran, along with all the other external protagonists in this struggle, if I were to be able to pull together a government with any prospect of enduring. Bill cautioned that direct contact with Iran was largely forbidden. I persisted and Powell subsequently gave me a green light for such discussions as long as I stuck to Afghan-related issues.

I called on Paul Wolfowitz, Rumsfeld's top deputy, and asked, as I had of McLaughlin at the CIA, that he assign someone to travel as part of my team. It was important that all the key players in Washington be kept apprised of my progress and that I be kept informed on theirs. I also raised the sensitive issue of an international peacekeeping force, noting that the Afghan expatriate leaders were unlikely to return to Kabul unless international troops were deployed for their protection. I knew Paul and his boss would be unenthusiastic about anything that looked like nation-building so only mentioned this in passing. Paul acknowledged the likelihood of such a request, which I took as reluctant acquiescence.

My last call in Washington was to see Rice and Hadley. Both received me warmly and were fully comfortable with my plan of action. I would next travel to New York to see Brahimi, join Powell for his meeting there with the regional powers and Russia, and then head out to the region. Rice promised to arrange military airlift for my in-theater travel.

Richard Haass and I traveled to New York to prepare for the "six plus two" ministers meeting. We were joined by Russian, Chinese, Pakistani, Uzbek, Turkmen, and Tajik officials. Haass pointed out to me the Iranian representative, Javad Zarif, who, he said, spoke better English than I did. Brahimi chaired the session. We reviewed a draft of the communiqué the ministers would issue the following Monday, and the Pakistani and Iranian representatives got into an obscure argument about a particular passage in the document. This took a while to sort out but we eventually agreed on a text calling for the United Nations to help the Afghans establish a broad-based, multi-ethnic, politically balanced, freely chosen alternative to the Taliban regime.

The meeting concluded, and I walked to the Waldorf Astoria on Park Avenue where President Bush would be arriving the following day. The hotel was already packed with American officials, including Zal Khalilzad, and we had dinner while we talked over the latest news from Afghanistan. He told me that the hitherto static ground campaign had finally broken open, and the northern city of Mazar-e-Sharif had fallen to rebel forces. The fight was now moving toward the capital, Kabul. This created a dilemma for Washington. Over the past several weeks, administration officials had argued about the limits of American assistance to the Northern Alliance. As its name suggested, this assemblage of insurgent groups was made up largely of Persian-speaking ethnic Tajik, Uzbek, and Hazara fighters from the north of the country. Taliban strength rested primarily with the Pashtu-speaking tribes located mostly in the south. Some Pashtun opponents of the Taliban, like Hamid Karzai, were trying to raise insurgent groups in the south, but so far with limited success. Yet Pashtuns represented at least half the country's population. Pakistan, under strong American pressure, had for the time being ceased to support the Taliban, but Pakistani officials were pressing the United States not to allow the Northern Alliance to move into Kabul or into the Pashtun-dominated areas in the south. At a principals meeting earlier in the day Powell had successfully argued that the United States should condition further support for the Northern Alliance on its not taking Kabul. Rather the Northern Alliance should await the arrival of a then-nonexistent United Nations peacekeeping force. Zal and I agreed that this bargain, even if struck, was unlikely to be honored.

I returned to UN headquarters the following morning where I brought Errera and several other European officials up-to-date on our plans. America's NATO allies had unanimously declared 9/11 to be an armed attack on the entire alliance. Despite this gesture of solidarity, the Bush administration was fending off most allied offers of assistance, and there were practical reasons for doing so. Most European governments had no capacity to deploy and sustain forces at such a great distance, but the attitude also reflected a post-Kosovo aversion to war by committee. For this I had no sympathy. If we did not need our allies now, we would need them soon enough.

I next met Brahimi for coffee in the staff cafeteria overlooking the East River. For some weeks the UN and the United States had each been trying to bring together the various elements of the anti-Taliban opposition, so far to no effect. I urged Brahimi to announce the date and locale of a conference that would form the next Afghan government, letting it be understood than any who chose not to attend would be left out of the resultant process. Brahimi wanted to be sure the most important factions would come before he announced a date and he looked to me to secure that agreement.

As we talked, it became clear that Brahimi and I had somewhat divergent visions of how this eventual conference would be structured. Brahimi wanted to sequester Afghan representatives away from any outside influence, much as he had done in mediating settlement of the Lebanese civil war twelve years earlier. I countered that, as had occurred with the Bosnia and Kosovo settlements, some of the most important bargains were likely to be struck between the external parties, and I did not see their exclusion as likely to be productive. Brahimi conceded that he could not succeed without American involvement, and he could not grant the United States access while excluding everyone else, so agreed to think about the matter further.

After spending Sunday with my family in Washington, I returned to New York for the six-plus-two minister's meeting. As I waited in front of UN headquarters for Powell to arrive, there was a sudden commotion. Word passed from mouth to mouth that an airliner had just crashed across the river in Queens. Joschka Fischer came over to wish me well on my mission. We both assumed this downed plane was the result of another terrorist attack.

Powell arrived moments later and we proceeded to our meeting, where Kofi Annan chaired. Each minister read a statement, and then they agreed to the communiqué we had prepared the previous Friday. The Iranian foreign minister, Kamal Kharazi, said Iran stood with the United States in the face of terrorist incidents such as the one that had just occurred that morning. One of his aides came over with a copy of Kharazi's prepared text, showing us where this additional remark had been inserted in the minister's own hand. At the conclusion of the meeting Powell went around the room shaking hands with each participant, including Kharazi, and this simple gesture proved the most newsworthy aspect of the session.

We emerged to learn all of Manhattan Island's bridges and tunnels had been closed. The city was on lockdown, and this was going to pose difficulties to catching my flight overseas that afternoon. I arranged to join Powell's police-escorted motorcade, and by the time we arrived at Kennedy the crash earlier in the day had been determined an accident, not a terrorist attack. My flight to Rome left on time, almost completely empty.

Our team assembled for the first time the next morning. From State I had Craig Karp, one of the few FSOs familiar with Afghanistan. The United States had closed its embassy in Kabul more than a decade earlier. The joint staff sent Colonel Jack Gill, a student of the Napoleonic Wars and also a South Asia expert. Two officials came from Rumsfeld's staff, Bill Luti and Larry Franklin. Luti was a former naval officer who had worked for House Speaker Newt Gingrich and, more briefly, Vice President Cheney. Franklin was a career civil servant. The CIA representative, Phil Mudd, had most recently been working for Khalilzad on the NSC staff. Phil and his colleagues would provide my only link to the opposition figures actually fighting inside Afghanistan.

Gathering at the embassy, we received the overnight news from Washington that the Northern Alliance had agreed not to enter Kabul. As a result, U.S. aircraft had begun pounding Taliban defenses around the former Soviet airbase at Bagram, just north of the city. Indications were that the Taliban planned to abandon rather than defend the capital.

We were in Rome to meet with the former king of Afghanistan, Zahir Shah. We intended to fly from Rome to Tajikistan to meet with the political leadership of the Northern Alliance, but as our team gathered for lunch at a floating restaurant moored in the Tiber we learned that the people we needed to see at our next stop were not going to be available, having all gone into Afghanistan to be closer to the fast moving frontlines. Scrambling to rearrange our itinerary, the six of us spent most of what should have been a pleasant meal in a lovely locale on our cell phones. Gill called the Pentagon's National Command Center to reroute our plane, Mudd spoke with the CIA task force asking them to track down key Afghan interlocutors, and Karp alerted the State Department's Operation Center to our changing plans. This was in the early days of mobile phones, before such boorish behavior became common, and the restaurant's other patrons looked with wonder at six Americans who spent an entire meal eating with one hand and holding a phone to their ear with the other.

That evening we motored out to see the former king at his suburban villa. After ruling Afghanistan for forty years Zahir was overthrown in 1973 and had resided in Italy ever since. He received us in his home, a comfortable but unpretentious house in a gated community, remarkable only for the squad of armed Carabinieri guarding it. We found the former king surrounded by a dozen or so family members and courtiers. Sitting around the coffee table in his living room, Zahir spoke to us of his desire to work with the Northern Alliance and other elements of the opposition to form a broadly based successor government. He pledged that his supporters would attend the conference Brahimi was intending to call.

Zahir was then eighty-seven years old. He was alert but frail, speaking in a soft, barely audible voice. He stressed that he was seeking no formal role for himself, but he was, nevertheless, the leader of an important component of the Afghan émigré community, one which favored a restoration of the monarchy. His commitment to be represented at Brahimi's conference was an important step in my effort to bring that meeting to pass.

The Italian authorities provided us a motorcycle escort that took us back into Rome at breakneck speed through evening rush hour; in the process we lost our side view mirror to a passing car. Over dinner our team continued to discuss our forthcoming mission, and I opined that success in forming a broadly based government would require the support of all the key regional states, including Iran. Bill Luti became agitated, protesting against any dealings with that government. I replied that Iran, Russia, and India were the major long-term supporters of the Northern Alliance, and until our recent entry into the conflict, they were the major opponents of the Taliban. Any one of these three governments probably had enough influence to sabotage our efforts if they chose. It made sense, therefore, to engage all of them. Luti would have none of this. His protestations soon became so loud as to disturb the other patrons, leading me to change the subject. Once again a group of boorish Americans were observed not giving an excellent meal the attention it deserved.

The following morning we flew to Ankara where we met with Turkish officials. One of these suggested that Hamid Karzai would make a good candidate to head the new Afghan government. Returning to the airport for our onward flight to Islamabad, we found that the Air Force had switched out our small Learjet for a C-17 military cargo plane large enough to accommodate an M1 Abrams tank or several hundred soldiers in full combat gear. With just our small group aboard, there seemed enough floor space for a game of full court basketball.

We arrived in Pakistan late that evening. While we had been in the air the Northern Alliance forces had entered Kabul despite their promise not to do so, and so we spent the following day listening to every unhappy Pakistani official. They predicted a violent Pashtun reaction and destructive fighting for control of the city, as had happened in the mid-nineties, the last time northern forces had taken the city. Pakistani officials insisted that Pashtuns were the majority in Afghanistan, that Pashtun rulers had always governed Afghanistan, and that they should continue to do so in the future. Unstated was the Pakistani insistence on a government in Kabul amenable to Pakistan's influence.

Mostly what we heard was complaints, but the head of Pakistan's Inter-Service Intelligence unit, the ISI, did have one constructive suggestion. Unprompted, he suggested Hamid Karzai as an acceptable candidate to head the next Afghan government.

The following day was spent in Peshawar, the capital of the Northwest Frontier Province. Several million Afghan refugees had taken up residence in Pakistan over the past couple of decades and many were settled in or near this city. We met with several of their most prominent figures, and from them we heard more of the same complaints about the Northern Alliance. On my return to the embassy Christina Rocca called from Washington to say Powell wanted me to go to Kabul. Tommy Franks called with the same message, but neither State nor Defense offered me any way to get there. In the end it was the CIA that did so.

Gary Berntsen, the CIA officer attached to the Northern Alliance leadership, had for several days been trying to persuade its foreign minister, Abdullah Abdullah, to meet with me. Phil Mudd reported that Abdullah would be available the following morning in Tashkent, the capital of Uzbekistan. We took our C-17 up and over the Afghan battlefields and then drove to the home of our ambassador in Tashkent for the meeting. Berntsen was the first to arrive. He was very intense, likely having been running on adrenaline for some time. Berntsen said Abdullah was a serious and influential figure within the Northern Alliance. He reported that things were quiet in Kabul and offered to fly us there, where we could all stay with his agency team.

Abdullah arrived a few minutes later. He was young, poised, and articulate, with a very precise delivery and carefully chosen words. We got right to business. Abdullah was anxious to explain why the Northern Alliance forces had entered Kabul despite their promise not to do so. He also wanted to complain about British troops showing up uninvited at Bagram airfield immediately after its capture by Northern Alliance troops. He expressed a willingness to attend Brahimi's conference but wanted it held in Kabul. He also objected to the Northern Alliance representatives being treated on a par with three other opposition groups largely made up of émigrés who had contributed nothing to the imminent fall of the Taliban.

As we proceeded through these issues, Abdullah struck a conciliatory note. The Northern Alliance had not anticipated the Taliban would abandon Kabul when they had agreed not to enter the city. Once it became apparent that the former regime had absconded, it became necessary for Northern Alliance military and police forces to enter the city to prevent looting and sectarian violence. In the event, the entry had, indeed, been orderly; there were no reports of looting, and the city was calm. I accepted this explanation without demure. Regarding the British arrival at Bagram, I said I was sure the lack of prior coordination was an oversight and promised that it would not be repeated.

On the key issue, whether the Northern Alliance would attend Brahimi's conference, Abdullah proved flexible. He said they preferred the meeting take place in Kabul, but would go elsewhere. They would resist being treated as one of four equal factions, but would not allow this to derail the meeting. In sum, I had what I had come for, a Northern Alliance commitment to join the royalist faction and other opposition figures at a UN-hosted meeting where a new government would be formed. To pin this down I suggested and Abdullah agreed that we hold a joint press conference to announce the accord.

Abdullah proposed that I fly with him back to Afghanistan the following morning to meet the rest of the Northern Alliance leadership. We left at dawn on a CIA-chartered transport otherwise filled with cargo. On the way Abdullah told me he and a couple of other key Northern Alliance leaders recognized that leadership of the new government would need to go to a Pashtun and a non-Northern Alliance figure, and he suggested Hamid Karzai for this role. It was at this point that I began to suspect my task might prove to be easier than I had anticipated. If both the ISI and the Northern Alliance foreign minister, otherwise mortal enemies, suggested the same individual to head the new government, how hard could it be to get wider agreement? Abdullah warned me, however, that

Northern Alliance president Rabbani and others in the leadership were likely to resist ceding the top job.

As we approached Bagram the head of my security team offered a piece of advice: "If it isn't paved, don't step on it." The airfield and its surrounding area had been a no man's land between the two sides until a few days ago, and it was still heavily mined. On arrival we were greeted by an Afghan honor guard and ushered into a couple of ancient Mercedes sedans for a brief drive, over an unpaved road, to one of the few buildings that still possessed a roof; no windows, but a roof. Inside I was introduced to President Rabbani, a dignified, white-bearded gentleman in traditional robes. The rest of the assembled leaders, all a generation younger, wore battledress or Western garb.

Rabbani expressed gratitude for American assistance. I responded by stressing the need to move quickly to form a more broadly based government. After our initial exchange Rabbani returned to Kabul, and our discussion continued; each of the remaining members of the leadership made a short statement, to which I replied, one after the other. Marshal Fahim, the defense minister, led by explaining, much as Abdullah had done the day before, why they had felt the need to move forces into Kabul despite having promised not to do so. Yunis Qanuni, the interior minister, repeated the various reservations regarding the location and participation in the proposed UN conference, but like Abdullah the day before he stressed that these were "concerns, not conditions." I took this as a firm commitment, expressed before the full Northern Alliance leadership, that their representatives would show up when and where Brahimi set his conference.

After about a dozen exchanges of this sort, we were shown to an adjoining room where a vast array of barbequed meats and vegetables was spread before us. It being Ramadan, the Afghans could not join in the repast. The sole exception was Fahim, who suffered from diabetes and had a religious dispensation due to his need for regular nourishment. While we lunched members of Berntsen's CIA team rounded up a couple of Western journalists, which allowed Abdullah and me to announce for a second time that the Northern Alliance was ready to attend the upcoming UN meeting.

On our return to the airfield a group of bearded soldiers in loose formation approached. I assumed it was another Afghan honor guard, a bit less snappy than the one for our arrival, and it was only when they approached within speaking distance that I realized these were American soldiers. They were led by Colonel John Mulholland, the senior U.S. American military officer in Afghanistan. He asked me to say a few words to his men, and I have seldom felt so unequal to the occasion. Here were the handful of soldiers who had just conducted one of the most daring and rapidly decisive military campaigns in history. I told them that America's role in Afghanistan was just beginning, but theirs would never be forgotten.

The CIA took us back to Tashkent where we rendezvoused with our C-17 and flew on to Washington, arriving Thanksgiving eve.

Brahimi accepted an offer from the German government to host his conference. The venue was to be the same government guesthouse on the Petersburg where Albright and I had negotiated the UN Security Council resolution that ended the Kosovo air war two years earlier. Since then, the German government and the American embassy had moved to Berlin. My old house across the river was now vacant, having been traded for property in Berlin.

Arriving a couple days early for the conference, I met individually with most of the external players. Thomas Matussek, who had been an aide to Hans-Dietrich Genscher during my years in Bonn, was in charge of arrangements for the meeting. His team would control access to the conference site. A major effort would be made to keep numbers down, but Matussek agreed that an exception would be made for the Americans, provided we were discreet.

The Indians sent a distinguished former diplomat who had been their ambassador to Pakistan, S. K. Lambah. The Russians were represented by the appropriately named Zamir Kabulov, a long-time Afghan expert from the foreign ministry. Iran was represented by its deputy foreign minister, Javad Zarif, whom I had seen but not spoken with in New York. The British representative was Robert Cooper, a diplomat attached to Prime Minister Blair's staff in the Cabinet Office.

Pakistan sent a relatively junior diplomat who had, until a few days earlier, headed its embassy to the Taliban regime in Kabul. His was a difficult task, representative to a conference otherwise almost entirely made up of Pakistan's regional and Afghan enemies. He spent most of the conference sitting by himself in a distant, otherwise unoccupied, lounge, shunned by most of the participants.

Lambah became the fourth person to suggest to me that Hamid Karzai would make a good candidate for leadership of the new government.

This idea had certainly achieved a certain momentum, it having already been suggested by the Turkish foreign ministry, the Pakistani ISI, and the Northern Alliances top diplomat. Comparing notes with Lambah over lunch I found American and Indian objectives for the meeting were similar. Subsequently I met with the Russian, Kabulov, who also cited Karzai as a good candidate, although he was pessimistic that the conference would agree on this or anything else of consequence.

My delegation again included Craig Karp from State, Jack Gill from the joint staff, and Phil Mudd from the CIA. Luti again represented Rumsfeld's office, and brought along another of his subordinates, Harold Rhode. In addition several officers from our missions in Pakistan and Central Asia joined us; they were familiar with most of the émigré Afghan participants in the conference and would help us keep abreast of discussions among the various factions. Finally, Zal Khalilzad from the NSC also joined the delegation. Zal had been raised in Afghanistan and spoke native Dari, the Afghan form of Persian spoken by the northern population and by educated Pashtuns. He had long-established relationships with most of the leading Afghans and would prove invaluable in the coming days.

Earlier, in New York, I had asked Brahimi to let the Iranians know I was ready to work with them. On the eve of the conference I received a message from that delegation inviting me to meet at their hotel. I asked Zal to join me, and Luti also wanted to come. I rebuffed his request, knowing how strongly he opposed any such conversations. Zarif had not yet arrived. We met with Mohammad Taherian, the Iranian ambassador to the Northern Alliance, and a couple of Zarif's subordinates from the foreign ministry. The Iranians presented their objectives for the conference in terms largely matching our own, and they, too, proposed Hamid Karzai as a potential leader of the new government. His bandwagon was definitely rolling.

The next morning I briefed my delegation on the meeting. Luti and Rhode grumbled and said they would be leaving the next day, I assumed to return to Washington. Six years later, on reading former CIA director George Tenet's memoirs, I discovered that Luti and Rhode went on to Rome, not back to the United States, where they met with violent opponents of the Iranian regime to discuss the possibility of Pentagon funding for an effort at its overthrow. According to Tenet, this initiative was taken behind the backs of the White House, the State Department, and the CIA, and was terminated, with difficulty, only after Tenet and Powell complained to Rice and Hadley. As Luti later took up a senior position on the NSC staff, the White House can't have been too displeased.

Larry Franklin, the Pentagon bureaucrat who accompanied Luti on our first trip, was later tried and convicted on espionage related charges for passing classified information about Iran to the Israeli government.

Brahimi had invited twenty-five leading Afghan personalities to the meeting, divided among four delegations, of which the Northern Alliance and the royalists, also known as the Rome Group, were the two most important. The other two factions represented were the Peshawar Group, drawn from émigrés based in Pakistan, and the Cyprus Group, made up of mostly younger émigrés who had met periodically in Cyprus and were said to have links to Teheran.

Watching these Afghans arrive at the Petersburg, I was impressed by the warmth with which delegates from the various factions greeted each other, often with hugs and what appeared to be genuine expressions of regard. This was my first inkling that the sectarian and factional passions in Afghanistan might not approach those we had observed in the former Yugoslavia or those we would later encounter in Iraq.

Brahimi had met me halfway with the arrangements for access to this conference. The non-Afghan observers would work, eat, and sleep in the same building as the Afghans. Thus all main external actors would be present, but we non-Afghans would not actually participate in the formal sessions, which would involve only Brahimi, his staff, and the Afghans.

The conference opened on November 27 with a welcoming speech by Joschka Fischer. Hamid Karzai was also invited to deliver remarks via satellite phone from the outskirts of Kandahar where Karzai and his recently raised rebel force were seeking to take the Taliban's home base and last bastion. Brahimi, who had arranged for this intervention, had also apparently gotten on the Karzai bandwagon.

The conference soon fell into a pattern. It was Ramadan and even the more cosmopolitan of the Afghans were being scrupulously observant of the daylong fast as well as the ban on alcohol. Recalling the festivities that had accompanied earlier diplomatic gatherings, most famously the Congress of Vienna in 1815, I wondered jokingly how a conference at which everyone was jet lagged, hungry, and sober could have any chance of success.

The Afghans worked late into the night and slept through the morning, reappearing only in late afternoon. We internationals, being excluded from these late-night sessions, kept more normal hours, spending the mornings consulting among ourselves and the afternoon lobbying the Afghans. As part of this routine, I had coffee and pastry each morning with the German, Italian, and Iranian representatives. (The Iranian delegation was postponing their fast until their return to Teheran.) On the third morning of the conference, we received a draft of the document Brahimi had circulated the previous evening that was to serve as the conference's final conclusions.

Zarif commented that this paper made no mention of democratic elections. "Don't you think the new Afghan regime should be committed to hold democratic elections?" he asked. I allowed that this seemed a reasonable suggestion, and Zarif, with a twinkle in his eye, went on to note that the document also made no mention of international terrorism. "Don't you think the Afghans should pledge to cooperate in combating such terrorists?" he asked. Again I agreed, sure at this point that Zarif was having a bit of fun at my expense, presenting Iran as the promoter of democracy and scourge of international terrorism. He was also making two significant points, however: that Iran was measurably more democratic than any of America's Arab allies and that Iran was opposed to the two extremist groups then of greatest concern to the United States, the Taliban and Al Qaeda.

For the first few days I confined myself to urging the various Afghan factions to converge while refraining from getting involved in the specifics. I also sought to keep as low a media profile as possible, speaking to the press only on background so as to keep the UN and the Afghans in the foreground. The last thing I wanted was to have a "made in the USA" label attached to the outcome of this meeting.

I had no written instructions and only the most general of oral guidance. My job was to get an agreement, and almost any agreement would do so long as it resulted in an Afghan government that could replace the Taliban, unite the opposition, secure international support, cooperate in hunting down Al Qaeda remnants, and relieve the United States of the need to occupy and run the country. No one in Washington had ever suggested that Karzai should be our candidate to head this government. On this and much else I was given a free hand.

I collaborated with Robert Cooper, the UK representative, in crafting language in the final declaration calling for a peacekeeping force. Many of the Afghan representatives wanted a countrywide international military presence, but Cooper and I knew that neither London nor Washington was ready to take on such a role. We, therefore, persuaded the Afghans to confine their request to a force that would secure Kabul. This would provide enough security to encourage the émigré leaders, who feared the Northern Alliance as much as they did the Taliban, to return to the capital. The final Bonn Declaration made only a very general reference, therefore, to the possibility of a wider mandate for this force at some future date.

Having floated this language I accosted Zarif at breakfast to complain about an article in that morning's *Paris Herald Tribune*. His foreign minister was quoted saying that a peacekeeping force for Kabul would not be necessary. "You and I agreed on the inclusion of a call for an international force in this agreement," I said. "Why is your foreign minister being quoted to the contrary?"

Zarif responded, "You can consider my minister's comments a gesture of solidarity with Don Rumsfeld. After all, Jim, you and I are both way out in front of our instructions on this one, aren't we?"

This was true enough. Zarif's agreement held, and there were no further difficulties from Teheran on this point.

The meeting was intended to last one week, and an association of dentists was scheduled to hold its convention in the facility upon our departure. As this deadline approached, the meeting deadlocked; the Afghans could not agree on who should lead the new government. They could not even agree on how such a person should be chosen. The Rome Group wanted Zahir Shah to head the government or at least to name its head, and this the Northern Alliance side would not accept. To break the deadlock I put forward a proposal, first to Brahimi and then, with his blessing, to each of the Afghan groups. Under its terms, the Rome Group would be accorded the privilege of nominating the leader, but their nominee would require the consent of the other three groups. I knew Karzai was a member in good standing of the royalist faction and the only one of its number the Northern Alliance would likely accept. So I figured this arrangement would satisfy the royalist sense of prerogative while ultimately producing Karzai as the consensus candidate. Khalilzad called the former king in Rome and secured his blessing for this arrangement.

This stratagem almost went awry when the royalists nominated, instead, someone the Northern Alliance did not want but would not block. The Rome Group's initial candidate was Abdul Sattar Sirat, the leader of their delegation. Sirat was a professor of Islamic law at a Saudi university.

He was old enough to have served as a minister in the king's government before his overthrow twenty-eight years earlier. A distinguished and highly respected individual, Sirat did not seem by age, temperament, or profession to be ideally suited to the task of leading a divided, war-torn country. I went to see Yunis Qanuni, the leader of the Northern Alliance group, who, I assumed, would veto this nomination, thereby requiring the Rome Group to nominate someone else. But when I inquired, Qanuni replied, "I can't do that. Sirat is my wife's cousin."

Eventually it fell to Brahimi, seconded by Matussek, the German host, to tell Sirat that he should withdraw his candidacy to open the way for someone with a wider appeal, and Sirat reluctantly did so. The Rome Group then nominated Karzai, who quickly secured the approval of the other three factions.

Hamid Karzai called me a couple of times during the conference, not to raise his own prospects but simply to update me on the progress of his efforts to expel the Taliban from Kandahar. His brother was in Bonn as a member of the Rome Group, so Hamid did not need me to tell him what was transpiring. His second call to me was made only moments after he had narrowly escaped death from an errant American bomb that killed three of his American Green Beret advisers and twenty-five of his Afghan followers. If he was shaken, he gave no sign of it.

With agreement on the head of the new provisional government, Brahimi went on to secure consensus on the final declaration. This document would provide an interim constitution while defining a path toward full democracy. All that remained was to agree on the actual composition of the new regime. Brahimi had asked the four groups to name their candidates to head various ministries, but the Northern Alliance refused to do so.

Qanuni told me President Rabbani and those who supported him were balking at the transfer of power and loss of position. He suggested the meeting adjourn for a couple of weeks so he could return to Kabul and secure the necessary authority, and I passed this proposal on to Washington. Enough had already been achieved that the meeting could be presented as at least a partial success, yet once the participants were dispersed, even existing areas of agreement could unravel, and it might also prove difficult to reassemble the group. Rich Armitage called back to say that Powell wanted us to soldier on until we had a fully agreed upon new government. While we labored on the Petersburg, Powell would begin working the telephone to mount further pressure on Rabbani and his colleagues in Kabul.

Qanuni was visibly relieved when I reported Powell's reaction. I briefed the Russian, Indian, Iranian, and other European representatives, stressing that the decisive moment had arrived and they all needed to join in the final push. I also met with Joschka Fischer who needed no prodding to join in the effort.

Khalilzad and I contacted the top Northern Alliance leaders in Afghanistan. I called Abdullah in Kabul to stress the need to break this deadlock, and when I passed a message via the CIA to Marshal Fahim to the same effect, he responded positively. Khalilzad spoke to two of the top Northern Alliance commanders, Abdul Rashid Dostum and Ismail Khan, and finally to Rabbani himself, stressing the dire consequences for Afghanistan if the Bonn meeting were to fail. I held my only on-the-record press briefing of the conference, putting the blame for the impasse squarely on Rabbani.

The logjam was finally broken by the Russian ambassador in Kabul, who interrupted a cabinet meeting there to deliver a message from Moscow warning that if the agreement on the table in Bonn was not accepted, the Northern Alliance could expect no further Russian assistance. This démarche, the product of a call by Powell to Foreign Minister Ivanov, caused Rabbani to relent and allow the cabinet selection process to go forward.

There was to be one more hurdle. Shortly after midnight on what was supposed to be the last day of the conference, Brahimi asked to see me. Gerhardt Schroeder, the chancellor of Germany, was due to arrive in a few hours to witness the signing of the Bonn Declaration, yet there was still no agreement on the composition of the new government. The Northern Alliance was insisting on filling eighteen of the twenty-six ministries, and the other three groups could not accept such an unbalanced division of portfolios. The resultant government would hardly be broadly based if the Northern Alliance, which represented maybe 30 or 40 percent of the population, occupied 75 percent of the cabinet posts, particularly since it was already accepted that Fahim, Qanuni, and Abdullah would retain the three most powerful portfolios: defense, interior, and foreign affairs.

I proposed to Brahimi that we invite the external representative likely to have the most influence with Qanuni to join us. Accordingly, at that early morning hour we roused Kabulov, Lambah, Zarif, and Matussek.

For two hours this group worked over Qanuni, each of us in turn insisting that he needed to give up several ministries, but Qanuni remained obdurate. Finally, Zarif took Qanuni aside and spoke quietly to him for a few moments, following which the Northern Alliance envoy returned to the table and said, "All right, I agree. We will give up two portfolios. And we can also create three further ministries, which the others can also have."

We had a deal. Schroeder arrived, the Bonn Declaration was signed, and Afghanistan had a new government. I did not remain for the ceremony, preferring that the UN, the Germans, and the Afghans share the spotlight. By the time Schroeder arrived, I was on my way to the airport and a flight back to Washington.

TWENTY-FIVE

Losing the Peace: Afghanistan

A WEEK LATER I WAS back in Afghanistan. We landed at Bagram in the middle of the night and rested in a tent with a few sleeping Green Berets till dawn. We then drove to Kabul, some thirty miles distant, passing disabled tanks and rusted-out antiaircraft guns, detouring around areas marked as mined and fording a shallow stream beside a bombed-out bridge. As we entered the city pedestrians were out and about, including a few unarmed soldiers. There was an occasional traffic cop, but no traffic save for a few battered taxis. When we arrived at the American Embassy, we found a company of U.S. Marines camped out there. The building had stood empty since its closure in 1989, and was without heat, electricity, and water. Twelve-year-old documents still lay in out-boxes, half-smoked cigars in ashtrays. A half-finished bottle of Scotch sat on the basement bar, and several late-1980s model cars were parked in the motor pool, one of which still started. A dozen State Department and USAID officials had preceded me by a few days and occupied a three-room underground bunker that somehow had power and plumbing. The men shared one small room, the women another. I was given the third room, which also contained our only desk, telephone, and computer. Our sole link to the outside world was by satellite telephone, and communication within the city was by runner. To arrange any meeting, one had to dispatch a messenger with a request and received the response similarly.

I called on Hamid Karzai, who was quartered as a guest of President Rabbani at the former royal palace. Kandahar had fallen and the Taliban were on the run everywhere. Karzai had arrived the day before on a U.S. Air Force transport, and when he stepped off the plane he was greeted by Marshal Fahim and a Northern Alliance honor guard. Seeing no one else deplane, Fahim asked Karzai "Where are your men?" Surely no Afghan warlord would travel without an armed entourage.

"You are my men," Karzai responded, pointing to Fahim and the assembled honor guard. When recounting this story, Karzai failed to add that the last time he had seen Fahim, Karzai had been a prisoner and Fahim had been his interrogator. Putting his life in the hands of an erstwhile adversary was an act of considerable statesmanship and courage.

The following day I met with President Rabbani, and he proved most gracious. There were no recriminations. He said he was committed to a peaceful and dignified transfer of power, and he proved as good as his word. I also called on Abdullah and Qanuni at the Foreign and Interior Ministries. Both were busy preparing for Karzai's inauguration.

On my way to Kabul I had stopped in London to discuss the creation of the peacekeeping force called for in the Bonn Declaration. British troops were to form its core, and it was to be called the International Security Assistance Force (ISAF). The word "assistance" had been inserted at the Pentagon's request to underline its limited responsibilities. Rumsfeld had also required that the force be confined to the Kabul city limits. Finally, and most oddly, the Pentagon insisted the force was not to report to the United Nations, to NATO, or even to the American military command in Afghanistan. It was to be entirely free-standing. These strictures reflected the aversion to peacekeeping, multilateralism, and nation-building that pervaded upper levels of the Pentagon and was shared to one degree or another elsewhere in the administration.

Rumsfeld made a short visit to Bagram. Karzai, Fahim, and I drove out to meet him. On arrival Rumsfeld asked me what Karzai would ask of him, and I said Karzai wanted ISAF to be expanded to cover the rest of the country. "What would that take?" Rumsfeld asked skeptically.

"The British believe that a force of about 5,000 will suffice for Kabul," I explained, "so perhaps another 20,000 might suffice to secure at least the other major cities." Rumsfeld looked skeptical and did not pursue the topic further.

The next day we held a ceremony formally reopening the American Embassy. Qanuni and Fahim both attended, as did Colonel Mulholland, the Special Forces commander who had greeted me a month earlier at Bagram. British General John McColl, the designated head of the soon-to-arrive international peacekeeping force, was also present.

Back in 1989, when the embassy was closing, the departing Marine guard detachment had carefully left behind the flag that had last flown over the embassy, along with a note for their successors, and twelve years later our Marines raised this same flag. I gave a short speech acknowledging how costly that American departure had been for both countries and pledging that the United States would not again abandon Afghanistan. Although I had no authorization to make such a commitment, the promise seemed a safe bet only a few weeks after 9/11.

Following the ceremony, at General McColl's request, I asked Qanuni and Fahim to stay behind for a discussion regarding the arrival of the British-led international force. These troops needed to be in place in time for Karzai's inauguration, then only five days off. Fahim had been trying to limit the size of this force and circumscribe its freedom of action. After some discussion Fahim gave way on all outstanding points but one. His troops were not prepared to pull out of the city, and, particularly, out of its historic Bala Hissar fortress, as provided for in the Bonn agreement. Qanuni, who had agreed to this provision in Bonn, offered me no support. For a few moments, I foresaw the whole arrangement coming apart, but fortunately General McColl intervened to say he could live with the continued presence of Fahim's troops within the city.

I made short visits to Islamabad and New Delhi, and arrived back in time for Karzai's inauguration. Abdullah and Qanuni had managed the logistic and security arrangements for the arrival of over a thousand celebrants from all over the country and, indeed, the world. Foreign ministers from Iran, Pakistan, and Europe were in attendance. Tommy Franks came, accompanied by his wife. As they and I drove together to the ceremony, I briefed Franks on a just-received news report of an American airstrike that had hit a column of tribal elders on their way to Kabul for the occasion. Franks said this was the first he had heard of the incident. On our arrival at the inaugural site, he immediately attracted a scrum of American and international journalists, and, when they asked him about the attack, he flatly denied any such incident had occurred.

Franks's denial helped prevent news of this attack overshadowing that of the inaugural. But the bombing had occurred, and a number of tribal elders had been killed as a result. This was the first of many such regrettable incidents, and it was only after several more instances of collateral damage to civilians—including an attack on an Afghan wedding party that killed thirty men, women, and children and wounded many more—that U.S. military authorities abandoned this "deny first, investigate later" reaction to such reports.

To my surprise the inauguration ceremony started on time. Rabbani, Brahimi, and Karzai spoke, as did Iranian foreign minister Kharazi and Belgian foreign minister Michel, representing the European Union. Luncheon for the more important guests was served at the palace, and General Dostum and Ismael Khan came over to introduce themselves and pledge support for the new regime. Dostum inquired of Franks, "Who do you want me to kill now?"

In his memoir Franks writes that he carried a concealed pistol throughout the day. Apparently he felt the occasion safe enough to bring his wife but dangerous enough to require a concealed weapon.

We drove out to Bagram together, where planes awaited us. Franks and his wife traveled on to spend Christmas with his troops elsewhere in the region, and I flew to Washington to spend it with my family.

I considered my Afghan adventure over. I had done everything asked of me. I had made clear that I did not want to be named ambassador to Afghanistan. I intended to resume preparations for retirement, but Rich Armitage tried to persuade me otherwise. He said Powell, Rice, and Hadley wanted me to assume responsibility for interagency management of Afghan issues. I said I did not think this job could be done effectively from the State Department—Defense was likely to be the dominant player in Afghanistan for some time, with the CIA not far behind, and State a distant third. Those other agencies, particularly Rumsfeld's Defense Department, were unlikely to accept guidance from anywhere but the White House, if then. Rich persisted and I agreed to take up the task for the next few months while I explored opportunities outside the government.

In early January I joined Powell in Tokyo for a conference of potential donors to Afghan reconstruction. The meeting raised $5 billion in pledged assistance, of which only $290 million was to come from the United States, little more than 5 percent of the total. Iran pledged $500 million. I pointed out to Powell that the United States had committed far larger sums to Balkan reconstruction, both in total amounts and as a proportion of the global total, and he responded with a pained grimace. This was all he had.

On the fringes of the larger meeting in Tokyo, I held a session with those governments interested in supporting the Afghan security sector. Aid donors tend to be more comfortable funding schools or hospitals than armies, police forces, or prisons, but security is the bedrock requirement for any enduring development. Abdullah and Brahimi joined me for the session, and the result was agreement that the United States would take the lead in building a new Afghan army. The Germans would do the same for the police. The British volunteered to take on the counternarcotics task, the Italians said they would lead assistance to the judicial sector, and Japan was ready to assume responsibility for the disarmament, demobilization, and reintegration of the many militias that had been raised to combat the Taliban.

This distribution of responsibility has been justly criticized. Over the next several years none of these lead nations, with the exception of Japan, delivered on their promises. Even the United States would prove remiss in its early efforts to build a new army. Yet there was at the time no real alternative to this lead nation arrangement. Washington did not want NATO to become involved. Brahimi wanted the UN to concentrate on implementing the political provisions of the Bonn agreement, which involved the drafting and adoption of a constitution, the holding of national elections, and the installation of a fully representative government. He did not want to see UN responsibilities widened. I introduced the lead nation arrangement not because it would work well, but because it was better than nothing.

The same leadership vacuum existed in the area of economic development. The United States was contributing too little assistance to claim the lead, and Brahimi resisted my suggestion that he coordinate economic reconstruction efforts. The new Afghan government was in no position to do so. In the end a laughably unwieldy steering group comprised of Japan,

Saudi Arabia, the United States, the World Bank, and the European Union was charged with overseeing donor coordination.

Brahimi proved brilliantly successful in securing implementation of the political aspects of the Bonn Declaration. By 2005 the country had a new constitution and a freely elected president and parliament, but other elements of the country's institutional development lagged badly.

In Washington I pressed for expansion of ISAF beyond Kabul; both Karzai and Brahimi were calling for such a move, and Powell had the issue put on the NSC agenda. In the run-up to this meeting the NSC staff circulated a paper arguing that peacekeeping was a failed concept, one proven not to work. This assertion was stunningly ill-informed. Whether a peacekeeping mission could succeed in Afghanistan was, indeed, debatable, but the preceding decade had seen successful peacekeeping operations in Bosnia, Kosovo, Sierra Leone, East Timor, Mozambique, Liberia, El Salvador, Namibia, Cambodia, Albania, and Macedonia. The NSC staff's counterfactual critique was yet another manifestation of the new administration's resistance to anything that smacked of nation-building.

When the principals assembled, George Tenet warned there was a danger of resumed fighting among the warlords who had collaborated in ousting the Taliban and were now squabbling among themselves for predominance. Rumsfeld countered that there were no potential contributors to a peacekeeping force, a particularly disingenuous argument. Rumsfeld had already spoken out publicly in opposition to such an expansion. What government was going to volunteer, unasked, to join a force in Afghanistan that the American defense secretary was known to oppose? Rumsfeld did offer that American forces already in-country, of which there were then less than 10,000, would use their influence to defuse confrontations among local militias. On this basis the meeting concluded, and ISAF remained confined to Kabul. American commanders would discourage local warlords from fighting each other, but public order would be left in the hands of a new Afghan government that had no national army and no police force.

Given the lack of security beyond Kabul, the State Department forbad government civilians from traveling outside the city. Other donor governments did the same. Reconstruction beyond the capital became very difficult. I suggested that State and USAID personnel should be located at U.S. bases in key provinces. Everyone agreed, but it took more than a year before the first Provincial Reconstruction Team was fielded, reflecting the inertia on Afghanistan issues that prevailed throughout Washington at the time.

In early February Hamid Karzai made his first official visit to Washington. The White House, eager to deflect his likely request for an expansion of ISAF, decided to make the U.S. offer to build a new Afghan army the centerpiece for the visit. I raised no objection to that; Afghanistan needed a national army. But I pointed out that there was no connection between what Karzai wanted and what the president was going to promise. Karzai wanted a security presence throughout the country now; we were promising to have one ready in four or five years. In fact, it took more than ten years before the Afghan army was ready to assume a countrywide security role.

Following the Karzai visit, the Pentagon informed me that it expected State to pay for training the new Afghan army. I dismissed this as ridiculous. State had neither the money nor the expertise, but the resultant argument consumed several weeks. Finally, the Pentagon agreed to fund the training program. Several weeks later I asked General Keith Chilton of the joint staff what was happening.

"We are sending a colonel and a Special Forces team to Kabul to begin the training," he replied.

"Who are they going to train?" I inquired.

"Whomever Defense Minister Fahim designates," he responded.

I pointed out that if it were left to Fahim the new army would be manned exclusively by Tajiks and officered solely by Northern Alliance veterans. "We will need to be involved not just in training, but in the recruitment, fielding, and sustainment of the new army if we are going to build anything that lasts," I insisted.

Chilton looked dubious, but said he would take this advice back to the Pentagon for consideration. Several weeks later I inquired again where things stood, and Chilton said they had informed the secretary of my view that the United States needed to work to ensure an ethnically balanced Afghan Army. "We're not going to do that," Rumsfeld had responded. "That would be social engineering!"

The result was a year of almost entirely wasted effort. The United States trained thousands of recruits supplied by Fahim and other Northern Alliance commanders, nearly all of whom promptly deserted.

In his first State of the Union address, on January 29, President Bush included Iran, along with North Korea and Iraq, in what he characterized as the "axis of evil." Despite this rebuff, the Iranians persisted in offering help on Afghanistan. In March I held a second meeting of governments interested in helping the Afghan security sector, this time in Geneva. At the conclusion of the plenary session, the Iranians asked to see me privately. We met in the lounge of our hotel, where they introduced me to a general of the Revolutionary Guard, who was dressed in full uniform.

"My government is prepared to participate in an American-led program of support for the new Afghan army," the general said. "Specifically, we are prepared to house, clothe, arm, and train up to 20,000 troops in a broader effort under your leadership."

"Well," I replied dubiously, "if you train some Afghan troops and we train some, might they not end up having two incompatible doctrines?"

The general smiled, "Don't worry; we are still using the manuals you left behind in 1979."

"All right," I conceded. "So maybe they would have compatible doctrines. But might they not develop conflicting loyalties?"

Considering this, the general responded, "Iran trained, equipped, and is still paying the Afghan troops your military is now using to hunt down remaining Al Qaeda elements. Are you having any difficulty with their loyalty?"

"No," I admitted. "Not that I know of."

Back home, I went to see Powell.

"Very interesting," he responded to my account of the conversation. "You need to see Condi."

I went to see Rice.

"Very interesting," she said. "You need to talk to Don."

Several days later Rice organized a meeting of NSC principals. I recounted my conversation with the Iranians. Rumsfeld shuffled through his papers and did not look up throughout my presentation. When I finished, he made no comment and asked no questions. Neither did anyone else. After a prolonged silence, Rice moved on to the next agenda item, and the Iranians never received a response.

Throughout these months I was disturbed by the lack of attention being paid by top levels of the administration to developments in a country we had just overrun and liberated. While working on Haiti, and later the Balkans, I had been hounded night and day by Berger, Albright, and Talbott for updates, status reports, and responses to the latest developments. From January through April 2002 I did not receive a single such inquiry.

Powell, Rice, and Hadley were readily available to meet on request, but there was no prodding to get things moving or to show results. From Karzai's inauguration in December until my departure in April, there were only two White House-chaired interagency meetings on Afghanistan. One of these decided against expanding ISAF, and the other chose to ignore the Iranian offer of assistance in building an Afghan army.

In early April a White House speechwriter called to ask whether it would be okay for the president to announce a Marshall Plan for Afghanistan in an upcoming speech. I readily agreed. Maybe this would lead to some greater effort. The president issued such a call on April 17 at the Virginia Military Institute, but there was no follow-up, no increase in U.S. assistance, and no effort to galvanize a broader international effort.

In its continued efforts to hunt down Al Qaeda and Taliban remnants, the U.S. military was inadvertently continuing to kill innocent civilians, sometimes in large number. The policy of deny first, investigate later had finally been abandoned, but the United States was still offering no assistance to those innocents it had maimed or rendered homeless, or to the families of those it had killed. I proposed that the United States should make *ex gratia* payments to such individuals, not because we were legally required to do so but because this was both the humanitarian and politically expedient thing to do. The Defense Department responded with the ultimate Washington stonewall: "We don't believe such payments are legal. Your lawyers will have to talk to our lawyers."

In November 2002, some months after I had left the government, an American AC-130 gunship attacked yet another Afghan wedding party, this time killing forty-eight celebrants and wounding a hundred others, and this tragedy finally overcame the Pentagon's legal qualms. *Ex gratia* payments to the victims or families of such incidents became the norm in Afghanistan and later in Iraq.

In late 2001 I was selected for promotion by the Foreign Service board that meets annually for this purpose. The list of those selected, comprising several hundred officers of all ranks, was sent to the Senate for confirmation, and Jesse Helms, still heading the Senate Foreign Relations Committee, told the department that no one within the Foreign Service would be promoted that year unless my name was deleted. The department removed my name and resubmitted the list.

I urged Powell and Rice to send Khalilzad to Kabul as ambassador. Unbeknownst to me, Zal contacted Jim Thomson, the president of the

RAND Corporation, where Zal had worked before entering the Bush administration, to urge that he recruit me to RAND. In due course I went to RAND and, a year later, Zal went to Kabul.

On the last day of April, in a retirement ceremony on the seventh floor of the State Department, before a group of family, friends, and colleagues, Colin Powell gave me a large medal and an affectionate hug.

TWENTY-SIX

Losing the Peace: Iraq

THE RAND CORPORATION GOT ITS start during World War II as a source of operational analysis for the U.S. Army Air Corps. Beginning in late 1940s it assembled the intellectual fathers of nuclear deterrence theory, including Herman Kahn, Albert Wohlstetter, and Thomas Shelling, who began to grapple with the place nuclear weapons should occupy in American strategy and statesmanship. Eventually some thirty Nobel Prize winners became associated with RAND at some stage in their careers, but perhaps the best known of RAND alumni was fictional. In Stanley Kubrick's classic Cold War satire, *Dr. Strangelove, or: How I Learned to Stop Worrying and Love the Bomb*, the title character, played by Peter Sellers, works for "the BLAND Corporation."

I spent my first six months at RAND's California headquarters. The trip to Santa Monica provided an excuse for our first family vacation in years and, with our now-grown sons, Toril and I drove across the country, stopping at numerous sites along the way. Once in California, we took an apartment overlooking the ocean a few blocks from the office. I bicycled to work on a path alongside the ocean, and colleagues played beach volleyball at lunch time. When it came time to leave California, it was hard to tear ourselves away from this land of perpetual sand, surf, and perfect weather. But friends, family, and professional contacts all called us back to RAND's Washington office.

For the next eleven years I was occupied with an agreeable mix of thinking, reading, writing, and helping guide others' work on national security policy. My experiences with Somalia, Haiti, Bosnia, Kosovo, and Afghanistan turned out to be far more relevant than my deeper exposure to issues of transatlantic and East-West relations. Europe was quiet, the Soviet Union was gone, and Russia was friendly. In contrast, nation-building, despite the Bush administration's determination to the contrary, proved a growth industry.

RAND provided the opportunity for reflection and dozens of super smart colleagues to help. The result was a series of volumes examining the American and broader international experience with peacekeeping, post-conflict reconstruction, and state-building from the end of World War II to the present. The first of these studies was completed just as the war in Iraq was launched.

As the invasion became more imminent, Zal Khalilzad, still at the White House, asked me to come see him. He explained the president had tasked him with forming a post-invasion Iraqi government, essentially the same mission we had worked on together a year and a half earlier for Afghanistan. Zal was looking to pull off something similar with Iraq and asked my advice. I said it would be difficult. The UN was unlikely to play as helpful a role this time around, as the Iraq intervention would not have a Security Council mandate. Even more important, there was no on-the-ground opposition to Saddam, no Iraqi equivalent of the Northern Alliance. All of Saddam's domestic opponents were either dead or in exile. Many of these émigré figures had been out of Iraq for decades. Finally, most of Iraq's neighbors were opposed to the invasion. These governments were unlikely to provide Zal the kind of support we had received in Bonn from the Indians, Russians, and Iranians. Zal acknowledged all these difficulties but was committed to giving it a try.

I found the administration's case for invading Iraq very weak. In the weeks immediately leading up to the intervention, international inspectors announced that Saddam had no nuclear arms nor had they found any evidence of an active program to develop such weapons. The Bush administration did not challenge this assessment, but continued to assert that

Saddam had "weapons of mass destruction." There was good reason to believe he probably retained chemical weapons acquired decades earlier. But so what? Why should the United States care so intensely about Iraq's chemical weapons in 2003 when it had done nothing about their use against Iran in the 1980s and, later, against Saddam's own population? As a practical matter the assertion that Saddam had WMD, or weapons of mass destruction, was being used to obscure the absence of any new or imminent threat from Iraq. Of course we now know that even those chemical weapons had long ago been destroyed. Saddam's unwillingness to confirm their destruction made the administration's charge plausible, even likely, but hardly an adequate basis for a war.

As the war approached, the Defense Department invited a number of outside analysts into the Pentagon for a briefing on its plans for post-invasion Iraq. Bill Luti, who had moved up to become Doug Feith's senior deputy, led off. Employing a series of PowerPoint slides, Luti described an American-led occupation of indeterminate duration to be headed initially by retired lieutenant Jay Garner, who was, in due course, likely to be superseded by a more senior personality, perhaps a former American governor or diplomat. Garner, who was present, acknowledged this point. After a while Rumsfeld arrived and offered to answer questions. Asked about American plans for post-Saddam Iraq, Rumsfeld said he favored the rapid creation of an indigenous government on the Afghan model, a stance clearly at variance with the briefing we had just been given.

These two alternative visions for post-Saddam Iraq, an occupation or the rapid creation of a sovereign Iraqi government, would continue to be debated within the Bush administration up to and beyond the actual invasion. The decision was made in favor of the former only after widespread rioting and looting broke out in the aftermath of the fall of Baghdad. Khalilzad's efforts to form an Iraqi government were terminated, Jerry Bremer was appointed to head the Coalition Provisional Authority (CPA), and the UN Security Council formally recognized an American-led occupation of Iraq.

Many proponents of the war have since argued that if the United States had immediately turned power over to the Iraqis the country would not have descended into civil war. Fourteen months later the United States did put in place a sovereign Iraq government only to see the situation deteriorate faster and further. It is not clear that doing this earlier would have produced a better result.

Bremer asked to see me the day after he was appointed. We had first worked together when he was Kissinger's top aide and I worked for Sonnenfeldt. Jerry asked me to come to Baghdad as his deputy. I declined, noting that I had been at RAND less than a year. I warned him that the United States had far too few troops in Iraq to secure the territory it had overrun, and noted that even as we spoke these numbers were being reduced and forces withdrawn. "You are going to be sent out with insufficient backing and left hanging in the wind when things fall apart," I predicted.

I left with Jerry the galley proofs of *America's Role in Nation Building: From Germany to Iraq*, the study on which I had been working since arriving at RAND. This book examined the American experience in post-conflict reconstruction from 1945 onward. It concluded with a chapter on Iraq, looking ahead at the challenges likely to face the United States in the aftermath of an invasion. Before leaving Washington Bremer raised with President Bush the problem of declining troop levels, specifically citing the study I had given him. He also sent a copy of the study to Rumsfeld. He did not get an increase in U.S. force levels, but at least the planned withdrawals were canceled.

Shortly after his arrival in Baghdad Bremer called to say he was desperately short of staff. If I would not come, could I at least send him some experienced people? Eventually nearly a dozen RAND analysts joined the CPA, including David Gompert, my colleague from the Ford, Carter, and Bush 41 administrations, who left RAND to take responsibility for building a new Iraqi army and reforming the police.

Over the succeeding months I watched the administration make the same mistakes in Iraq as it had in Afghanistan, this time with even more devastating effect. As soon as Baghdad fell the United States began pulling forces out of Iraq. The Pentagon's plan was to be down to 30,000 troops by year's end, and when widespread looting broke out, eventually stripping nearly every government building in the country to the bare walls, American troops stood by passively. In the run-up to the war, the administration had assured Congress that the reconstruction of Iraq would be self-financing. Half a year passed before Congress was asked to provide funding for this purpose. Meanwhile, violent resistance emerged almost immediately. It grew quickly throughout the CPA's existence and intensified further thereafter.

After the CPA closed down, I was able to secure RAND access to its voluminous archives. That organization was so poorly resourced that it had almost no capacity to operate classified systems, so virtually its entire output was unclassified. Based on more than 100,000 internal CPA memos, along with numerous interviews, we produced the first and still only documented history of the occupation.* This concluded that the CPA had achieved a good deal more than generally appreciated. During its fourteen-month existence, the CPA successfully restored Iraq's essential public services to near or beyond their prewar level, instituted reforms in the Iraqi judiciary and penal systems, introduced a new currency, dramatically reduced inflation, promoted rapid economic growth, put in place barriers to corruption, began reform of the civil service, promoted the development of the most liberal constitution in the Middle East, and set the stage for a series of free elections.

Despite these economic and social accomplishments the United States failed to stem Iraq's descent in bitter sectarian civil war. Bremer and his team garnered much of the blame for this failure, largely on the basis of two early decisions: the dismissal of Baath party civil servants and the disbandment of the Iraqi Army.

The decision to outlaw the Baath party had been made in Washington before Bremer was named and was implemented by him on his arrival in Baghdad. Bremer's own misstep, which he has acknowledged, was to turn implementation of de-Baathification over to the anti-Baathist émigré figures that Rumsfeld and others in Washington had hoped would form the initial post-Saddam government. These politicians sought a far more rigorous purge than Bremer or Washington had intended. Indeed, had Khalilzad's effort to form an Iraqi government early in 2003 been pursued to success, the de-Baathification process would probably have been even more draconian.

The Iraqi Army had been dispersed by the U.S. military. During the march on Baghdad leaflets were dropped that threatened soldiers with death if they remained under arms and in uniform, instructing them to, instead, drop their weapons, change their clothes, and go home. This avoided the need to intern the defeated soldiers and establish POW camps,

---

Occupying Iraq: A History of the Coalition Provisional Authority, Dobbins and others, RAND, 2009.

but it meant the Iraqi Army had been effectively disbanded by the time Bremer arrived. He proceeded to formally dissolve it, and then delayed for several weeks on a decision to pay pensions.

These early actions contributed to the occupation's subsequent difficulties. The more basic problem, however, was that the Bush team had made a conscious decision to reject the lessons on force sizing and regional diplomacy learned by the Clinton administration through a costly eight years of trial and error. NATO had committed 50,000 troops to stabilize Kosovo, a society of two million, 90 percent of whom were wildly pro-American. The Bush administration planned to commit only 30,000 troops to stabilize Iraq, a society fifteen times more numerous than Kosovo, and a lot less friendly. The Clinton administration accepted the need to provide for public order and to use NATO military and international police for that purpose from the first day of the Kosovo intervention. The Bush administration made no such plans or provisions. The Kosovo air campaign and the subsequent reconstruction effort had strong regional as well as broader international support. The United States invaded Iraq against the advice and contrary to the perceived interests of nearly all that country's neighbors and several of America's closest allies. Then, when the absence of WMD became apparent, Washington advanced a new rationale for the endeavor, one bound to antagonize nearly every government in the Middle East. American officials declared Iraq was to become a model democracy that would foster comparable political change throughout the Middle East. Neighboring regimes, needless to say, had little interest in advancing such program. Several did their best to subvert it.

Donald Rumsfeld was explicit in rejecting the Clinton model for nation-building. He wrote and spoke in support of what he characterized as the low profile, small footprint approach to post-conflict reconstruction. He argued that by flooding Bosnia and, subsequently, Kosovo with military manpower and economic assistance the United States and its NATO allies had turned these two societies into permanent wards of the international community. To avoid this outcome in Afghanistan and Iraq he advocated committing a minimum of both manpower and money to their stabilization and reconstruction so these countries could become self-sufficient much more quickly.

Rumsfeld was employing the dependency argument advanced during the previous decade's domestic American debate over welfare reform. The analogy could not have been more inapt. By minimizing troop deployments, refusing to accept responsibility for public order, and stint-ing on reconstruction aid, the United States provided time and space for violent resistance movements to emerge, organize, recruit, fundraise, in-timidate the population, and begin an insurgency. In both Afghanistan and Iraq the American troop presence was reinforced only after the initial commitment was proven inadequate. This turned out to be a vastly more expensive approach to stabilization than the initially supersized NATO interventions in Bosnia and Kosovo. Consolidating the peace in Afghani-stan or Iraq was always going to be more difficult than pacifying those other two smaller, more developed, more Western, and less hostile socie-ties. But the Bush administration's refusal to learn from those earlier expe-riences made these later efforts much harder than they needed to be.

As the Iraq operation faltered I was called repeatedly to testify before the Senate and House committees. I spent an hour with Senator Biden on a train trip from his home in Wilmington to Washington explaining why things were going so badly in Iraq, and I was asked to address the entire Democratic Caucus of the House of Representatives on the topic. In 2004 I wrote an article for *Foreign Affairs* magazine titled "Winning the Unwin-nable War." In it I urged adoption of classic counterinsurgency doctrine. Eighteen months later, as Iraq descended further into bloody chaos, I wrote a follow-on article provocatively entitled, "Who Lost Iraq?"

That judgment proved premature. Like the Clinton administration be-fore it, the Bush team got better over time. By his second term President Bush was embracing nation-building with all the zeal of a new convert. The Pentagon issued a directive making stabilization and reconstruction operations a core mission of the American military, on par with major combat, and the State Department created an office to support its role in such operations. The president named Lieutenant General Doug Lute as the White House "war czar." NATO was invited to take command of ISAF, which was no longer limited to Kabul, but expanded countrywide. Troop levels were increased in Afghanistan and even more substantially in Iraq. General David Petraeus wrote a new counterinsurgency doctrine for the U.S. military and was sent to Baghdad to put it into effect. Iraq was not lost after all; at least not yet.

The highly controversial decision by President Bush to surge additional forces into Iraq in 2008, the production and application by General David Petraeus of the newly updated counterinsurgency doctrine, and the Ameri-can outreach to elements of the Sunni community ready to resist Al Qaeda all combined to produce a substantial decrease in violence throughout Iraq. But despite these advances, America's patience was wearing thin.

A few weeks after assuming office, Vice President Biden invited me to dinner at his residence to talk about Afghanistan. Dick Holbrooke, who had just been named the administration's special representative for Afghanistan and Pakistan, was there along with a couple of other experts on Afghanistan. Biden asked each of us for our advice. At the conclusion of my remarks, Biden looked a bit puzzled. "He's talking about counterinsurgency," Dick explained in a somewhat dismissive manner. I don't think Dick disagreed with me, but clearly he thought Biden was likely to. Only weeks into the new administration, nation-building was once again falling into disfavor.

We know from Bob Woodward's account of the Obama administration's initial internal debates that this was the case. Counterinsurgency had been dropped from the national tool kit in the wake of Vietnam. It enjoyed a brief return to respectability during George W. Bush's second term, but now the tide was turning again. President Obama did send additional troops, additional civilians, and additional economic assistance to Afghanistan throughout 2009. He insisted nation-building was not part of the mission, even though he explicitly cited protection for the upcoming Afghan elections as a main reason for this reinforcement. In announcing the last tranche of these reinforcements Obama set an eighteen-month deadline for their withdrawal. He subsequently promised to have all American forces out of that country by the end of his second term.

There had been periodic efforts to lure me back into government. Colin Powell called a couple of times to see if I would take up the Afghan portfolio again. His successor, Condi Rice, asked me to head our embassy in Pakistan. On her last days in the Senate, Hillary Clinton asked to see me, and inquired whether I would head State's Office of Stabilization and Reconstruction. I had no qualms refusing these offers. Life as an analyst, author, and commentator had settled into a comfortable routine, and my position at RAND gave me a measure of control over my schedule, a luxury few in government enjoy, along with abundant opportunities to learn, write, and travel. It also allowed Toril and me to remain near our children and first grandchild.

In 2009 Toril was diagnosed with advanced breast cancer; she died three years later. A month before her death she traveled to Norway to say goodbye to her ninety-five-year-old father. He passed away the day after

her visit. Toril faced the inevitable with great courage and tranquility, concerned above all to minimize distress to friends and family.

On a Saturday morning several months later the State Department's
operation center caught me at home to say Secretary of State John Kerry
wanted to speak to me. "Will you come see me when I get back to Washington?" he asked. "I need someone to take over the Af/Pak portfolio.
Everyone says you are the only person for the job."

This was essentially the same position I had filled once before and had
subsequently turned down twice. This time I accepted. I knew Kerry was
likely the last secretary of state to call, and this the last opportunity to
serve in my chosen profession. Toril's passing also left a space that I thought
extra work might help to fill.

TWENTY-SEVEN

Afghanistan Again

RETURNING TO STATE AFTER MORE than a decade I found everyone much younger except the few people I knew, who seemed much older. Attending Kerry's morning staff meeting I was astonished to encounter more than 100 other participants. Kerry held a smaller staff meeting later in the week, which numbered only some thirty attendees, still more than double the number that had sat around Jim Baker's conference table, or the two dozen who met with Colin Powell. A few days later I participated in a National Security Council meeting with the president and found the same thing. The White House Situation Room had been remodeled and significantly enlarged. Attendance had kept pace, with a dozen or more White House staffers lining the table and back row, in some meetings outnumbering all the agency representatives combined.

My own office was a prominent example of this growth, representing as it did the largest of several dozen independent and, in principle, temporary fiefdoms tacked on to the Department's permanent establishment. My responsibilities were similar to those I had back in 2002, but I commanded much greater resources. For this I could thank Dick Holbrooke, who had created a substantial bureaucratic power base and recruited a talented staff numbering almost 100. I brought with me a single colleague from RAND. Otherwise I was more than pleased to rely upon the first-rate team Dick had assembled. Our embassies in Kabul and Islamabad were also much enlarged; indeed they were now among the biggest diplomatic posts in the world. These two countries now received a substantial share of the U.S. government's development and security assistance budgets, a sharp contrast to the relative penury of my operation back in 2002.

Holbrooke's appointment as special representative for Afghanistan and Pakistan (SRAP) had caused several dozen other countries to create similar positions. The German Foreign Ministry volunteered to organize regular meetings bringing together these officials from capitals to compare notes and coordinate policy. Two days after being sworn in, I was on my way to Brussels for one such gathering. Entering the room set aside for the meeting, I was astounded to see over fifty national delegations, each seated behind its flag, a true mini-United Nations. Attending were representatives of all NATO and EU member states as well as all Afghanistan's neighbors and near-neighbors. We heard reports from the Afghan government, the UN, and NATO, with a particular emphasis on preparations for the upcoming Afghan presidential election. Participants were also keen to size up the new American SRAP and hear where the Obama administration was headed.

I reported that negotiations on a bilateral security agreement between the United States and Afghanistan were moving forward. Current American and NATO military operations were scheduled to conclude by the end of 2014, and everyone wanted to know what would come next. There was little I could say, as Washington was just beginning to weigh the options and President Obama was in no hurry to make a decision.

Participants were also eager to hear about prospects for peace negotiations with the Taliban. Again I had little to report. American officials had begun talking to Taliban representatives in late 2010. These discussions continued through early 2012, at which point the Taliban had broken off contact. We were working through Pakistan and a couple of other governments to bring the Taliban back to the table, so far without response.

This was about to change. Upon my return to Washington I was alerted from several sources, including the government of Qatar, that the Taliban were ready to resume talking. This led me to begin digging more deeply into the history of these efforts.

As early as 2001 there had been opportunities for a negotiated peace in Afghanistan. Mullah Omar, then still defending Kandahar, had approached Hamid Karzai with an offer to surrender provided he was granted immunity. American officials advised Karzai to refuse such a deal. In 2002 a Taliban delegation came to Kabul but, again, American officials discouraged Karzai from negotiating. Later that year the United States imprisoned the former Taliban foreign minister when he came to Kabul. By 2003 the Taliban had shifted their focus back to the battlefield.

The first of these early approaches had occurred while I was working on Afghanistan. It was rebuffed without reference to me or, as far as I know, anyone else at State or the White House. Had I been consulted, I am not sure how I would have responded. At the time I regarded the Taliban as a spent force, so discredited by their behavior in government and their rapid overthrow that they would be unlikely to reemerge as a threat. In this I was wrong. Nevertheless it would have been better had these early Taliban overtures been carefully evaluated and debated within the administration rather than rejected out of hand.

With the arrival of the Obama administration the American attitude on negotiating with the Taliban began to change, largely thanks to Dick Holbrooke. When we met at the vice president's residence in early 2009 Dick told me he had brought Barney Rubin, the top American academic expert on Afghanistan, onto his staff. Barney had been a member of Brahimi's team on the Petersburg in 2001 and was an early and persistent advocate for peace talks. Holbrooke spent the next couple of years pushing for negotiations. In 2010 he got the Bush-era ban on contacts with the Taliban lifted. President Karzai established a High Peace Council headed by former president Rabbani to build domestic support for "reconciliation," as the goal of those peace talks became known. In November of that year the first meeting between U.S. officials and Taliban representatives took place in Germany. One month later, on the verge of what might have been an important opening, Dick Holbrook died, the result of a torn aorta. His last recorded words were "end this war in Afghanistan."

Coincident with Holbrooke's outreach, the White House encouraged the Century Foundation to put together an international fact-finding group, headed by Lakhdar Brahimi and including Tom Pickering and myself, to explore the possibilities for peace talks. In visits to Afghanistan and Pakistan we were able to talk to past and present Taliban representatives. We also met with President Karzai, General David Petraeus, then the American commander in Kabul, and the leaders of Pakistan's military intelligence agency, the directorate general for Inter-Service Intelligence, or ISI. On our return we published a report indicating that the Taliban was interested in negotiations and recommended the appointment of an international mediator to get talks started. The White House liked this idea, so Lieutenant General Doug Lute, the top NSC official handling Afghanistan, travelled to Paris to ask Brahimi if he would take on this task. Secretary Clinton intervened, however, arguing that involving a third party like Brahimi would be "contracting out American diplomacy." As a result the idea of an international mediator was dropped in favor of direct U.S.-Taliban talks.

Holbrooke's efforts to push reconciliation forward were slowed by bureaucratic resistance within the administration. This was occasioned, in part, by his difficult relationship with our ambassador and our commanding general in Kabul and with the White House back home. Dick's successor, Marc Grossman, was more collegial, but he continued to face hesitancy in the Defense Department and indecision in the White House. Pickering and I had discussed prospects for reconciliation with General Petraeus while we were in Kabul. He was not opposed to peace talks in principle, but preferred to establish a stronger position on the battlefield first. The Pentagon exhibited similar caution. The president was unwilling to press the debate to a timely conclusion, and as a result the United States missed the opportunity to launch negotiations at the peak of its combat strength in Afghanistan.

In 2011 American and Taliban representatives discussed several possible confidence-building measures that might accompany the launch of peace negotiations. These measures included the transfer of several Taliban detainees captured in the early days of the American intervention in exchange for an American soldier, Sergeant Bowe Bergdahl, being held by the Taliban. Such an exchange had been agreed to in principal when Afghan president Karzai raised a more fundamental objection.

Karzai had been an early proponent of talking to the Taliban. For years he had been dissuaded from doing so by American officials. As Washington's interest in such talks waxed, however, Karzai's waned. Karzai wanted an Afghan-centered peace process, with the Kabul government and the Taliban inside the room and everyone else out. Washington said it also wanted an Afghan-led negotiation, but Karzai no longer trusted the United States. Confidence had eroded over the years as successive American officials listened politely to his concerns and then ignored his advice, requests, and directives. It had taken a further steep dive when Senator Biden, elected but not yet inaugurated as vice president, stalked out of a dinner with Karzai after a heated exchange about corruption. Then Obama decided to discontinue the monthly video conferences Bush had held with Afghan and Iraqi leaders. Relations with Karzai reached a nadir in 2009 when Dick Holbrooke began encouraging prominent Afghans to run against him in that year's presidential election. The Afghan leader concluded Dick was leading an effort to replace him, and this was not paranoia. The head of the UN mission in Kabul, Kai Eide, and American Secretary of Defense Bob Gates had both levied the same charge. When controversy arose over the results of the 2009 vote, Holbrooke urged Karzai to agree to a second round of balloting, further enraging the Afghan president. Senator Kerry, then chair of the Senate Foreign Relations Committee, was flown in to calm Karzai, who eventually agreed to a second round only to see his opponent Abdullah Abdullah withdraw.

It was against this background of suspicion and hostility that Karzai viewed the prospect of U.S.-Taliban talks. In early 2012 the Taliban was ready to negotiate with the United States but not with Karzai or his representatives. Karzai insisted talks should not proceed without his government's participation. Washington did not think it could proceed with peace talks over the open opposition of the Afghan government. Apprised of Karzai's condition, the Taliban broke off further contact with the United States.

This was the situation when I took over from Grossman a year later. But within weeks of my arrival Qatar, Pakistan, and two other Western governments all reported to us that the insurgent leadership was ready to open talks with both the United States and the government in Kabul.

Preparation for such talks became the main focus of my activity. The first step was to revive agreement in Washington on the proposal, which Grossman had first put to the Taliban representatives in early 2012. This envisaged the opening of a Taliban office in the Qatari capital for the purpose of talking to American and Afghan representatives, on the understanding that the first item on the agenda for the U.S.-Taliban conversations would be the exchange of five Taliban detainees from Guantanamo for the American soldier held by the Taliban. Before putting this proposal to the Taliban, I needed to make sure Kerry and Secretary of Defense Hagel, neither of whom had been in office in early 2012 when this scheme was first devised, were on board. Then I would need to do the same with Karzai.

The issue was put on the agenda for a meeting of the National Security Council, my first exposure to Obama. I found him very much at ease and quite familiar with the issues. In fact, he was clearly the most relaxed person in the room; he was the president, after all. Still I was struck by the contrast between the cabinet secretaries and their equivalents sitting up straight and looking very businesslike while Obama at the head of the table casually leaned back and crossed his legs.

Kerry was on the road and so participated via secure video. I had sent him a memo and we had spoken for a few minutes by phone, but we had not been in the same city for several weeks. I was disconcerted to find him taking a line divergent from what I had advised. This wasn't the last time I would discover we differed only when we both showed up in the White House Situation Room. This did not seem to faze Kerry, who, during one later White House meeting, engaged me in an extended exchange regarding some point at issue while everyone else waited to see what State position would emerge. For my part, I would have been a lot more comfortable if there had been time to hash out these possible differences beforehand, but there seldom was.

The president and Tom Donilon, who was in his last weeks as national security adviser, were strongly in favor of proceeding along the lines mapped out a year earlier, so there was enough of a Washington consensus to put a proposal to Karzai. I set out on my first trip to Afghanistan and Pakistan since the Century Foundation visit three years earlier, and Doug Lute joined me, along with several members of my own staff. Lute had joined the Bush White House as its war czar during the darkest days of the Iraq conflict and stayed on into the Obama administration, remaining responsible for Afghanistan after the American military withdrawal from Iraq. His support for the president's decision to end the American presence in Iraq and to draw down troop levels in Afghanistan put him at odds with the Pentagon, and this had effectively ended his military career short of the fourth star that should have rewarded his service to two presidents and the management of two wars. Instead, Obama nominated Doug to become the U.S. ambassador to NATO. His name was then put before the Senate.

Lute and Holbrooke did not get on. Dick had sought to move the locus of interagency coordination on Af/Pak issues from the White House to

State. Lute resisted, and the two individuals and their subordinates entered into trench warfare. Remnants of this bad blood lingered several years later. Survivors of those earlier battles on my staff warned me to be careful, but I had known Lute for years and felt we could work together smoothly, as generally proved to be the case.

We took a plane from Andrews Air Force base, overnighted in the UK, and then flew on to Kabul, where we met with President Karzai. I hoped, based on my earlier association with the president, to smooth over some of the irritations that had developed between him and the Obama administration. Karzai greeted me warmly, but we almost immediately fell into disagreement. I explained that the Taliban was now ready for direct talks with his representatives as well as with the United States and proposed we proceed along the lines that had been agreed on between our two governments in 2012, permitting the opening of a Taliban office in Doha and the beginning of parallel U.S.-Taliban and Afghan-Taliban talks. Karzai asked how we could be sure the Taliban representatives in Doha would confine their activities to these talks rather than seek to function as an all-purpose embassy to the world of an alternative Afghan government. I responded that we had negotiated an exchange of diplomatic notes with Qatar committing that government to enforce limits to the activities of the Taliban office that would preclude such behavior. Karzai said that any such commitment by Qatar should be made to him, not the United States.

Karzai then turned to his foreign minister, Zalmai Rassoul, and instructed him to fly forthwith to Doha and conclude such an agreement. Rassoul sighed resignedly, recognizing a mission impossible, but nodded his assent.

Lute and I went on to Islamabad to meet with Pakistan's army chief, General Ashfaq Parvez Kayani. Kerry had cultivated Kayani, meeting with him several times and speaking regularly by telephone. This treatment reflected the fact that the army, not the foreign ministry, president, or prime minister ran Pakistani foreign policy. Kayani had promised to be helpful in bringing the Taliban to the table, and it now looked like he was about to deliver. We met at army headquarters, located in a lush green British Raj-era cantonment with acres of manicured lawn dotted with well-kept bungalows, an environment in stark contrast with the rundown, sun baked city all around it.

Kayani had the annoying habit of chain smoking throughout meetings and mumbling in a low, barely comprehensible voice. I found him eager to be complimented on his success in bringing the Taliban to the table; once, indeed twice, was not often enough. He was already jealous about the Qatari role, and I had to stress that Qatar was only the host, not the mediator for these prospective talks. I assured him that we still considered Pakistan our most important partner in promoting peace processes and suggested he assign someone to Doha with whom we could consult regularly as talks proceeded. He agreed, turning to his intelligence chief, Lieutenant General Zaheer-ul-Islam, to so direct.

Later in the day I telephoned the outgoing president, Asif Ali Zardari, who was in Karachi. We then took a helicopter to Lahore, some 200 miles distant, to meet with the prime minister-elect, Nawaz Sharif. The helo, an updated version of the Vietnam-era Huey, had been originally provided to Pakistan by the United States for use in counternarcotics operations. The weather was very hot, the afternoon sun beating down on the open-sided cockpit, and the landscape below was densely populated and parched. Lahore, when we arrived, was something of a relief; it is reputed to be the greenest of Pakistani cities.

We drove to Sharif's estate on the outskirts of town. Sharif had spent several years in exile in Saudi Arabia following his overthrow by the army in 1999, and I had been warned to expect opulence. The decor of his home was, indeed, like something one might find in the *Arabian Nights*. Two stuffed lions stood guard in the entry hall, and a six-foot circular table was covered with a mountain of assorted chocolates. Sharif greeted us warmly and introduced half a dozen of his advisers, several of whom were about to become ministers in his government. We then arranged ourselves in a crescent, which I always find annoying, as it requires the two principals to shift sideways in their seats to talk to each other while those at the far ends strain to hear.

Sharif had just won a general election, his party having achieved an absolute majority in the parliament. He spoke briefly and generally about his intentions, but mostly listened and asked questions. I explained where we were on reconciliation and what we hoped for from Pakistan in that regard. Sharif spoke warmly about his relationship with Dick Holbrooke, saying Dick had shared his enthusiasm for large, monumental infrastructure projects. Recalling his own role in building the freeway linking Islamabad and Lahore, he suggested the United States build a subway system for Karachi, the country's largest city. The conversation was not very substantive, but Sharif made clear his desire for a close relationship with Washington.

We flew that evening from Lahore to Turkey for a meeting the next day with Qatari Deputy Foreign Minister Khalid-Al-Attiyah. Istanbul is the most beautiful city in the world, and any excuse to visit will do, but this meeting was important. I explained to Al-Attiyah that Karzai wanted to conclude a written agreement with Qatar spelling out the conditions under which the Taliban could operate in Doha. I understood his government was not likely to accord Karzai this kind of oversight and recognized the Taliban would rather abandon talks and the office rather than accept any such arrangement. I, nevertheless, urged that the Qataris find some way of meeting Karzai halfway.

That evening my team had dinner on a glittering barge in the middle of the Bosporus. Barney Rubin, a connoisseur and bon vivant, ordered the meal, consisting principally of several different fresh fishes chosen live from tanks. We were all in a buoyant mood, hopeful that long-sought peace talks would commence within a few weeks. Someone discovered this was my birthday, and the evening concluded with a cake topped, in lieu of candles, with half a dozen sparklers.

The Qataris refused, as we anticipated, to negotiate an agreement with Kabul regarding its treatment of the Taliban representatives. But the emir did invite Karzai for a visit, which went so well that Karzai agreed to drop his demand and move ahead with opening the Taliban office. We, for our part, completed the exchange of notes with the Qataris detailing the limits under which the Taliban office would operate. The most important of these restrictions was that the Taliban representatives should present themselves only as the political office of the Taliban movement, not as the representatives of the so-called Islamic Emirate, the name under which the Taliban had once governed Afghanistan.

The ceremonial opening of the office took place on June 18. It closed several hours later. The Taliban representatives had done exactly what Karzai had feared and what we had agreed with Qatar they should not be allowed to do. The televised opening of the office, in the presence of Qatari officials, took place beneath the flag of the Islamic Emirate in a walled compound bearing the sign "Office of the Islamic Emirate." Kerry immediately telephoned the emir to protest. The flag and sign came down, but the damage had been done. Karzai made a great fuss, stoking protests across the political spectrum in Afghanistan. The Taliban, for its part, felt it had been humiliated and declared the office closed.

Kerry and I traveled to Doha that weekend. We sought an explanation as to how this had been allowed to happen. The emir, flanked by a distant relative who had been handling relations with the local Taliban representatives, claimed that U.S. officials, in discussions more than a year earlier, had told them that the Taliban representatives could label themselves as they pleased as long as they understood that others would not accept the Islamic Emirate title. I responded that surely the memorandum of understanding we had concluded on this topic a week earlier superseded anything that might have been said a year ago. The emir brushed this aside, asking why we were showing such deference to Karzai, whose regime was not likely to last very long. This remark betrayed the emir's real attitude toward the Kabul government and his distant cousin's consequent tilt toward the Taliban.

At the conclusion of the meeting Al-Attiyah gave me a lift to my own vehicle, which was sitting in the sun only a few hundred yards distant. But the temperature was 115 degrees and there was no shade. He told me he would be moving up to become foreign minister in a few days and that the Taliban dossier would be moved to the Foreign Ministry, where it would be handled more professionally. He did become foreign minister, but the Taliban dossier continued to be held by a junior member of the royal family.

I went to see the Qatari attorney general with whom my predecessor, Marc Grossman, had negotiated the relevant memorandum of understanding. He, too, alleged that Marc had, a year earlier, said he did not care how the Taliban described itself as long as they understood that others would not follow suit. I expressed doubt Marc ever said any such thing, but insisted that, in any case, this was irrelevant since we had just concluded a written agreement that said otherwise.

Meanwhile, the Taliban representatives continued to insist they would not meet with American or Afghan government representatives without their flag and their sign. They did meet quietly with a couple of other Western government officials, and it was through those channels that their side of the story emerged. The Taliban representatives insisted the Qataris had told them it was okay to present themselves as representing the Islamic Emirate. The Qataris had even procured the flag and constructed the offending sign for them. "It wasn't our idea to have these symbols," the Taliban representatives insisted, "but once having raised the flag and posted the sign, we cannot now proceed without them."

From Doha I went on to Kabul. Karzai was always available and welcoming on these visits, but full of complaints and fantastic allegations. Responding to the mishandled opening of the Taliban's Qatar office, Karzai had already stated publicly that he would not conclude the bilateral security agreement (BSA) with the United States until the Americans brought the Taliban into peace talks.

On its face this was a ludicrous proposition. The BSA was intended to provide the legal basis for a continued American military presence beyond 2014. The Taliban were, naturally, opposed to such a presence and, thus, to such an agreement. By stating that he would not conclude this agreement until the Taliban came to the peace table, Karzai effectively provided the Taliban a veto over the accord and, thus, a means to force an American withdrawal.

There was, nevertheless, a perverted logic to Karzai's stance. He claimed, and perhaps believed, that the United States was intentionally prolonging the war in Afghanistan to perpetuate its military presence in the region. He insisted that Pakistan controlled the Taliban, that the United States controlled Pakistan, and that the United States could, therefore, bring the Taliban to the peace table if it chose. Pakistan did tolerate the Taliban's use of its territory, and did actually facilitate Taliban activities. So Pakistan did have considerable influence, if not control, over the Taliban. The United States also had influence with Pakistan by virtue of a very large economic and military assistance program.

Karzai and I argued over these issues repeatedly throughout the following year. The discussions were spirited, even heated, but usually good humored. Karzai did not mind being contradicted, and could take a joke, but he seldom gave ground. Exasperated after his umpteenth insistence that we could move Pakistan if only we would, I finally responded, "Mr. President, I cannot get you to do what I want. Why do you think I can Pakistan? Afghanistan is, after all, far more dependent on the United States than is Pakistan." Karzai smiled, acknowledging the debating point, but returned to his position in our next conversation.

I shared Karzai's frustration with Pakistani behavior. In 2001, Islamabad had abandoned the Taliban regime, but not the Taliban movement, which was given time, space, and even some assistance within Pakistan as it regrouped, resupplied, recruited, retrained, and began to project power back into Afghanistan. Admiral Mike Mullen, chair of the joint chiefs from 2007 to 2011, had visited Pakistan twenty-seven times in an effort to cultivate General Kayani and wean Pakistan from its tolerance of and support for Afghan militant groups. In the end, Mullen admitted defeat.

I spend my time in office in a similar effort with not much more to show for it. The problem was that the United States wanted several things from Pakistan. The first of these was help in tracking down remaining Al Qaeda operatives. We also needed to use Pakistani air space, ports, and roads to supply our forces in Afghanistan. We were urging restraint in the growth of Pakistan's nuclear arsenal. Help combating the Taliban was only one objective among several, and unfortunately not always Washington's top priority.

My next stop was Islamabad, where Prime Minister Sharif again asked to see me. Kayani was in attendance, and I noticed he neither smoked nor mumbled in the prime minister's presence. I urged Sharif to reach out to Karzai and make an effort to repair the relationship between the two governments. Sharif expressed concern about the threat Pakistan faced from its own version of the Taliban, the Tehrik-e Taliban Pakistan (TTP) or Pakistani Taliban. "We have no strategy for dealing with them," he said. "What should we do?" Was reconciliation, as we were trying in Afghanistan, the answer, he wondered. I responded that the Pakistani Taliban would have to come under a great deal more military pressure before they were likely to enter serious negotiations.

Sharif took my first piece of advice but did just the opposite regarding the second. Later that same day he telephoned Karzai and invited him to Islamabad, but for an entire year he forbade any military action against the TTP while he sought to engage them in negotiations. Only once he had demonstrated conclusively to the public and parliament that the TTP was not ready for meaningful talks did he authorize a military offensive into the wild border region the militants had long dominated.

This campaign proved broadly successful, leading eventually to a significant decrease in militant violence throughout Pakistan. The offensive also garnered wide public support, which it would not have done had he taken my advice and launched the attack before trying to negotiate. Delay came at some cost, however. American and NATO troops had been drawn down substantially over that same year, and Afghan forces were severely stretched as a result. Thousands of the militants forced out of Pakistan by the army offensive simply moved into neighboring Afghanistan and continued operating from there. Had the offensive been launched a year earlier, these militants would have been caught between American and Pakistani forces. Instead they found unimpeded sanctuary on the Afghan side of the border.

Following the meeting with Sharif, Kayani and I went to an adjoining room where we were joined by Jalil Jilani, the number two at the Foreign Ministry (and later ambassador to Washington). Kayani was naturally disappointed at the failure to launch the Doha talks that he had been instrumental in arranging. Jilani, hearing I was going on to New Delhi, asked that I urge the Indians to resume their "composite dialogue" with Pakistan, which had been interrupted because of ceasefire violations along the line of control in divided Kashmir.

Our embassy found it notable that Kayani had attended the meeting with the prime minister, something he had not bothered to do under the previous government. They were similarly struck by Kayani inviting the foreign ministry to join his own meeting with me. These were taken as encouraging signs of some shift in the civil-military relationship in favor of the former. Unfortunately this proved to be largely wishful thinking. Sharif and his ministers were a bit more active in the national security field than their immediate predecessors, but the army continued to dominate policy on all issues of importance to Washington.

In New Delhi, the Indians were quite interested in Afghanistan, but not in improving relations with Islamabad. They did not question Sharif's good faith but doubted his ability to overcome the army's collusion with anti-Indian and anti-Afghan militant groups. This attitude, encountered repeatedly over the following year, was grounded in bitter experience but was, nevertheless, deeply frustrating, as it foreclosed any prospect of improvement. Insanity has been defined as repeatedly doing the same thing and expecting different results, but in diplomacy, if one does not keep trying to solve intractable problems, there is zero chance of success. Indian officials were right to be skeptical about the capacity of Pakistan's civilian leaders to follow through on any commitments made, but it would have been more productive to have tested some of these openings rather than regard them as meaningless.

Kerry visited Islamabad a month later, following which Sharif came to Washington. I pushed on both occasions to put the Afghan Taliban safe havens in Pakistan at the top of our list of objectives. There was a good deal of competition. The CIA and some in the Pentagon were still focused heavily on Al Qaeda targets. One senior Defense Department official suggested we stop pushing the Pakistan army to clean out the militant-dominated tribal area of North Waziristan on the grounds that doing so might make it more difficult for us to track down remaining Al Qaeda leaders. The use of Pakistani roads and ports remained essential for the supply of our forces in Afghanistan. Demonstrations had succeeded in closing these border crossings to U.S. and NATO cargoes for some weeks in protest over continued drone strikes on the Pakistani side of the border.

Kerry and the rest of the administration were also concerned about the growth of the Pakistani nuclear inventory and wanted to urge restraint both in numbers and types of weapons. I thought this a wasted expenditure of influence, as the Pakistani's were largely paralleling the sorts of things we had done during the Cold War and were unlikely to pay much heed to our urging them to "do what we say, not what we did."

Both Kerry and the president did feature the issue of "cross border militancy" prominently in their meetings and, in Kerry's case, in his public remarks in Islamabad. I suggested employing the term "cross border militancy" to stress that the phenomenon was now cutting both ways, with sanctuaries on both sides of the border from which attacks were launched on the other. Nor was the Afghan intelligence service immune from playing the same game as the ISI, working with the TTP just as the ISI was working with the Afghan Taliban. Nevertheless the volume of militant infiltration from Pakistan into Afghanistan far exceeded the reverse flow.

The response from Sharif and his civilian advisers was positive. They accepted the legitimacy of U.S. concerns and did not refute—in fact, privately acknowledged—that their military was doing just what the United States alleged. They promised it would stop but cautioned it would take time.

The military line changed as well, particularly after Kayani's retirement. When pressed to do something about the Afghan Taliban and, in particular, the Haqqani network, Kayani's response had been that the army had to concentrate on the militant groups of greatest threat to Pakistan. It could not afford to drive the Afghan and Pakistani Taliban closer together. Kayani's successor, Raheel Sharif (no relationship with the prime minister), promised, in contrast, that the army was going to treat all militants equally as soon as the prime minister authorized an offensive into North Waziristan.

Unfortunately, the follow-through on these promises was disappointing. In June 2014, after a year of unproductive attempts at dialogue with the TTP, the Pakistani army swept into North Waziristan and began cleaning out TTP strongholds, largely emptying the area of civilians as well. Afghan Taliban elements were allowed to flee unhindered with the civilians, and the Haqqani network simply relocated elsewhere in the border region. Its operations against targets in Afghanistan were temporarily disrupted but eventually renewed, and nothing was done to make the life of the Taliban top leadership, which made its home in the adjoining province of Baluchistan, more difficult.

Pakistan's tolerance and support for the Afghan Taliban began as a calculated means of power projection in its regional competition with India. Increasingly this relationship became a defensive measure, designed to avoid adding one more extremist adversary to the several already seeking to subvert the Pakistani state. What started as an offensive measure to gain influence became a defensive measure to avoid damage. But the effect upon Afghanistan and American forces there was unchanged.

In retrospect, Kayani's frank acknowledgment that the army was not prepared to antagonize the Afghan Taliban was preferable to General Sharif's insincere assurances that the army would. It is virtually impossible to negotiate with someone who says he agrees with you but does not. Successful negotiation requires the two sides to acknowledge their differences and then try to narrow them. Assent, however insincere, pretty much ends any discussion.

Relations with Karzai continued to deteriorate to the point that several European leaders reported to Obama that Karzai was accusing the United States of perpetuating the war and intentionally sabotaging prospects for peace. Incensed, the president arranged a video conference with Karzai to rebut these charges, but when confronted with what he was alleged to have said, Karzai did not back down. Rather he stoutly reaffirmed these views, and the discussion became heated. Obama asked everyone to leave the video conference rooms in Washington and Kabul, and the two presidents spoke further for most of an hour. Of course, the conversation was monitored in the White House, and presumably in Kabul as well. Karzai gave no ground and the conversation ended with no resolution of their differences.

Lute called me in New Delhi to inform me of this exchange. He said Obama had instructed him to have Jim Cunningham, our ambassador in

Kabul, deliver to Karzai a message recalling a number of things the two presidents had agreed on during Karzai's January visit to Washington and asking pointedly for assurances that Karzai still intended to follow through. I was annoyed that this video conference between Obama and Karzai had taken place and would certainly have counseled against it had I been asked. I was even more annoyed that Lute had sent instructions directly to Cunningham rather than through the department and, thus, me. I was even more upset when I saw what he sent, which had the appearance of an ultimatum. I was sure Lute accurately reflected the heated tone of the president's instructions, but I was equally sure Karzai was no more likely to be browbeaten into line with written complaints than he had been in direct conversation with Obama.

Ambassadors are instructed not to accept directions from anywhere but the State Department, with the sole exception of instructions that come to them from the president personally, and this one did not. I called Cunningham to remonstrate and was somewhat mollified when he assured me he had not delivered the message as received, but had, in more neutral language, listed the previous points of agreement and asked Karzai whether they remained valid. Not surprisingly the Afghan president never responded.

There was no improvement in Karzai's behavior and the whole exchange had just further poisoned the relationship. In fact, this episode opened a yearlong clash of wills between Obama and Karzai. Obama insisted Karzai conclude the bilateral security agreement before he, Obama, would decide whether to retain U.S. forces in Afghanistan. Karzai refused to conclude the BSA until the United States persuaded the Taliban to begin peace talks with his government. The Taliban, observing this public confrontation, naturally declined to come to the table.

Obama's position in this dispute was not much more logical than Karzai's. The United States already had a perfectly satisfactory status of forces agreement with Afghanistan. This document had been concluded in 2002 with the then-unelected provisional government headed by Karzai, and that agreement had no expiration date. It gave American forces complete freedom of action. It was Karzai who had asked that a new accord be drawn up, one that would give greater weight to Afghan sovereignty and impose more limits on the activities of American forces. Obama had agreed, and so my office had been assigned responsibility for negotiating the new accord, which was, by this time, largely completed. The White

House argument that we needed a new agreement to keep troops in Afghanistan was completely specious. Obama's converting something the Afghans wanted into something the United Stated needed made no sense unless the president was looking for an excuse to withdraw from Afghanistan entirely. He had, after all, withdrawn American forces from Iraq in 2011 on precisely the same grounds, the absence of a status of forces agreement. I thought Obama was unlikely to repeat this action in Afghanistan, but there seemed to be elements in the White House who were keeping that option open.

Karzai, for his part, felt safe refusing to conclude the BSA because he really believed Washington had larger geopolitical reasons for wanting to retain military bases in Afghanistan having to do with its competition with China, Russia, and Iran and, therefore, wanted to stay indefinitely. One of his predecessors, the nineteenth-century Shah Shuja, had concluded a similar agreement with the British and was overthrown as a result. Karzai wasn't worried about being overthrown, but he was concerned about his legacy and did not want to be remembered as the leader who invited a permanent American occupation. Tactically, the very fact that Obama was insisting on the BSA gave Karzai leverage only so long as he resisted. The effect of this foolish and wholly counterproductive confrontation was to greatly increase uncertainty regarding American and NATO intentions within the American government, within the NATO alliance, and most damaging, among the Afghan public. This occurred just as Western troops began leaving, the Afghan economy slowed, the war heated up, national elections approached, and the country prepared for the first democratic transfer of power in its history. Obama was stubborn, Karzai delusional, and both leaders were behaving badly.

Karzai won this particular face-off. He never did conclude the BSA, and Obama finally agreed to keep American troops in Afghanistan for at least two more years. This was not because Obama wanted a permanent U.S. presence. Quite the contrary, he clearly would have preferred to leave. But in the end Obama was rational and responsible and Karzai was neither, which gave the latter the advantage in such a pointless game of chicken.

For the next several months we continued to work on the BSA text. Eventually Kerry flew to Kabul and spent a long day and a half closing out the remaining issues. Karzai intended to submit the resultant text to a grand council, or *loya jirga*, that he had called especially to review the document. Tensions were high and the discussion occasionally quite sharp.

Kerry threatened to walk away several times, and Ashraf Ghani, then an adviser to Karzai, and I both intervened at different points to get things back on track. General Joseph Dunford, our commander in Afghanistan, contributed constructively to overcome several roadblocks. Then just when we thought we had an agreed-upon final text Karzai balked, saying he disagreed with some points that he had accepted an hour earlier. He said he would submit the text as it stood to the *loya jirga* but would not recommend approval.

Shortly thereafter 2,500 prominent figures from all over the country assembled in Kabul to review the draft agreement. Their number included all members of parliament and a number of locally elected officials. Karzai made the opening presentation. It contained some tendentious language, but he was generally positive about the agreement without explicitly recommending approval. After two days of debate, the *jirga* overwhelmingly endorsed the accord, with only a couple dozen members dissenting.

The assembly went further; it explicitly called on Karzai to sign the agreement before the end of the year. This he had not expected. Karzai addressed the group a second time, announcing he would not sign the agreement but would, rather, leave this task to his successor, who was not to be elected until spring of the following year at the earliest.

For its part, the White House kept announcing new deadlines, threatening that all American forces would leave the country at the end of 2014 if the BSA was not concluded by September of 2013, and when that date had passed, by November, then by the end of the year. Ultimately the agreement was not signed until a full year later, on September 29, 2014, and not by Karzai.

Throughout this period of uncertainty, I was called several times to testify before the House and Senate Foreign Affairs and Defense Committees and to confidentially brief the House and Senate leadership in smaller settings. I found most members of both houses and both parties supportive of a continued American military commitment and critical of the president for delaying a decision on its duration and extent. Many members, Democrat as well as Republican, had visited Afghanistan repeatedly over the years and had a sense of what was at stake. Even Nancy Pelosi, Democratic Leader of the House, came up to me after one such session to express her concern that we not abandon the women of Afghanistan.

Asked in testimony before the Senate Foreign Relations Committee whether there was a real prospect of the zero option for Afghanistan that the White House kept threatening, I said I thought not. Polling through-out Afghanistan showed strong support for a continued American and NATO presence. All the likely candidates to succeed Karzai in the up-coming elections had indicated they would sign the BSA as soon as they took office. I expressed confidence that one way or another the agree-ment would be concluded, opening the way for a continued American engagement.

Someone in the White House didn't like this response and brought it to the president's attention. Tony Blinken, the deputy national security ad-viser, called to warn me. The next day the National Security Council met to discuss a proposal from Jim Cunningham, our ambassador in Kabul. After consulting with me Jim had sent a telegram urging that the presi-dent should announce troop levels for 2015 in advance of the upcoming Afghan presidential elections, even if the BSA had not yet been signed. Ben Rhodes, who managed White House messaging on national security issues and was the main purveyor of the zero option threat, argued that this would undercut the credibility of our deadline, which at that point had already been passed once. The president asked my view, and I agreed with Cunningham. The vice president said any decision to retain American forces in Afghanistan was going to be very unpopular on the Hill to which I responded that, on the contrary, I had encountered broad satisfaction when I reassured members that the BSA would ultimately be signed. The president turned to me to say that this reassurance was not consistent with the current administration line. He proceeded, politely but firmly, to dress me down for breaking ranks.

Cunningham's proposal was rejected. The size, mission, and disposi-tion of American forces for 2015 and beyond remained uncertain for an-other seven months, and this created similar uncertainty for more than a dozen other allies, who would stay if we did and leave if we did not stay.

In January, the NSC met again. The president heard an intelligence community assessment that the size of the residual American presence being recommended by General Dunford for 2015 was probably the mini-mum necessary to hold the country together for even a few more years. Kerry said the choice was clear-cut, but the president disagreed, challenging the assessment. He and Biden again got into a mutually reinforcing ex-change about American public opinion.

"You know," the president said, "that Afghanistan today has become more unpopular than Vietnam ever was." This was jaw-dropping stuff.

Seated to the president's left was former lieutenant John Kerry, USN, and to Biden's right, former sergeant Chuck Hagel, USA, both of whom were old enough to know from personal experience how ludicrously untrue this assertion was. No one said anything, however. The president sent us all back to revise our assessments and refine the options some more.

As the months passed, the costs of delay began to mount. Bases began to close and people to leave whom the Pentagon and other agencies were recommending should stay. Meanwhile Afghan attitudes were clear. Of the eleven candidates for president, ten campaigned on a promise to sign the BSA immediately upon assuming office. The eleventh privately promised to do the same. In the second round of voting, the two remaining candidates repeated the same promise. Signing the BSA and keeping American forces in-country was clearly a vote winner in Afghanistan.

Finally, in late May 2014, Obama announced his decision to retain 9,800 American troops in Afghanistan in 2015, to reduce that to 5,500 by 2016 and to zero by 2017. The figure for 2015 was within a few hundred of Dunford's recommendation. The lower figure for 2016 and zero beyond were not condition-based but simply reflected a decision to close out American involvement in the conflict by the end of the president's term in office.

One week after this announcement the Iraqi army collapsed. Islamic State fighters swarmed out of Syria, captured Mosul, and advanced to within sight of Baghdad, underscoring rather dramatically the consequences of premature withdrawal. Disastrous as this development was, I was relieved, knowing that the president would not now carry out his announced intention to withdraw entirely from Afghanistan before the end of his term.

In the fall of 2013 our line to the Taliban lit up again. The Qataris reported that Taliban representatives were willing to resume discussions regarding a prisoner swap. Kerry agreed we should respond positively, and when Cunningham and I raised it with Karzai, he had no objection. My military and civilian colleagues at Defense were positive, but Hagel had doubts. At his request, we met, and he expressed his concern that Karzai would use any U.S. contact with the Taliban as yet another excuse not to conclude the BSA. I replied that the opposite was more likely. Having made a peace process his condition for signing the BSA, a failure to take up this Taliban offer of talks would only reinforce Karzai in his refusal to conclude that agreement. Hagel pronounced himself satisfied and approved our going ahead, but the next day I was told he had changed his mind. Officials in his office intimated to the White House that Hagel felt I had misled him. I called Jim Miller, the head of Hagel's policy staff, to say I could not continue in my position if I had lost the confidence of the secretary of defense. Shortly thereafter I received a call from Mark Lippert, Hagel's chief aide, assuring me the secretary did not feel in any way misled, but had simply reconsidered his position.

The issue continued to be debated, and in early 2014 Hagel indicated his agreement to the swap. By the time we were ready to engage, however, the Taliban had withdrawn its offer of direct talks, having woken up to the import of Karzai's statement that he would not conclude an agreement providing for a continuing American military presence in the absence of peace talks and to Obama's repeated statements that the United States would not stay beyond 2014 without such an agreement.

While not willing to engage directly, the Taliban did agree to work on the Bergdahl exchange through the Qataris. This time both sides avoided a repetition of the June 2014 misunderstandings by communicating exclusively in writing, with the Qataris simply passing texts back and forth. Several months were required to complete negotiations by way of this laborious process, but on May 31, Bergdahl was returned to U.S. custody and five Taliban detainees were transferred from Guantanamo to Qatar, where they were to remain for at least a year.

The swap provoked loud protests from Congress. The most serious complaint was that the administration had failed to provide the forty-five-day notice to Congress required by law for any intended transfers out of Guantanamo. The president had chosen not to do so because of concern that if public notice was given of the Taliban's intention to release Bergdahl forty-five days in advance of his actual move, the agreement and Bergdahl himself would be at risk. Some members of Congress asked us why we could not have let them know in confidence about the intended transfer, but others said quite plainly that, had they been informed, they would have done their utmost to block it.

The issue of notification aside many members simply didn't like the five-for-one swap. They characterized Bergdahl as a deserter and the five Taliban detainees as "the worst of the worst." Actually the Taliban detainees in question had been captured or had surrendered soon after American entry into Afghanistan. Most of them had nothing whatsoever to do with the ensuing insurgency and none had any connection with 9/11. The charge that they would "return to the battlefield" was overblown, since most of them had never been on the battlefield. They were mostly mid-level and now late- to middle-age officials of which the Taliban had no shortage, and they weren't going back to Afghanistan anytime soon.

The White House compounded its difficulties by the manner in which it handled the announcement of Bergdahl's return. The president held a Rose Garden ceremony with Bergdahl's parents, which gave the mistaken impression that the administration regarded Bergdahl as a returning hero. Susan Rice's subsequent statement on a Sunday talk show that Bergdahl had "served honorably" compounded this impression.

Bergdahl had, in fact, been a good soldier until the day he left his post, but the circumstances of that departure remained unexplained. Bergdahl had also endured five years of brutal captivity, including months confined blindfolded in a small iron cage. He had made a couple of serious attempts to escape, one of which was briefly successful. So the congressional rush to judgment regarding his behavior seemed to me unfair and certainly prejudicial to the eventual handling of his case by the military authorities.

Our principal preoccupation through the first half of 2014 was the Afghan presidential election. The process started off well but then went badly off track. All the institutional and legislative requirements had been met in good time: an electoral law had been passed, an election commission was appointed following the consultative procedures set out in that law, ballots were printed, and elaborate security arrangements were put in place. Twenty-seven candidates presented themselves and sixteen were disqualified by the electoral commission. Three more dropped out as election day approached, throwing their support to one or another of the remaining candidates. The remaining eight contenders participated in rallies throughout the country, all of which went off peacefully. Afghan television broadcast multiple debates, and campaign rhetoric was generally responsible and issue-oriented, without divisive sectarian appeals. The first round of voting was held on schedule, on April 5, and eight million Afghans voted, defying significant Taliban efforts to disrupt the balloting. The Afghan army and police provided all the security; NATO forces remaining in the background and largely on their bases. Abdullah Abdullah, Karzai's first foreign minister, received 45 percent of the vote and Ashraf Ghani, an Afghan American former World Bank official and Karzai's first finance minister, came in second with 34 percent. Since neither received an absolute majority, a second round of voting was scheduled.

Karzai played a puzzling role throughout the campaign. He was almost universally suspected of maneuvering to stay in office, but he neither said nor did anything to substantiate this accusation. On the contrary he encouraged several prominent figures to join the race and provided advice to a number of candidates. For instance, it was he who urged Ghani to choose Abdul Rashid Dostum as his running mate. This was an odd coupling. Dostum, who was widely regarded as the most brutal of Afghan warlords, had earlier been characterized by Ghani himself as a "known killer." Yet he brought with him the Uzbek vote and this, ultimately, provided Ghani his margin of victory.

I believed Karzai was sincere in wanting to oversee a peaceful and democratic transfer of power. His constant maneuvering among the candidates betrayed an eagerness to remain relevant and avoid lame duck status as long as he could, and he may also have wanted to ensure that whoever won would be in his debt. In the end, however, even this master politician lost control of the situation and had to call on us for help.

The second round was scheduled for June 14. On June 6, an attack on Abdullah's motorcade killed three of his bodyguards, but the candidate was unhurt. Vigorous campaigning resumed countrywide, again with little further violence.

I ordered a series of nine opinion polls to be conducted throughout the campaign, funded by the United States but organized by several nonpartisan Afghan civil society groups. My experience with the Serbian elections in 2000 had demonstrated that opinion polling could play an important role in countering electoral fraud. I thought such polls might also help discredit the usual response of losers in third world elections, who invariably allege that they were robbed, no matter how great their margin of loss.

Unfortunately, in a low trust society like Afghanistan, no one accepts the neutrality of anyone else. Our first poll showed Abdullah ahead. Ghani's team immediately alleged that the United States was trying to throw the race to Abdullah. The next of our polls showed Ghani gaining. Abdullah's team launched an immediate attack on the validity of the survey. Karzai also began muttering about foreign interference. At Cunningham's urging, I canceled the remaining polls. Ghani's camp then commissioned its own poll, which showed him gaining on Abdullah.

The second-round results raised eyebrows in several respects. Participation was considerably higher than the first, leading to charges of ballot box stuffing. Many of these additional votes came from rather insecure areas where it was difficult for independent observers to validate the claimed participation. Having been eleven points behind in the first round, Ghani came out several points ahead in the second. Concerns were further raised when Abdullah released voice recordings of the electoral commission's chief operating officer conspiring to stuff ballot boxes in favor of Ghani.

Having over the previous year been repeatedly subjected to Karzai's bitter complaints about Holbrooke's prominent role in the 2009 presidential campaign, I chose to keep a low profile throughout this campaign. In the aftermath of this dubious and loudly protested second-round result, however, it was clear the United States would have to step in and help broker some acceptable way forward. In a remarkable turnaround from his 2009 performance, Karzai actually begged me to do so.

I traveled to Kabul ten days after the second-round balloting. Results had not been officially announced, but it was widely known that the count showed Ghani with a substantial lead. Abdullah was just beginning to release excerpts of the recordings, probably made by the Afghan intelligence service, of the chief electoral officer plotting to skew the results, and tensions were rising. Ghani might have the votes but Abdullah had the guns. Most of the army and police leadership favored him, as did several of the most powerful provincial governors. I met first with President Karzai, who admitted he was no longer able to control developments. He told me it was now up to the United States and the rest of the international community to retrieve the situation, and he promised to cooperate with us in so doing. At the conclusion of our conversation I noted that, for the first time in over a year, we had gotten through an entire meeting without a single argument. Karzai smiled and promised that until this electoral crisis had been surmounted the truce would continue, and he was true to his word.

I met with both candidates in their private homes. Each insisted he had won and the other was trying to steal the election. Abdullah was calm, friendly, and unthreatening, but embassy reporting made clear that some of his supporters were less so. Ghani began our conversation by laying out his plans on assuming office. I had to remind him that he was not yet president. Ghani, a smart and charming man, was also known to have a short fuse, and at a couple of points in our conversation he visibly restrained himself. My message to both candidates was that they were going to have to work together to bring the country out of this dangerous crisis.

I met with Jan Kubis, the head of the UN mission, and relayed President Karzai's appeal for the international community to broker a solution to the crisis. The two of us met jointly with all the Western ambassadors, and then separately with the most important regional representatives, those from Pakistan, Russia, Iran, India, and China, to explain what was going on and what we thought needed to be done. Everyone agreed on the need to recount the second-round ballots. This would be overseen by the UN, who brought in additional personnel for the effort. But whatever the result of that recount, I felt the balloting had been too tainted by irregularities to provide a clear and unassailable result. The two candidates were going to have to be cajoled into some sort of coalition government if the country was not to descend into civil war. I was particularly anxious to encourage the former backers of the Northern Alliance—Russia, Iran, and India—to urge restraint on Abdullah and his supporters.

Kubis and I met with Ahmad Nuristani, the chair of the electoral commission. We urged that he not announce any results and that he cooperate in the UN-supervised recount. This he agreed to do despite pressure from other commission members.

Shortly following my return to Washington I was alerted that a coup d'état was underway. Elements loyal to Abdullah had taken over a number of Kabul police stations and a march on the presidential palace was being organized. Kerry immediately telephoned both candidates, and Secretary of Defense Hagel, Chair of the Joint Chiefs Dempsey, and CIA Director Brennan called their Afghan counterparts.

Later that night Obama himself called Karzai and then the two candidates. Obama made clear that there would be no American assistance to either side of a divided Afghanistan. He said he was directing Kerry to fly to Kabul and urged the candidates to ensure their people did nothing precipitate until the secretary arrived. The next morning Abdullah attended a large meeting of his supporters, which was televised. With some visible difficulty Abdullah was able to persuade his colleagues to stand down and await Kerry.

John Kerry is an impressive negotiator. He uses his physical stature, commanding presence, long familiarity with the actors and issues, and the power of his office to great effect, as I had witnessed in his successful completion of the BSA negotiations. Here, once again, in a couple of days of difficult bargaining with the candidates separately and, eventually, together, he patched together an agreed power sharing arrangement. Both candidates pledged in writing that, depending on how the UN-supervised recount went, one would become president and the other the government's chief executive officer, that other cabinet appointments would be shared equally between them, and that within two years they would work to have the Afghan constitution amended to provide for the office of an "executive prime minister."

Ten days later I visited Kabul again and made the same rounds, seeing Karzai, the candidates, the UN ambassadors, and the electoral commission. Accompanied by the chair of the electoral commission, I went to watch the vote recount. In two airplane hangar-size buildings perhaps a thousand people sat at dozens of tables individually reviewing eight million ballots one at a time. Each table had a staffer of the electoral commission, an official from the UN, someone from civil society, and representatives of both candidates. The hubbub was enormous as each table argued about one ballot at a time. Fighting occasionally broke out, happily not lethal. This was the largest vote recount ever handled by the United Nations, and it was clear to me that the process, while essential, was never going to allay suspicions whatever outcome it eventually produced.

I also found out that the candidates themselves were making no progress toward putting together a coalition government, but were still bargaining over the CEO's job description, responsibilities, and authority. Kerry had to make another visit at the end of August to consolidate the deal on what became the "national unity government." Ghani was inaugurated as president and Abdullah sworn in as chief executive officer, and the BSA was signed the day after. Abdullah acknowledged Ghani as the winner, but he insisted that the actual vote count never be announced. This was a reasonable demand, as the recount process had been imperfect, and while the resultant total had reduced Ghani's vote significantly, it probably still overcounted it.

In my judgment this was the best possible outcome for a close election in an impoverished country in the midst of a civil war that had never in its history experienced a democratic transfer of power. Every one of the country's eight million voters had voted for either Ghani or Abdullah. They had been selected democratically from a much wider field. They were both successful politicians and skilled technocrats with substantial government experience. There were no significant ideological or policy differences between them. They had been colleagues in Karzai's first government and had no history of bad blood. If anyone could hold the country together, it should be these two.

By late summer of 2014 Afghanistan had a new government, the BSA had been signed, and a continued American and NATO military presence was assured, at least through President Obama's term of office. For me it had been a hectic and often frustrating sixteen months, and I was pleased to return to the more relaxed and ordered life of analyst and author.

TWENTY-EIGHT

Reflections

CONFLICT, CONFLICT RESOLUTION, AND POST-CONFLICT recon-struction have occupied much of my professional life. Throughout the Vietnam War I had little responsibility and no influence, but I was able to witness several stages in the war's evolution: conning an aircraft carrier on Yankee Station; monitoring the communications between two nearby de-stroyers as they engaged a phantom enemy in what became the second Tonkin Gulf incident; inadvertently aborting a covert penetration of North Vietnam; participating in the opening phase of the Vietnam peace talks; and then, once back at home, witnessing the social upheaval that ultimately compelled President Nixon to resign and the United States to abandon South Vietnam.

The roughly coincident collapse of South Vietnam and the Nixon pres-idency were shocking. Within a single year the United States had lost its first war and driven its first president from office. Yet from the perspective of the State Department's seventh floor there was remarkably little evi-dence that American influence had been diminished as a result. This was partly a tribute to Henry Kissinger's resilience and energy but also to the inexhaustible abundance of American power. In 1975 the "American century" heralded by Herney Luce in 1941 was not even half over. There was a brief flirtation with retrenchment during the Carter administration, but by the end of his term Jimmy Carter had brokered peace between Egypt and Israel, committed the United States to the defense of the Persian Gulf, begun a covert program to support the anti-communist insurgents in Afghanistan, and secured European support for the deployment of hundreds of nuclear-armed missiles capable of reaching Moscow. Only five short years after the fall of Saigon Ronald Reagan was elected and it was morning in America again.

The year I spent with Sonnenfeldt and Kissinger left me a convert to détente and arms control. I accepted the logic of nuclear deterrence, but I also understood that any system that could fail would do so given enough time. I knew that when mutual assured destruction failed the result would be just that. My next decade was spent working to sustain deterrence at lower levels of risk. This put me on the dovish side of bureaucratic battles between Kissinger and Schlesinger, Vance and Brzezinski, Shultz and Weinberger, to the point that Reaganauts might regard me as a "flaming liberal," although few liberals of that time would have numbered me among their company.

Détente did not end the Cold War, but it did help keep the peace in Central Europe, that conflict's epicenter, the only place where a cold war might turn hot. Kissinger was wedded to the concept of "linkage" and hoped the Soviet Union could be brought to help the United States withdraw from Vietnam with honor. But détente never progressed far beyond Europe. When diplomacy proved unable to blunt Soviet moves in the third world, détente appeared to have failed, but it had served its most important function. Whereas the United States might actually go to war with the USSR over Berlin, it was never going to do so over Angola, El Salvador, or Afghanistan. Enhanced stability in Europe was well worth détente's modest price, while the greater openness that resulted also eventually eased the way for Gorbachev, glasnost, and perestroika.

We now know that by the time Ronald Reagan entered office the Soviet Union was a diminishing, not a growing, threat. Those were the years during which Soviet leaders were dropping like flies: Brezhnev in 1982, Andropov in 1984, and Chernenko in 1985. Aboard Air Force Two, taking Vice President Bush to the third of these funerals, some wag posted a sign: "You Die, We Fly!"

My experience at the time did not accord with those, including Henry Kissinger, who see Reagan's first and second terms as all of a piece, reflecting a core strategy that Reagan followed throughout his presidency. Seen from within, Reagan's first term was chaotic and occasionally quite dangerous. Inexperienced White House advisers and a largely aloof president failed to moderate disputes between the bitterly antagonistic secretaries of defense and state and between the hardline and moderate factions within the administration as personified by the likes of Richard Perle and Richard Burt. It was only after the departure of Cap Weinberger and the arrival of Frank Carlucci as national security adviser and then as secretary of defense, along with the replacement of Don Regan as White House chief of staff by Howard Baker that things settled down, and it took the Iran-Contra debacle to bring about this shake-up. Absent the arrival of this more moderate and collegial set of chief advisers I doubt Reagan would have been able to capitalize on Gorbachev's arrival as successfully as he did.

The Soviet system did not collapse because the United States outspent it militarily but because it had failed to compete with the West in almost every sector of human endeavor. President Reagan did not pursue his fanciful dream of a space-based missile shield as a ploy to bring Moscow to the negotiating table. In fact he insisted on pushing ahead with this unrealizable objective even when Gorbachev offered to abandon nuclear weapons altogether if only Reagan would also abandon this program.

American hawks credit harsh rhetoric, lavish military spending, and a visionary new weapons system for the Soviet Union's collapse. Doves cite gross inefficiencies in the Soviet system, growing recognition of the gulf opening between East and West, particularly in the economic sphere, enlightened policies by a new generation of Soviet leaders, and the skillful engagement of these leaders by their Western interlocutors. I expect both sides deserve some credit. The hawk–dove tensions in American society worked to keep U.S. policy on a relatively steady course, never veering too far from the mean.

Reagan and Shultz seized the opportunity Gorbachev presented to wind down the Cold War; George H. W. Bush, Jim Baker, and Brent Scowcroft brought this process to a conclusion with a tour de force of traditional diplomacy. That team then took the first step toward establishing the "new world order" by leading an unprecedentedly broad international coalition to victory over Saddam Hussein, only to then take half a step backward by standing aside while the Balkans descended into a decade of conflict. The collapse of Yugoslavia was probably inevitable, but stronger, more direct and consistent U.S. involvement alongside the Europeans could have softened that landing.

By the early 1990s the post-Cold War world looked anything but ordered. Famine in Somalia, genocide in Rwanda, and ethnic cleansing in the Balkans were just the most visible of some forty civil wars then raging around the world. Much of the following decade was spent extinguishing these conflicts. Some, like the civil wars in Cambodia, El Salvador, and Mozambique, were fueled by competition between the two superpowers and were quickly ended by United Nations diplomacy and peacekeeping missions supported from both Washington and Moscow. Other societies, notably Yugoslavia and Somalia, had actually been held together by Cold War pressures, and fell apart when these external sources of support were withdrawn.

At RAND we examined twenty international military interventions that took place from the end of the Cold War until 2004. These included all the larger American-led efforts plus a number of operations organized by the UN and others. Fourteen of these interventions produced lasting peace. The people of Bosnia, Kosovo, Croatia, Albania, Macedonia, Sierra Leone, East Timor, Mozambique, Liberia, El Salvador, Namibia, Cambodia, Cote d'Ivoire, and the Solomon Islands are all living in peace today because international troops arrived in the aftermath of a conflict to provide security, oversee disarmament, support reconstruction, help organize elections, and install new governments, and then remained long enough to consolidate the new regimes.* So much for the oft-heard claim that nation building never works.

After two decades of involvement in first world diplomacy, I found myself thrown into these unfamiliar realms, first in trying unsuccessfully to forestall the violent breakup of Yugoslavia, then trying, again unsuccessfully, to end conflict in Somalia. My efforts to devise some American response to the Rwandan genocide were cut short by President Clinton's decision to focus on Haiti instead. By the end of his presidency, the U.S. government had evolved an effective approach to post-conflict stabilization and reconstruction, which was put to the test in Bosnia and Kosovo. Unfortunately, Clinton's successor, George W. Bush, rejected the main elements of that approach. His administration failed, first in Afghanistan

---

Overcoming Obstacles to Peace, Dobbins and others, RAND, 2013.

and then in Iraq, to deploy a large and capable stabilization force, to move quickly to provide for public security, to deter the emergence of violent opposition, to secure the cooperation of neighboring states, and to move to reconcile former adversaries. Stabilizing Afghanistan and Iraq was always going be more difficult than pacifying the much smaller and more Westernized societies of Bosnia and Kosovo, but the failure to apply the lessons of the 1990s in the decade that followed made this task much harder than it needed to be.

Unfortunately, the failure to stabilize both Afghanistan and Iraq has not resulted in an American determination to do better next time. Rather these setbacks have solidified an aversion to the whole nation-building paradigm. In the course of the 1990s the combination of UN peacekeeping and American-led peace enforcement operations steadily reduced the number of conflicts worldwide. But failed efforts to stabilize Afghanistan and Iraq ultimately led the Obama administration to adopt an attitude toward nation-building operations very much akin to that of early George W. Bush and Don Rumsfeld. The Obama administration formally stated that it was not planning for, and would not prepare for, large-scale stability operations. In 1999 the three-month Kosovo air campaign gave way to a sixteen-year commitment of American and NATO boots on the ground. The six-month Libyan air campaign gave way to no such follow-up, but rather five years (and still running) of chaos, conflict, and radicalization. Obama's 2011 withdrawal from Iraq only compounded the original error of invading that country. American efforts to end the civil war in Syria also have been limited and ineffectual.

Democracy promotion, like nation-building, has also fallen out of fashion. Yet here, too, the record is a good deal better than generally appreciated. Beginning in the mid-1970s with Portugal and Spain, democracy spread rapidly across Latin America, Asia, Central Europe, and Africa, exempting only the Arab world. Over a thirty-year period the number of democracies increased from thirty-nine to 123. The last decade has seen this process slow and even, in some societies, reverse. Yet Freedom House still rates 145 countries as partially or fully free.

My experience in this field began with Portugal and then Spain, the last West European countries to emerge from dictatorship. There followed transitions throughout Central and Eastern Europe. We had less success with Russia and the other states emerging from the former Soviet Union. Haiti proved deeply resistant to reform. Democracy advanced elsewhere in the Western Hemisphere, however. The Balkans today are still the poorest and most poorly governed part of Europe, and Bosnia and Kosovo are still Europe's least developed societies. But they and the region as a whole are more prosperous, better governed, and more democratic than at any time in their history. In 2000, Serbia experienced the first of what, subsequently, came to be labeled "color revolutions," in which Western support for civil society and democratic opposition forces allowed the peaceful overthrow of an entrenched, illiberal regime. To say Afghan democracy is a work in progress is an understatement. But Afghanistan is today much more democratic than at any time in its history and is also more democratic than any of its six neighbors: China, Iran, Turkmenistan, Uzbekistan, Tajikistan, and Pakistan. In my personal experience, therefore, democracy promotion has a pretty good record.

One of the reasons the Obama administration has found itself embroiled in so many conflicts is because it has not been able to bring any to a conclusion. Obama had hoped to end the wars in Iraq and Afghanistan, leaving behind governments capable of dealing with their own security challenges. But wars are not over because one says they are. In retrospect it is clear that we left Iraq too early and deescalated in Afghanistan too abruptly. Obama himself acknowledges failing to follow through on his intervention in Libya, and America's half-hearted engagement in Syria has served only to prolong the conflict.

Bill Clinton was careful to take on no more than one military intervention at a time. This led him to abandon the field in Somalia before intervening in Haiti, to largely wrap up that operation before committing troops to Bosnia, and to turn to Kosovo only once Bosnia had been stabilized. This "one war at a time" policy was not motivated by any shortage of military assets, as these interventions were all comparatively small. Rather it reflected an implicit understanding that top policymakers would not be able to devote the time and political capital necessary to optimize American performance across multiple missions during their most complex and demanding phases.

Obama's very reluctant and incremental approach to military commitments has allowed crises to pile up. As a result he is passing on to his successor American military engagements in half a dozen ongoing conflicts, including Afghanistan, Iraq, Syria, Libya, Somalia, and Nigeria. To be fair, the original sin in this regard was George W. Bush's decision to invade Iraq before making any serious effort to stabilize Afghanistan.

Those two simultaneous conflicts stretched American capabilities nearly to breaking, prevented either war from being successfully terminated, and contributed to the inadequate American response in Libya and Syria. Invading Iraq was, thus, the original overstretch from which we are still suffering.

The price of democracy is a certain degree of amateurism. Nowhere is this truer than in the realm of national security. Modern American presidents are chosen principally for what they promise to do for the economy, over which they have limited sway, rather than for how they propose to conduct foreign and defense policy, over which they have near total control. This is in stark contrast to the early years of the America republic, when our presidents were almost invariably victorious generals or diplomats of distinction. In the twentieth-century only Dwight Eisenhower and George H. W. Bush have approached this standard.

Fortunately, presidential performance generally improves over time. Franklin Roosevelt, Harry Truman, and George H. W. Bush were the most positively consequential of twentieth-century presidents. Roosevelt's major national security accomplishments came during his third term in office. Truman finished Roosevelt's fourth term and went on to head the fifth successive Democratic administration, drawing on many of Roosevelt's top officials. George H. W. Bush was a third Republican-term president, succeeding Ronald Reagan, after having himself been a two-term vice president, a genuine war hero, the U.S. envoy to China, ambassador to the United Nations, and director of the CIA.

In the modern era, most other new presidents have been inexperienced in the exercise of national power and, consequently, prone to costly mistakes. Think of Kennedy's Bay of Pigs, Johnson's Vietnam buildup, Clinton's Black Hawk Down, and, most costly of all, George W. Bush's invasion of Iraq. For his part, Ronald Reagan almost blundered into a nuclear war with the Soviet Union in 1983, but handled his relations with Gorbachev deftly during his second term. Clinton stumbled in Somalia, barely recovered in Haiti, but racked up solid accomplishments in Bosnia and Kosovo. In his second term George W. Bush courageously and wisely moved to reverse a catastrophically deteriorating situation in Iraq.

In his first term Obama largely avoided neophyte errors by keeping key elements of Bush's second-term national security team in place, including Bob Gates as secretary of defense, Doug Lute as the White House war czar, and David Petraeus as our top general in the field. This level of continuity from one administration to a successor from a different party is unparalleled. As time passed, however, Obama's own predilections came to the fore, as evidenced in the withdrawal from Iraq, the rapid drawdown in Afghanistan, and the much advertised pivot to Asia.

Following defeat in Vietnam the United States turned with some relief from Southeast Asia to the more congenial mission of defending West Germany, and the American military quickly erased any institutional memory of counterinsurgency. Obama's decision to shift attention from the Middle to the Far East had a similar quality, moving from a chaotic and frustratingly resistant region to one more orderly, familiar, arguably much more important and more threatening, but also much more peaceful.

Since 1980 East Asia has been largely free of both interstate conflicts and serious civil wars. Deterring a rising China and reassuring its neighbors are important missions, but announcing that this was going to be done at the expense of Europe and the Middle East turned out to be both bad policy and flawed public diplomacy. The Obama team may be forgiven for not foreseeing Russia's aggression in Ukraine, but the fragility of Libya, Syria, and Iraq was already evident in late 2011 when the pivot was first announced.

Obama was the tenth president under whom I served, and Kerry the thirteenth secretary. Obama was the most intellectual and probably the smartest but also the most controlling. If the record of George W. Bush's first term might be caricatured as policy without reflection, the Obama White House often seemed committed to reflection without policy, as the interagency machinery minced issues ever more finely before eventually spitting out a decision. Even Richard Nixon allowed Henry Kissinger more scope than Obama gave his principal subordinates.

Obama participated personally in NSC deliberations more frequently than most of his predecessors. I found this tended to dampen rather than animate debate. The president was quick to express dissent when the conversation took a turn with which he disagreed, and it became hard to pursue a contrary line of argument thereafter. Meetings at the principals and deputies levels were also dominated by White House staff. Agency attendance in these meetings was usually limited to one or two persons, whereas there would typically be a dozen White House staffers present. Often enough there were more White House staff sitting around the Situation Room table than all of the agency representatives combined, something I had never seen in any prior administration.

These meetings were elaborately prepared, with detailed discussion papers provided in advance, although these often appeared only minutes before the meeting in question. When lower level meetings challenged existing policy, that consensus was not always reported upward. The White House also imposed an unprecedented uniformity of public messaging. In prior administrations agency spokespersons looked primarily to their own agency leadership for guidance. Under Obama they looked most exclusively to the White House media operation.

Many presidential decisions were reached in discussion between the president and his immediate staff, leaving the agencies without input and also without any way of determining whether the directions coming from the White House staff truly reflected the president's considered judgment. In prior administrations presidential decisions were usually conveyed in confidence to the relevant cabinet officers before becoming public. Under Obama the first agencies learned about such decisions was often in some public announcement. This gave the administration spin masters inordinate power, with policy formulation being driven by policy explication rather than the reverse. It also diminished the prestige and, therefore, the influence of the president's principal cabinet officers.

Micromanagement on this scale requires extra manpower, and the Obama NSC staff grew accordingly, doubling in size over that of the early George W. Bush administration. There are, admittedly, some valid reasons for this growth. The twenty-four-hour news cycle and the expectation that the White House publicly react to world events in real time requires a high degree of both agility and discipline. The post-9/11 focus on homeland security and counterterrorist operations abroad created a whole new sector of government activity that needs oversight, just as do the actual wars in Afghanistan and Iraq.

Unhappiness with an overweening White House staff has been attested to by more authoritative sources than me, to include the first three of Obama's secretaries of defense, all of whom registered such complaints. At the same time, I, like others, found Obama thoughtful, careful, cautious, and courteous, even while reprimanding me for assuring Congress that he was not going to carry out his threatened withdrawal from Afghanistan.

Many point to the George H. W. Bush administration as the model of a well-run national security system. This had a lot to do with the experience of the team. Both Baker and Cheney had previously served as White House chief of staff. Scowcroft had previously served as national security adviser. And it was the president who had the most extensive national security resume. Previous and subsequent presidents spent their early years in the White House learning on the job, often making costly mistakes in the process, but George H. W. Bush was prepared to take charge from day one.

Brent Scowcroft is almost universally regarded as the model national security adviser. He ran an orderly, professional interagency process under one of our least knowledgeable modern presidents, Gerald Ford, and our most experienced, George H. W. Bush. Scowcroft managed to hold his own while working with two tremendously powerful secretaries of state, Henry Kissinger and James Baker. I was also impressed with Sandy Berger, Clinton's second-term national security adviser. Whereas Brent was cool and often reserved in judgment, Sandy was hot, intense, impatient, and decisive. He was an equal participant in NSC principals discussions, not just a mediator, but he, nevertheless, was able to run a collegial system. I particularly admired the way in which he and John Podesta, Clinton's chief of staff throughout the impeachment crisis, steered the White House and the country through that turbulent period, maintaining staff morale and keeping a professional focus on the nation's business.

Shultz, Baker, and Kerry were strong negotiators. Shultz may have been the best poker player, his countenance famously unreadable. Baker employed grace, wit, and a sharp mind. Kerry used his height, commanding presence, tenacity, and long familiarity with the issues and personalities to good effect. He also tended to wield the power of his office frontally, while Baker's style was subtler. Both men had a feel for power and how to use it. Kerry was dogged in the pursuit of important objectives even when the chances of success were slim, whereas Baker picked his battles more carefully. Baker had more power by reason of his much closer relationship with the president. He also had the largest opportunities and, thus, the greatest accomplishments.

The secretary I most enjoyed working with was Madeleine Albright. I admired the strength of her convictions, her common sense, and her ability to employ rather than suppress her femininity to make her way in what was otherwise still exclusively a man's world. As the Kosovo air campaign has been labeled Madeleine's war, so can the relative tranquility that has reigned throughout the Balkans ever since justly be called Madeleine's peace.

Albright told me some years after leaving office that the one thing she regretted was not having established a better relationship with the Foreign Service. Rich Armitage, Talbott's successor as deputy secretary of state, was quoted claiming he and Powell were repairing the department after sixteen years of neglect, thus including Baker and Christopher as well as Albright in his criticism. Colin Powell was, indeed, much more attuned to the importance of institutional development than his predecessors. His emphasis on stewardship was likely a product of his military background. He was, as a result, the more beloved chief if not the more consequential.

I regret not having worked with Hillary Clinton. I traveled with her as First Lady and briefed her for a trip to Haiti, but these exposures left only a superficial impression. I was surprised to observe from a distance how thoroughly she won over the State Department, generating intense loyalty from many of the professionals who worked with her there. I was even more surprised when she called a couple of months into my SRAP tenure to ask how things were going. She had worked closely with my predecessors, Dick Holbrooke and Marc Grossman, and wanted to keep abreast of developments. Clinton asked knowledgeable questions and provided insightful advice. She called back several times over the following year, showing a seriousness and commitment that I found remarkable.

I had with her the sort of conversations I would have liked to have had with Kerry. He was always available when I needed his help, which was fairly often, but his long familiarity with the issues and personalities of my region tended to make him impatient when told things he thought he already knew. This was a reflection of the whirlwind pace Kerry maintained, more intense than any prior secretary. Kerry accommodated himself to a White House-centric policy process by focusing on the representational and negotiating aspects of the job. I admired his tenacity and could always count on him to reinforce my efforts with the Afghan and Pakistani leadership. With the White House, not so much.

I have often wondered how my life might have unfolded if I had responded differently to Congressman Burton's question back in 1996. I would likely have gone out as ambassador to Argentina rather than working on war and peace in the Balkans. Again, in 2000, I would likely have gone to the Philippines and missed service on Afghanistan. By being compelled to remain in Washington, I became available to play a part in what were the dominant diplomatic dramas of the day: the Kosovo war, the stabilization of Bosnia, the democratic transitions of Serbia and Croatia, and the invasion of Afghanistan. On leaving the service I was able to draw on those still-topical experiences as an analyst and author for more than a decade before being recalled to government service and Afghanistan. Much as I hate to admit it, and much as they would hate to hear it, Dan Burton and Jesse Helms probably did me a favor.

Index